PRAIRIE WILDFLOWERS

A Guide to Flowering Plants from the Midwest to the Great Plains

DON KURZ

D1560044

FALCON GUIDES

GUILFORD, CONNECTICUT
HELENA, MONTANA

FALCONGUIDES®

An imprint of The Rowman & Littlefield Publishing Group, Inc.
4501 Forbes Blvd., Ste. 200
Lanham, MD 20706
www.rowman.com
Falcon and FalconGuides are registered trademarks and Make Adventure Your Story is a trademark of The Rowman & Littlefield Publishing Group, Inc.

Distributed by NATIONAL BOOK NETWORK

Copyright © 2019 The Rowman & Littlefield Publishing Group, Inc.

Photos by Don Kurz

Maps by Melissa Baker

British Library Cataloguing in Publication Information available

Library of Congress Cataloging-in-Publication Data available

ISBN 978-1-4930-3636-3 (paperback)
ISBN 978-1-4930-3637-0 (e-book)

∞™ The paper used in this publication meets the minimum requirements of American National Standard for Information Sciences—Permanence of Paper for Printed Library Materials, ANSI/NISO Z39.48-1992.

Printed in the United States of America

PRAIRIE WILDFLOWERS

THIS BOOK IS DEDICATED TO ALL THE PRAIRIE AND GRASSLAND MANAGERS AND STAFF, BOTH PUBLIC AND PRIVATE; TO THE PRAIRIE ENTHUSIASTS, EDUCATORS, AND VOLUNTEERS; AND TO ALL THAT HAVE WORKED TIRELESSLY TO IDENTIFY, PURCHASE, PRESERVE, DEDICATE, RESTORE, AND ESTABLISH PRAIRIE AND RELATED ECOSYSTEMS.

CONTENTS

APPROXIMATE PRESETTLEMENT RANGE OF THE TALLGRASS PRAIRIE

The range of the original tallgrass prairie is represented in green. Tan indicates the former expanse of smaller, more scattered prairies, large areas of savanna, and open oak woodlands; all have remnants that can still be visited today along with opportunities to see a variety of prairie wildflowers. Prairies also occurred in scattered locations eastward and along the southern part of Texas and Louisiana; these were known as coastal prairies, some of which still exist.

INTRODUCTION

For wildflower enthusiasts, there is no better place to see such a vast array of colors, shapes, and sizes of native flowering plants than the tallgrass prairie. Blooming starts in March with such ground-hugging plants as pasqueflower, prairie smoke, and early buttercup. As the growing season progresses, the variety of shapes and sizes of prairie wildflowers changes every two to three weeks as different species come into bloom. This parade of shifting colors continues through the summer, with large displays of coneflowers, blazing stars, and sunflowers, and ends in the fall, with asters closing out the season in October. Few other ecosystems produce such a continuous spectacle of wildflower blooms throughout the growing season.

Prairie wildflowers are generally known as "forbs," which distinguishes them from other categories such as grasses, sedges, shrubs, and trees. "Forb" is derived from the Greek *phorbe*, for pasture or fodder. These wildflowers or forbs are part of a complex formation of plants and animals that inhabit what is known as a "prairie." "Prairie" is the French word for *meadow*, but the ultimate root is the Latin *pratum*, which has the same meaning.

What initially set the stage for prairies to develop dates back to the formation of the Rocky Mountains. From 80 million to 55 million years ago, a number of plates began sliding underneath the North American Plate. The angle of those sliding plates was shallow, creating an uplift of a section of the North American Plate that stretches more than 3,000 miles from the northernmost part of British Columbia, in western Canada, to New Mexico, in the southwestern United States. The presence of the mountain range then created a rain shadow, which is when the mountains block the passage of rain-producing weather systems and cast a "shadow" of dryness behind them.

The initial emergence of extensive prairie probably began 7 to 5 million years ago during a very dry period, which restricted forests and woodlands, and encouraged evolution and expansion of grasses and forbs. During the fluctuation of the Pleistocene or glacial period over the past 2 million years, the cooling and warming intervals caused the prairie to expand and recede. When the last glacial period ended about 11,000 years ago, a warming trend began, and about 8,000 years ago, the prairies greatly expanded all the way to what is now Ohio.

There are three main prairie types or ecoregions in the United States. They are shortgrass, mixed-grass, and tallgrass, and they are classified by the amount of rainfall they receive and the types of grasses that grow there. The **shortgrass prairie** is the westernmost prairie region and begins on the foothills of the Rocky Mountains and extends eastward into the Great Plains to the western third of Nebraska, north into southern

Saskatchewan and Alberta, Canada, and south into northwestern Texas. This region receives from 10 to 24 inches of rain annually and favors more drought-resistant, short grasses such as blue grama and buffalo grass, which are less than 2 feet tall.

The **mixed-grass prairie** is an ecotone, a transition between the two other prairie types. It occurs in the central portion of the Great Plains and central Nebraska, north into southern Saskatchewan, and south into north Texas. Rainfall ranges from 24 to 30 inches a year, with grasses that range from 2 to 5 feet, such as little bluestem, side-oats grama, western wheatgrass, and sand dropseed.

The third type, and the subject of this book, is the **tallgrass prairie**. It is found along the eastern part of the Great Plains and extends eastward into Indiana and Ohio, north into southern Manitoba, and south into the east-central part of Texas. Rainfall ranges from 30 to 40 inches annually, greatly influenced by moisture-laden northerly winds from the Gulf of Mexico. Dominant prairie grasses are over 5 feet tall and include big bluestem, Indian grass, switchgrass, prairie cordgrass, and eastern gamagrass.

The tallgrass prairie once covered more than 400,000 square miles, but today, the few remaining tallgrass prairies occupy less than 1 percent of that former range. Imagine what it must have been like exploring this region for the first time. Caleb Atwater, in 1831, wrote of his experiences in Ohio's tallgrass prairie: "Sometimes I traveled, during four or five hours, either by day or by night, across some prairies, without seeing even a bush, or a tree— above me were the widespread and lofty heavens, while the prairie, with its grasses and flowers, extended in all directions around me, far beyond the reach of my vision."

A major factor in maintaining such extensive expanses of prairie was the influence of fire. As biomass, particularly that from grasses, became more prominent after the last ice age, its ignition became more frequent and extensive. This was due to the occasional lightning strike or intentional fire setting by Native Americans. They saw the value of burning prairies in order to stimulate new growth to attract game, enable easier travel, and to initiate acts of warfare. Grazing by bison, pronghorn antelope, and deer also helped to keep the prairies in a healthy, open condition, but their influence was mainly concentrated in the mixed-grass and shortgrass regions.

Unfortunately, most of the tallgrass prairie has been eliminated. Over 99 percent of this landscape has been converted to growing crops, intensive grazing, and development, while many of the remaining prairies are seriously degraded due to fire suppression and invasive nonnative species. Those prairies in private ownership grow fewer every year, but many of the largest and the best remaining prairies have been protected by state and federal natural resource agencies, county park boards, colleges and universities, and private organizations such as The Nature Conservancy and the National Audubon Society. For public access information to these protected prairies, refer to the Tallgrass Prairie Directory in the back of this book.

Tallgrass Prairie Natural Communities

Wildflowers, as well as grasses, sedges, shrubs, trees, and animals, can be found to occupy one or more prairie types or natural communities. These classes of prairies are determined by the type of soil substrate, soil moisture, and landscape position. Presented in this section are some broad classifications that will aid in determining what type of prairie wildflower is being encountered.

Wet prairies occur on floodplains of rivers and sometimes in small depressions of upland prairies. The soils are poorly drained and become saturated with standing water during the spring and winter or after heavy rains. Perennial grasses, often up to 7 feet tall by midsummer, dominate the prairie, along with a mixture of

Wet Prairie

prairie wildflowers and sedges. Typical prairie plants include prairie cordgrass, bluejoint grass, swamp milkweed, common ironweed, blue flag, various asters, and numerous sedges. Agricultural practices, wetland drainage, channelization, and woody encroachment have drastically reduced the occurrence of wet prairies across the prairie region.

Mesic prairies occupy moderately well-drained sites. They are found on broad, level hills, plains, and lower gentle slopes. This is a more common prairie type in the northern parts of the prairie region. Relatively high soil moisture content and deep soils allow for a wide diversity and density of prairie plants, which provides a very

Mesic Prairie

3

showy display rivaling the other prairie types. Dominant grasses include big bluestem, Indian grass, switch grass, and prairie dropseed. Typical wildflowers are compass plant, prairie dock, lead plant, tall blazing star, purple prairie clover, and rattlesnake master. Mesic prairies have greatly declined across the region due to agricultural practices, invasion by exotic species, woody encroachment, and fire suppression.

Dry prairies occur on a wide range of well-drained substrates. They are found on broad hills, slopes, and plains. This is a common prairie type in the western and southern parts of the prairie region. Dry prairies with more moisture content are referred to as dry-mesic prairies. Soils can be relatively deep, but in others, bedrock can be found

Dry Prairie

at or near the surface. The dominant grass is typically little bluestem. Other grasses include prairie dropseed, side-oats grama, big bluestem, and Indian grass. Prairie wildflowers include pale purple coneflower, round-headed bush clover, New Jersey tea, purple and white prairie clovers, flowering spurge, bird's foot violet, rosinweed, and white wild indigo. Dry prairies, although greatly diminished in total acreage, represent the most commonly encountered prairie type today. This is primarily due to dry prairies being less suitable for plowing due to shallower soils. Haying and cattle grazing account for much of the dry-prairie acreage that remains today, and the level of that usage greatly influences the natural quality of the prairie.

Hill prairies are a type of dry prairie but found on steep to moderately steep hills and tops of bluffs. The typically south- to west-facing exposures trigger accelerated soil moisture evaporation and excessive heat levels that favor drought-tolerant plants. Hill prairies occur on large deposits of gravels from glaciers, on narrow ridges above bluffs

Hill Prairie

and cliffs, and from windblown glacial soil or loess (pronounced luss) that accumulated on the windward side of broad river valleys. The dominant grasses include little bluestem, side-oats grama, hairy grama, and plains muhly. Prairie wildflowers include purple prairie clover, narrow-leaved bluets, thimbleweed, pasqueflower, prairie smoke, and aromatic aster. Hill prairies have greatly deteriorated over time due to quarrying, poor grazing practices, invasion by nonnative invasive plant species, and woody encroachment due to fire suppression.

Sand prairies occur on extensive sand deposits left when glaciers retreated and can be found along floodplains of rivers and shorelines of lakes. Sand prairies also formed on sand dunes that were sculpted into hills by the power of the wind, such as along Lake Michigan. The soils are well-drained, nutrient-poor, easily

Sand Prairie

eroded or shifting, and droughty. Sand prairies often contain up to 50 percent bare sand on the surface. Clump-forming grasses occur, such as little bluestem, broom sedge, splitbeard bluestem, junegrass, and sand dropseed. Wildflowers include prickly pear cactus, clasping milkweed, sessile-leaved tick trefoil, lanceleaf coreopsis, Carolina puccoon, butterfly weed, and prairie rose. Sand prairies have typically been uncommon due to their restricted habitat, but they are continuing to decline due to conversion to cropland and development, altered hydrology, and sand and gravel mining.

Savannas occur in a transition zone between prairies and forest where fire plays a critical role. A higher frequency and intensity of fires tends to favor prairie while the opposite allows trees to expand and eventually succeed to forest. Savannas occur on loamy or sandy soils and in the northern part of the prairie region include bur oak

Savanna

and black oak trees, while post oak and black oak trees dominate in the southern region. The canopy cover is usually less than 50 percent, which then provides enough sunlight for grasses and wildflowers to flourish. Plants that can be found in savannas include grasses like little bluestem, big bluestem, and Indian grass, and wildflowers such as goat's rue, hoary puccoon, rattlesnake master, Culver's root, purple milkweed, and sky blue aster. Few remaining savannas exist today due to fire suppression, logging, and grazing.

Plant Identification

Sometimes, recognizing wildflowers by their color and shape alone is not enough. There may be more subtle differences that distinguish one plant from another, so some knowledge of basic plant parts and terms is helpful. In this wildflower guide, technical terms are kept to a minimum; however, a list of terms is included in the glossary at the back of this book.

Many Ozark prairie plants are **perennial**, which means they can live from a few years to well over a hundred years. Perennial plants can be divided into **woody** plants, such as trees and shrubs, and **herbaceous** plants that die back to the underground roots or stems by winter. The perennial wildflowers in this book are the herbaceous type, except for New Jersey tea, leadplant, and roses, which are all woody but could be taken for herbaceous upon first glance. **Biennials** have a two-year life cycle. The plant, in its first year, usually produces a basal set of leaves. During the second year, the plant sends up a stalk that produces flowers and fruits and then dies; its seed then produces future plants. **Annuals** complete their life cycle in one growing season. Some annuals produce seeds that germinate in the spring, whereas some species, called **winter annuals**, germinate in the autumn, overwinter as small, leafy rosettes, and continue their growth in the spring. Having a head start, they are usually some of the first plants to flower in the spring.

Sometimes it is difficult to determine which plants are perennial. These usually have well-developed underground roots in the forms of bulbs or tuberous roots, often with next year's growing buds visible. Annual plants typically have a small system of fibrous roots. All of the wildflowers in this book are perennial unless otherwise noted.

Leaves are important in identifying wildflowers. A variety of technical terms is used to describe leaf shapes, but in this book, simple terms are used. Features to note about leaves include: Are the leaves **opposite** each other (figure 1), or **alternate** along the stem (figure 2), or **whorled** at a particular point on the stem (figure 3)? Are the leaves

Figure 1

pointed at the tip or blunt? Are the leaf bases tapering, heart-shaped, rounded, or clasping the stem? Is the leaf texture thick, leathery, or thin? Are the leaf margins smooth, toothed, lobed, or wavy? Do the leaves have stalks attaching them to the stem, or are they stalk-less? Are there leafy **wings**, which are thin strips of tissue, attached edgewise along the stalk or stem? Note also that many plants produce **basal** leaves that form rosettes at the base of the plant (figure 4). These leaves are often larger than the leaves along the stem.

Figure 2

Figure 3

Figure 4

Leaves are characterized as either simple or compound. A **simple** leaf has a blade that is usually in one piece and may or may not be attached to a leaf stalk (figure 5). A **compound** leaf has a blade that is attached to a leaf stalk and is divided into leaflets that are either opposite each other or spreading like the fingers of a hand (figures 6–7). Determining whether a leaf-like structure counts as a whole leaf or

Figure 5

Figure 6

Figure 7

a leaflet requires examination of the leaf's attachment to the plant. True leaves, whether simple or compound, have buds arising at their point of attachment to the stem; individual leaflets of compound leaves do not.

Sometimes where the leaf stalk attaches to the stem, there is a pair of appendages called **stipules**. These may be large or tiny and scale-like, and they may fall off soon after the leaf opens.

Bracts are another kind of leaf-like structure, and they are often associated with and usually found just below the flowers. Some are miniature versions of the leaves, whereas others may be colored and resemble the petals of a flower.

Becoming familiar with flower parts is important in the identification of plants. The characteristic of flower color is less reliable than the actual floral structures, because one species of wildflower may have flowers in two or more different colors, and the colors of flowers sometimes change with age. A diagram of a generalized flower is given in figure 8. The variation and number of lower parts are key characters for the identification of most plants. Flowers generally have an outer series of flower parts, called **sepals**, that surrounds the base of the flower. The sepals together are called the **calyx**.

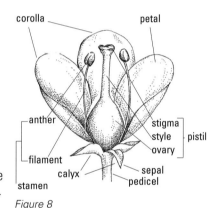

Figure 8

Inside the calyx of most flowers are a series of usually showy parts called **petals**. Petals also vary in size, shape, and color, and may be separate or fused. The petals together, whether separate or fused, form the **corolla**. Depending on the kind of plant, there may be no petals, with only sepals present, or the petals and sepals may look exactly alike.

Within the corolla are the **stamens**, which are the pollen-producing structures. The stamens have long, thread-like stalks called **filaments**, each of which support a club-like or elongated structure—the **anther**—which holds the pollen. Stamens vary in number from 1 to over 100 per flower, depending on the species.

Also within the corolla is the seed-producing part of the flower: the **pistil**, which normally consists of the stigma, style, and ovary. The **stigma** receives the pollen; it is supported by a column called the **style**. Below the style, the **ovary**, which is usually swollen, contains the developing seed after it is fertilized. In some plants, the style may be absent. Whereas most plants have both male (stamen) and female (pistil) parts in the same flower, some species have separate male and female flowers on the same plant, whereas others may have male and female flowers on separate plants.

Two families of plants that occur quite often in the tallgrass prairie deserve special attention: the bean family (Fabaceae) and the aster family (Asteraceae). The bean family has five modified petals, which are shown in figure 9. The **banner** is erect, spreading, and usually the largest of the five. The two side petals, or **wings**, closely surround the **keel**, which are the two fused lowest petals.

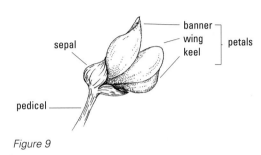

Figure 9

Members of the aster family (Asteraceae) have **flower heads** that look like single flowers but are actually composed of a cluster of a few to several hundred tiny flowers. This head of flowers is usually surrounded at the base by a series of bracts; these bracts are usually tightly clustered and overlap each other in rows. The calyx for each tiny flower is absent or reduced to bristles, scales, or hairs. In general, each flower head can produce two kinds of flower: **ray flowers** (figure 10) and **disk flowers** (figure 11). A typical aster family flower head is illustrated in figure 12. Each outer ray flower has a single colorful petal that is strap-like. The central disk flower has a small, tubular corolla, usually with five lobes on the end. Depending on the species, a flower head may have all ray flowers, all disk flowers, or a combination of both.

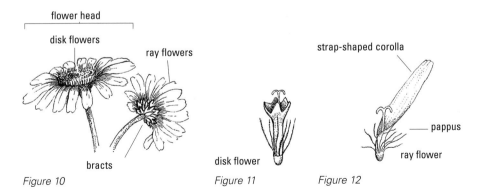

Figure 10

Figure 11

Figure 12

Using This Guide

Within the large and varied landscape of the tallgrass prairie region is a great diversity of plant life, including well over 1,000 species of plants. Within this group, a lesser number are considered wildflowers, a term that lacks a precise definition. It is generally understood, however, that certain plants have flowers that are eye-catching because of their color, shape, and/or size. In this book, 350 wildflowers are represented. These include wildflowers that are more commonly encountered in the tallgrass prairie region, as well as a few uncommon types that are particularly showy and characteristic of an area. Also, a few rare or uncommon plants are represented that are of conservation concern, to help bring awareness to their situation.

When a closely related species might be encountered, it is briefly described in the **Comments** section, which adds another 68 species to this guide. Also, a selection of more prevalent exotic or weedy plants is included in the **Weeds** section. Although their flowers can be showy, it is important to distinguish them from the native flora so one can gain a better understanding of native plants and the habitats in which they are found.

For ease and speed in identifying plants, wildflowers with similar color are grouped together. This is not a perfect method, however, because some wildflowers vary in color shades, especially where lighter pinks and blues sometimes grade into white. When a plant has flowers with two colors, the most noticeable color is the one determining its placement in this book. Within each color group, plants are arranged by their family and then by genus, all in alphabetical order, except for a few, mostly asters and goldenrods, where some have been reclassified and placed in a new or different genus. In those cases, the plants are moved out of alphabetical order in the chapter so they can be placed with former related species in the older genus. This results in fewer pages to flip through and a faster identification.

Each photograph is accompanied by text, beginning with the plant's **common name**. Often, each wildflower has several common names, so an attempt was made to select the name most widely used in a majority of the tallgrass prairie region. Because of the general confusion surrounding multiple common names, the scientific name is also presented. These names, rendered in Latin and Greek, are more reliable and universally accepted. The scientific name consists of two words that appear in italics. The first word, the **genus**, is the name of a group of plants with similar general characteristics, such as sunflowers, which are in the genus *Helianthus*. Note the first letter of the genus name is always a capital letter. The second part of the scientific name is the **specific epithet**, or species name, which identifies the particular species of a plant, such as the *mollis*. Note that the first letter of the species name is always a lowercase letter. So the correct presentation would be *Helianthus mollis*. The specific epithet may honor a person who may have first found the plant; it could refer to a geographic location; or it could describe some characteristic of the plant.

In a few instances, a plant has a scientific name with a third part, preceded by **variety**, which is typically listed with the abbreviation **var.** In either case, italics are not used. In this book, the abbreviation is not used. The variety is added when a set of plants differs slightly but consistently from other plants of the same species; these plants often have distinct ranges. The scientific names used in this book are from the most recently published references for these plants.

Next, the **family** name is listed. For example, the milkweed family has the scientific name of Asclepiadaceae. (Family names always end with the suffix –*aceae*.) Families are grouped according to similarities in their structure and biology. As one becomes more familiar with plants, this grouping by family characteristics becomes more obvious.

Each plant has a brief **Description** section that provides information on the size and shape of the plant and important characteristics of leaves, flowers, and sometimes fruits. It is not intended to describe a plant completely, but rather to provide those features that readily distinguish it from other plants without getting very technical. Sometimes identification, especially when examining flower parts and hairs, can be aided by the use of a magnifying glass or hand lens, preferably with a magnification power of 10.

The **Habitat/Range** section provides information on relative abundance of plants, using such terms as *common*, *locally frequent*, *uncommon*, and *rare*. This gives the reader a general perspective on the plant's status in the tallgrass prairie region. Many of the plants selected for this book have a wide range of distribution. A few, however, are found only in a part of the region, especially those that may be on the edge of their range and are found more commonly elsewhere, such as in the mixed-grass prairie region.

Finally, the **Comments** section provides an opportunity to describe closely related species and mention alternative common names, as well as scientific names by which the plant may have once been known. In addition, to increase interest and appreciation of plants, historical information on how plants have been used for food or medicine is presented. This information is based on written reports and should not be read as promotions for using wild plants as a food source or for medical or herbal prescriptions for self-healing. Those interested in historical or modern herbalism, homeopathy, or flower essences can search on the Internet. As you probably know, there is an amazing amount of information out there.

WHITE FLOWERS

Melanthium virginicum

This section includes flowers that are mostly white. Off-white flowers can grade into light colors of yellow, green, pink, and blue, so those sections should also be checked.

WATER HEMLOCK
Cicuta maculata
Parsley family (Apiaceae)

Description: A biennial, hairless plant up to 6' tall with several branches holding umbrella-shaped clusters of tiny white flowers. The stem is streaked or spotted with purple and is hollow toward the base. The leaves are alternate on the stem, up to 12" long, and divided into numerous, sharply toothed leaflets. The umbrella-shaped flower heads contain tiny 5-petaled, white flowers, each less than ⅛" wide.

Bloom Season: Mid-spring–fall

Habitat/Range: Common in wet sites along edges of streams and ponds, in roadside ditches, in marshes, and in wet depressions in prairies; found throughout the prairie region.

Comments: This plant is highly poisonous. Members of many Native American tribes used the root to commit suicide. Children have been poisoned by using the hollow stems as peashooters. A walnut-sized piece of the root is enough to kill a cow.

RATTLESNAKE MASTER
Eryngium yuccifolium
Parsley family (Apiaceae)

Description: This stout-stemmed, hairless plant can grow to a height of 5', with bluish-green leaves at the base that resemble a yucca. The leaves are up to 2' long, 1½" wide, with pointed tips, and small, soft, needle-like bristles scattered along the margin. The flowers, each with 5 tiny, white petals, are tightly packed in round balls up to 1" across. Whitish bracts stick out sharply from the flowers, which gives the flower head a rough, prickly feel and appearance.

Bloom Season: Summer

Habitat/Range: Occasional in prairies and savannas throughout the prairie region.

Comments: The Meskwaki used the leaves and fruit in their rattlesnake medicine song and dance. They used the root for treating bladder problems and poisons, including rattlesnake bites. They also used the roots mashed in cold water to make a drink for relieving muscular pains.

COWBANE

Oxypolis rigidior

Parsley family (Apiaceae)

Description: A slender, hairless plant, up to 5' tall, with alternate leaves along the stem that are divided into 5–9 narrow leaflets. These leaflets are smooth and up to 5" long and 1½" wide on the lower part of the stem, and smaller toward the top. The leaflets can be smooth or irregularly toothed along the margins. The flowers are in flat, dome-shaped clusters, up to 6" wide. Each tiny white flower has 5 petals.

Bloom Season: Mid- to late summer

Habitat/Range: Common in marshes, wet prairies, depressions in mesic prairies, and in wet soils along streams; found throughout the prairie region, except for the western part.

Comments: The roots and leaves of cowbane are poisonous and have been known to poison cattle. Skin contact with the plant can cause dermatitis among some individuals. Cowbane has smooth to irregularly toothed leaflets, while water parsnip has finely and regularly toothed leaflets.

WATER PARSNIP

Sium suave

Parsley family (Apiaceae)

Description: A tall plant, up to 6' tall, with a sturdy, smooth stem that is hollow toward the base. The alternate leaves are divided into 7–17 leaflets, each up to 4" long. The leaflets are toothed along the margin and have a pointed tip. Each leaf has a wide stipule sheathing the base of the leaf stalk. There are several umbrella-shaped flower clusters, up to 3" across, at the top of the stems. Each small flower is about ⅛" across, with 5 white petals.

Bloom Season: Summer

Habitat/Range: Shallow water of marshes, ponds, wet ditches, along streams, shallow water in wet prairies, and wet depressions in upland prairies; found throughout the prairie region, except for the western part.

Comments: Native Americans boiled the root and leaves for food. Because of its similarity to cowbane and poison hemlock, water parsnip should be avoided as a food plant.

INDIAN HEMP
Apocynum cannabinum
Dogbane family (Apocynaceae)

Description: The shrub-like plants are up to 4' tall, often with reddish stems, milky sap, and upright leaves with white to red veins. The leaves are opposite, widest at the middle, pointed at the tip, with smooth margins, and up to 6" long and 3" wide. The flower clusters are usually overtopped by the side branches. The flowers are small, less than ¼" wide, and bell-shaped with 5 tiny, white lobes. The seed pods are in pairs, slender, long-pointed at the tip, and up to 6" long, with seeds that have silky hairs attached at one end.

Bloom Season: Late spring–midsummer

Habitat/Range: Common in prairies, old fields, pastures, and along roadsides; found throughout the prairie region.

Comments: Indian hemp fibers have been found in fabric from the early Archaic period, from 3,000 to 4,000 years ago. The fibers were also used for rope and nets. Root tea was used to treat colds, dropsy (an abnormal accumulation of blood in the body; edema), fever, headache, and sore throat. Another species, spreading dogbane (*Apocynum androsaemifolium*), differs by having flowers that are pink or sometimes white, with the inside red, the lobes of the bell-shaped flowers noticeably spreading, and with drooping leaves. Habitat and range similar to Indian hemp.

TALL GREEN MILKWEED
Asclepias hirtella
Milkweed family (Asclepiadaceae)

Description: Stout-stemmed plants, up to 3' tall, with white, milky sap. The leaves are mostly alternate, hairy, and narrow, up to 6" long and 1" wide, with pointed tips. Several flower clusters arise on stalks up to 1½" long from the upper leaf axils. Each flower is up to ½" long and greenish-white, with 5 petals bent backwards and sometimes white-edged or purple-tipped, and 5 greenish-white structures called "hoods." The seed pods are smooth, slender, and up to 4" long and 1" thick.

Bloom Season: Late spring–summer

Habitat/Range: Occasional in upland prairies, becoming rare and local north and eastward.

Comments: Although not as showy as some of the other milkweeds, this tall, narrow-leaved milkweed casts a stately appearance. The flowers are pollinated mostly by long-tongued bees and wasps.

MEAD'S MILKWEED
Asclepias meadii
Milkweed family (Asclepiadaceae)

Description: Short, slender plants usually with a single stem less than 2' tall, with white, milky sap. The leaves are opposite along the stem, up to 3" long and up to 1½" wide, broadest at the base, tapering to a pointed tip. The leaves are stalkless, smooth, sometimes with wavy margins. There is one drooping flower cluster at the tip of the stem with less than 23 greenish-white flowers, each less than ½" long. The flowers have 5 reflexed petals and 5 cup-like hoods. The seed pods are slender, up to 4" long and ½" thick.

Bloom Season: Late spring–early summer

Habitat/Range: Rare and local in dry prairies in eastern Kansas, Iowa, Illinois, and Missouri.

Comments: Mead's milkweed is a very rare prairie plant and is federally listed as a threatened species due to habitat destruction throughout its former range. Unfortunately, even in protected sites, this milkweed continues to decline.

NARROW-LEAVED MILKWEED
Asclepias stenophylla
Milkweed family (Asclepiadaceae)

Description: A graceful, slender-stemmed plant, up to 3' tall, with milky sap and very long, narrow leaves. The leaves are mostly opposite, up to 8" long, and less than ½" wide. The flowers are in rounded clusters and arise from the leaf axils along the upper part of the plant. Each cluster has up to 25 white flowers, each less than ½" long, with 5 spreading petals surrounding 5 hoods. The seed pods are smooth, up to 5" long, and less than ½" wide.

Bloom Season: Early summer–midsummer

Habitat/Range: Occasional in dry prairies from the western to central prairie region.

Comments: The Lakota fed the root to their children when they refused to eat in order to regain their appetite.

WHORLED MILKWEED
Asclepias verticillata
Milkweed family (Asclepiadaceae)

Description: Slender plants, sparingly branched, up to 2½' tall, with milky sap. The soft, thread-like leaves, up to 3" long and less than ⅛" wide, are mostly in whorls along the stem. The flowers are arranged in clusters of 2–14, with less than 20 flowers in each cluster. There are 5 reflexed, greenish-white petals and 5 white hoods. The seed pods are smooth, narrow, and about 3" long.

Bloom Season: Mid-spring–late summer

Habitat/Range: Common in dry prairies, savannas, old fields, pastures, and along roadsides; found throughout the prairie region.

Comments: A tea from the whole plant was given to Lakota mothers unable to produce milk. The theory behind this practice is similar to the medieval concept of the doctrine of signatures—the belief that certain characteristics of a plant signify its uses. In this case, the milky sap was thought to signify that the milkweed would promote the production of milk. This milkweed is poisonous to cattle but is rarely taken in enough quantity to cause problems.

SPIDER MILKWEED
Asclepias viridis
Milkweed family (Asclepiadaceae)

Description: A large, somewhat sprawling plant, up to 2' tall, with thick stems and milky sap. The leaves are alternate, fleshy, up to 5" long and 2" wide, with wavy margins. The flowers appear in a large cluster, up to 5" across, at the top of the stem. Each flower has 5 whitish-green petals, ½–⅝" long, that spread upward, unlike other milkweeds where the petals are reflexed. Inside the flower are 5 purple hoods arranged in a star-like fashion that together are taller than they are wide. The seed pods are relatively smooth, up to 6" long and 1" thick, with each seed tipped with a tuft of long, white hairs.

Bloom Season: Late spring–midsummer

Habitat/Range: Common in dry or rocky prairies through the southern half of the prairie region, becoming uncommon eastward.

Comments: Spider milkweed has the largest flowers of the milkweeds found in the prairie region. The common name is given for the presence of crab spiders hunting for insect prey around the flowers. A similar species, antelope horns (*Asclepias asperula*), differs by being somewhat shorter, less than 12" tall, with smaller petals, ¼–⅜" long, and hoods that together are wider than they are tall. Occurs in dry or rocky prairies in the southwestern part of the prairie region. Known as antelope horns for the small antelope horn–like appearance of the seed pods, a trait that is also shared with spider milkweed.

GREEN MILKWEED
Asclepias viridiflora
Milkweed family (Asclepiadaceae)

Description: Plants with unbranched, hairy stems, up to 2' tall, with milky sap and opposite leaves. The leaves are thick and vary from narrow to broadly oval, up to 5" long and 2½" wide, with wavy margins. There are from 1 to several dense flower clusters arising from the leaf margins. Each greenish-white flower is about ½" long, with 5 petals bent backward and 5 erect hoods. The smooth, narrow seed pods are up to 6" long and 1" wide.

Bloom Season: Late spring–midsummer

Habitat/Range: Occasional in dry or sandy prairies throughout the prairie region.

Comments: The Lakota gave the pulverized roots of green milkweed to children with diarrhea. The Blackfeet chewed the root to relieve sore throat, and also applied the root to swellings and rashes. In the nonflowering vegetative state, stems of green milkweed can sometimes be mistaken for the very rare Mead's milkweed. Another similar-looking species, woolly milkweed (*Asclepias lanuginosa*), differs by having fine, woolly hairs on both leaf surfaces and a single flower cluster arising at the top of the stem. A very rare milkweed, it occurs on dry, rocky prairies and in open woods; found in the northwestern part of the prairie region and Kansas.

WESTERN RAGWEED
Ambrosia psilostachya
Aster family (Asteraceae)

Description: A colonial plant from 12–30" tall, with widely creeping rhizomes, and hairy stems and leaves. Lower leaves are opposite but the upper leaves are often alternate, up to 5" long, 2" wide, and deeply divided into many narrow lobes that are again further lobed. The hairy leaves are denser underneath giving the leaves a gray-green appearance. The flowers are tiny, drab, creamy white to greenish yellow, with the male flowers on spikes that are from 1–6" long, while the female flowers are in small clusters at the bases of the upper leaves.

Bloom Season: Midsummer–fall.

Habitat/Range: Common in dry prairies, loess hill prairies, and sand prairies; also roadsides, and sandy, open, disturbed ground; found in the western part of the prairie region but less frequent from Wisconsin and Illinois eastward.

Comments: Western ragweed along with the other ragweeds, are notorious for causing hay fever with their windborne pollen. The Cheyenne drank a tea made from a pinch of finely ground leaves and stems to treat bowel cramps and colds. The Kiowa boiled small pieces to make a medicine that was rubbed on sours. A tea was a remedy for "worm holes," a skin disease of horses, and for sores that were slow in healing. Another ragweed, common ragweed, *Ambrosia artemisiifolia*, is similar to western ragweed but differs by being an annual, with a taproot instead of rhizomes, stems much more heavily branched, less hairy overall, and more finely divided, fern-like leaves. Common ragweed is common in prairies, savannas, and often disturbed ground; found throughout the prairie region.

YARROW
Achillea millefolium
Aster family (Asteraceae)

Description: Single-stalked, strongly scented, hairy plants up to 2' tall, with alternate fern-like leaves and flat-topped flower clusters. The lower leaves are up to 10" long on stalks; the upper leaves are smaller and without stalks. Numerous flower heads are arranged in a branching, flat-topped flower cluster. Each head is about ¼" across with 4–6 white ray flowers surrounding a central disk of up to 20 yellow disk flowers.

Bloom Season: Mid-spring–fall

Habitat/Range: Common in prairies, fields, pastures, disturbed sites, and along roadsides; considered a native of both Europe and North America, yarrow is found throughout the prairie region.

Comments: Fossil records reveal yarrow pollen in Neanderthal burial caves. More recently, yarrow has been used in a wide variety of medicinal treatments by at least 58 Native American tribes as a stimulant, laxative, painkiller, diuretic, wound healer, antiseptic, and tonic, to name a few.

FIELD PUSSYTOES
Antennaria neglecta
Aster family (Asteraceae)

Description: A slender plant, spreading by underground runners to form large colonies. The densely hairy stems can eventually reach up to 8" when the fruit develops. The basal leaves are ½–2½" long and less than ¾" wide, with smooth edges, pointed tips, and narrowing bases. The lower surface is silvery white from dense, matted hairs and with a single prominent vein along its length. Flower stalks are white-hairy, with small, alternate, hairy leaves. There are separate male and female flowers on separate plants. The female flowers are white, about ⅜" long, and look like shaving brushes. The male flowers are also white, somewhat smaller, and have brown stamens.

Bloom Season: Spring

Habitat/Range: Common in dry prairies, savannas, and open woods; found throughout the prairie region.

Comments: The woolly, female flower heads account for the plant's common name. Early folk medicine sometimes prescribed a tea of pussytoe leaves taken every day for two weeks after childbirth to keep the mother from getting sick. An extract from the plant was once used to treat stomach disorders, and the flowers have been used to make cough syrup.

PARLIN'S PUSSYTOES
Antennaria parlinii
Aster family (Asteraceae)

Description: A slender plant, spreading by underground runners to form large colonies. The densely hairy stems can eventually reach up to 12" when the fruit develops. The basal leaves are 1–3¾" long and up to 1¾" wide, with smooth edges and rounded tips. The lower surface is silvery white from densely matted hairs, and the upper surface is gray-green and hairless to woolly hairy. There are 3–5 prominent veins on the lower surface. Flower stalks are white-hairy, with small, alternate, hairy leaves. There are separate male and female flowers on separate plants. The female flowers are white, about ½–¾" long, and look like shaving brushes with pink to yellowish tips. The male flowers are also white and somewhat smaller, with brown stamens.

Bloom Season: Spring

Habitat/Range: Fairly common in dry prairies, savannas, and open woods; found throughout the prairie region but absent in North Dakota.

Comments: A similar species, plantain-leaved pussytoes (*Antennaria plantaginifolia*), differs by usually having a woollier and gray-green upper leaf surface. The flowers are also smaller, with female and male flowers around ¼" long. They occur less frequently in prairies and savannas than Parlin's pussytoes and prefer open woods. Plantain-leaved pussytoes are found in the central and eastern part of the prairie region. The easiest identifiable field character that differentiates between field pussytoes and the other 2 species is that the former has 1 prominent vein on the leaf undersurface, while the latter 2 have 3–5 prominent veins. Past medicinal uses for both of these pussytoes are similar to field pussytoes.

PALE INDIAN PLANTAIN
Arnoglossum atriplicifolium
Aster family (Asteraceae)

Description: This plant has a smooth, whitish cast and widely spaced leaves, growing to a height of 4–6', but sometimes to 8'. The leaves are alternate on the stem and have a whitish coating on the underside. The lower leaves are long-stalked, large, 8" long, 6–8" wide, and broadly triangular, with shallow lobes and large teeth. Numerous flower heads form a somewhat flattened top, with the flower in the center of the cluster opening first. Each flower is less than ¼" wide, lacks petals, and includes 5 whitish, tubular disk flowers.

Bloom Season: Summer–early fall

Habitat/Range: In the mid- to eastern prairie region, it is found growing in prairies, savannas, and open woodlands, while on the western edge, it only in open woodlands.

Comments: The common name, Indian plantain, also refers to another species in this genus, *Arnoglossum plantagineum*, which has plantain-shaped leaves. "Pale" refers to the whitish cast of the plant. The leaves have been used as a poultice for cuts, bruises, and cancers, and also to draw out blood or poisonous materials.

PRAIRIE INDIAN PLANTAIN
Arnoglossum plantagineum
Aster family (Asteraceae)

Description: This plant has large, thick, distinctive basal leaves and a flowering stalk up to 5' tall, but it's usually less. The single stem is smooth and angled and grooved along the surface. The basal leaves are large, up to 8" long and 4" wide, with smooth but sometimes shallow-toothed margins, with distinct parallel veins along the leaf and long leaf stalks. The leaves along the stem are few, alternate, small, and lack teeth along the margins. The flower heads are numerous in open branches forming a flat-topped cluster. Each head is up to 1" tall, containing 5 white tubular flowers and no disk flowers.

Bloom Season: Late spring–midsummer

Habitat/Range: Common in wet to mesic prairies; found throughout the prairie region.

Comments: The name of the plant refers to the similarity of its leaves to that of a plantain. Native Americans applied mashed leaves to the skin to treat cancers, cuts, and bruises, and to draw out blood or poisonous substances.

WHITE SAGE
Artemisia ludoviciana
Aster family (Asteraceae)

Description: Narrow, strongly aromatic when bruised, densely white-hairy plants up to 3' tall, with branching occurring above the upper half of the stems. The leaves are very narrow, stalkless, pointed at the tips, and up to 4" long and ¾" wide. The leaves are smooth along the margins but occasionally may have teeth or even lobes. The underside of the leaves is densely hairy, giving the plant a bright white appearance. The flowers are numerous and occur in small clusters along the upper parts of the stem. Each flower head is less than ⅛" across, tubular, and contains several disk flowers.

Bloom Season: Summer–fall

Habitat/Range: Common in dry to mesic upland prairies, sand prairies, hill prairies, pastures, old fields, and roadsides; found in the western half of the prairie region; introduced eastward.

Comments: White sage has been used extensively by Native Americans for medicinal and ceremonial purposes. Its properties and powers were used to treat sore throat, coughs, stomach troubles, and several other ailments, and also to drive away mosquitoes, evil spirits, and bad luck.

FALSE ASTER
Boltonia asteroides
Aster family (Asteraceae)

Description: A much-branched plant, smooth, up to 6' tall, with alternate leaves along the stem. The leaves are narrow, up to 6" long and ¾" wide, reduced in size upward along the stem. The flower heads are numerous, each about ¾" across, with about 60 white petal-like ray flowers surrounding numerous yellow disk flowers.

Bloom Season: Midsummer–fall

Habitat/Range: Common in wet prairies, areas subject to flooding, stream banks, and marshes; found throughout the prairie region.

Comments: The genus name is in honor of James Bolton, an 18th-century English naturalist, botanist, mycologist, and illustrator. The seeds are commonly eaten by waterfowl.

FALSE BONESET
Brickellia eupatorioides
Aster family (Asteraceae)

Description: One or more often-reddish stems emerge from the base of this whitish or cream-colored plant to a height of 3'. The somewhat hairy leaves are alternate, up to 4" long and 1½" wide, with prominent raised veins and one central vein on the underside. The small, 7–21, yellowish-white disk flowers occur in clusters at the tips of branches. The styles extend beyond the flower, giving them a fringed look.

Bloom Season: Summer–early fall

Habitat/Range: Frequent in dry prairies, as well as rocky or sandy prairies, hill prairies, and savannas; found throughout the prairie region.

Comments: Great Plains Indians used false boneset to reduce swelling. Its bitter taste restricted its use as a medicine or food plant. The dried seed head has been used in winter flower arrangements. False boneset is sometimes confused with tall boneset (*Eupatorium altissimum*). False boneset has alternate leaves with one central vein, whereas tall boneset has opposite leaves with 3 veins.

HORSEWEED
Conyza canadensis
Aster family (Asteraceae)

Description: A tall annual with a single stem to a height of 7'. The slender leaves, 2–3" long and ¼–½" wide, are alternate along the stem and hairy. The flower heads are small, numerous, and up to ¼" long. There are 20–40 white ray flowers surrounding 8–28 disk flowers.

Bloom Season: Summer–fall

Habitat/Range: Common in upland prairies, sand prairies, banks of streams and rivers, pastures, fallow fields, crop fields, and along roadsides; found throughout the prairie region.

Comments: Native Americans and early settlers boiled the leaves and drank the liquid to treat dysentery. Native Americans also used the tops in their sauna bath, sprinkling them on the hot rocks. An oil obtained by distilling the plant has been used to treat diarrhea, hemorrhoids, and pulmonary problems. The pollen is an irritant to some hay fever sufferers, and the plant can cause skin irritation.

DAISY FLEABANE
Erigeron strigosus
Aster family (Asteraceae)

Description: An annual or rarely biennial plant, with stems to 2½' tall, with small, daisy-like flowers. The stems have scattered hairs lying flat against the stem. Leaves are narrow, less than 1" wide; the basal leaves are toothed and on stalks, and the stem leaves are alternate, without teeth, and stalkless. The flowers are in spreading clusters at the top of branched stems. The flower heads are about 1" across, with over 40 white, thread-like, ray flowers surrounding a yellow center of densely packed disk flowers.

Bloom Season: Mid-spring–early fall

Habitat: Common in dry to mesic prairies, pastures, old fields, and along roadsides; found throughout the prairie region.

Comments: A closely related species, annual fleabane (*Erigeron annuus*), differs by having spreading, rigid hairs on the stem and wider, sharply toothed leaves; it occurs in more disturbed prairies, fields, and pastures. Annual fleabane was used by the Lakota to make tea to treat children who had sore mouths and adults who had difficulty urinating.

TALL BONESET
Eupatorium altissimum
Aster family (Asteraceae)

Description: Hairy plants, 3–6' tall, with a single stem that branches toward the top. The opposite leaves are narrowly tapering at the base and typically stalkless. The leaves are up to 5" long and 1½" wide, with 3 prominent veins along the length of the blade and a few widely spaced small teeth on the upper half of the leaf. Narrow, flattish clusters of flower heads branch at the top of the stem. Each flower head has 5–7 white tubular flowers, each about ⅛" wide.

Bloom Season: Late summer–fall

Habitat/Range: Common in prairies, hill prairies, savannas, pastures, old fields, and roadsides; found throughout the prairie region.

Comments: The genus, *Eupatorium*, is named for the Greek Mithridates Eupator, king of Pontus from about 120–63 BC. There are up to about 60 species in this genus worldwide.

COMMON BONESET
Eupatorium perfoliatum
Aster family (Asteraceae)

Description: A plant up to 4' tall, with noticeable spreading hairs on the stem and leaves. The leaves are up to 8" long and opposite, with their bases joining and circling the stem. Infrequently, some plants will have leaves in whorls of 3 rather than opposite. The leaves taper toward the end, and the margins are toothed. The dome-shaped flower clusters have white flower heads each about ¼" tall that contain 9–23 small disk flowers but no ray flowers.

Bloom Season: Midsummer–fall

Habitat/Range: Common in wet prairies, moist depressions of upland prairies, marshes, along streams, and moist roadsides; found throughout the prairie region.

Comments: Early settlers called boneset "Indian sage" because it was widely used by Native Americans, who considered it a panacea for all ills, aches, and pains. The settlers' use of the name "boneset" is confusing, because it refers to its use in treating flu rather than in treating bones (a flu that caused severe body aches was called a "breakbone fever").

LATE BONESET
Eupatorium serotinum
Aster family (Asteraceae)

Description: Plants up to 4' tall, densely short-hairy in the upper part, with opposite leaves that are coarsely toothed along the margins. The leaves are 5" long and 2" wide, widest near the base, tapering to long pointed tips, and stalks ⅜–1¼" long. There are numerous branched flower clusters near the top. Each flower head is about ⅛" wide, with 9–15 white tubular disk flowers.

Bloom Season: Midsummer–fall

Habitat/Range: Occasional in dry prairies, hill prairies, pastures, old fields, roadsides, and disturbed areas; found throughout the prairie region.

Comments: The species name *serotinum* is Latin for "late" (flowering).

OLD PLAINSMAN
Hymenopappus scabiosaeus
Aster family (Asteraceae)

Description: A biennial plant with stems up to 5' tall and freely branching near the top. The stems are nearly smooth to woolly. Leaves are alternate, stalked, up to 6" long, up to 3" wide, and finely divided into segments, giving them a feathery appearance. Flowers are numerous, with globular-shaped flower heads about ¾" across containing several creamy white disk flowers; ray flowers are absent.

Bloom Season: Mid-spring–midsummer

Habitat/Range: Common on dry prairies, rocky prairies, and sandy areas; found in the western part of the prairie region from Nebraska to Texas, Missouri, and Arkansas; also introduced in Illinois and Indiana.

Comments: Old plainsman is an unusual name for a wildflower, but its woolly appearance and occurrence in dry, open prairies in the western prairie region must have inspired someone to give it that evocative title.

WHITE UPLAND ASTER
Oligoneuron album
Aster family (Asteraceae)

Description: Slender, branching plants to 2' tall. The leaves are narrow, alternate, and widely spaced along the stem. The lower leaves are up to 8" long and ½" wide, often with 3 fine veins running along the length of the leaf. The flower heads form an open, flat-topped cluster, with each head about ¾" across, up to 25 white, petal-like ray flowers, and a pale yellow central disk.

Bloom Season: Midsummer–fall

Habitat/Range: Occasional in dry prairies, hill prairies, pastures, railroads, and roadsides; found in the southern and northwestern prairie region; local and scattered elsewhere.

Comments: White upland aster is now considered to be more closely related to goldenrods because it has been found to hybridize with them.

SWEET EVERLASTING
Pseudognaphalium obtusifolium
Aster family (Asteraceae)

Description: An annual to biennial plant, up to 2½' tall, with felt-like hairs on the stems and undersides of leaves that give it a whitish cast. The leaves are alternate, narrow, up to 4" long and ½" wide, green on the top, white below, and lacking teeth along the margins. Numerous small flower heads occur on branches near the top. Each flower head is about ¼" tall, with white papery bracts surrounding a narrow tubular head of yellowish-white disk flowers.

Bloom Season: Midsummer–fall

Habitat/Range: Common in prairies, degraded prairies, old fields, pastures, and roadsides in the western half of the prairie region and scattered in the eastern half.

Comments: Dried plants have a maple or balsam fragrance. Pillows filled with dried flowers were used to quiet coughing. Plants laid in drawers and wardrobes kept away moths. Meskwaki burned sweet everlasting as a smudge to restore consciousness or to treat insanity. Other tribes used it for colds, fever, and other infirmities. When chewed, it increases saliva flow.

WILD QUININE
Parthenium integrifolium
Aster family (Asteraceae)

Description: The sometimes-branched stems are smooth in the lower portion, rough, with a few hairs in the upper portion, and up to 3' tall. The basal leaves are up to 8" long and 4" wide and taper into long stalks; the stem leaves are alternate, smaller, lacking stalks, hairy, and toothed along the margin. The flowers are numerous in flat-topped or slightly rounded clusters. Each individual flower head is ⅓" wide, with 5 tiny, petal-like ray flowers with stamens that surround a thick head of sterile disk flowers.

Bloom Season: Late spring–summer

Habitat/Range: Common in dry to mesic prairies and savannas; found throughout the prairie region, except for the northwestern part.

Comments: This plant is also known as American feverfew. The flowering tops of wild quinine were once used for intermittent fevers, such as malaria. This plant served as a substitute when the tropical supply of quinine from the bark of the cinchona tree was cut off during World War I. The roots were used as a diuretic for kidney and bladder ailments. A close relative, also known as wild quinine (*Parthenium hispidum*), has somewhat shorter stems with noticeable spreading rough hairs, and long hairs on the lower surfaces of leaves. Found in dry prairies and savannas—except for the eastern one-fourth of the prairie region.

ROUGH WHITE LETTUCE
Prenanthes aspera
Aster family (Asteraceae)

Description: Tall, slender plants, up to 6'
in height, with unbranched, hairy leaves and
stems, and milky sap. The leaves are alternate,
up to 4" long, 1¾" wide, and somewhat toothed
along the margins. The lower leaves are stalked,
whereas the upper leaves are smaller and lack
stalks, with the leaf bases often clasping the
stem. The flowers are clustered along the upper
portion of the stem. Each cylindrical flower
head is up to ¾" tall, with 10–14 creamy white,
fragrant flowers. Each petal-like ray flower has
5 small teeth at the tip.

Bloom Season: Summer–early fall

Habitat/Range: Occasional in prairies and
savannas; found throughout the prairie region.

Comments: Also known as *Nabalus albus*. One
feature that easily distinguishes rough white
lettuce from glaucous white lettuce is that the
former has basal and lowermost stem leaves,
usually withered or absent by flowering time,
while the latter has basal leaves persisting at
flowering. The Choctaw made a tea of the roots
and tops to increase urine flow and to relieve
pain. The bitter roots of this plant were once
used to treat snakebite; hence, its other name,
"rattlesnake root."

FLAT-TOPPED ASTER
Doellingeria umbellata
Aster family (Asteraceae)

Description: Plants, usually with one stem,
are up to 5' tall, with mostly hairless stems.
The leaves are alternate along the stem, up
to 3" (and rarely, 6") long, less than 1½" wide,
broadest at the middle, with toothless margins.
Flower heads are numerous at the ends of
branches forming a nearly flat-topped crown.
Each flower head is about 1" across, with 4–12
white, petal-like ray flowers surrounding a
yellow disk.

Bloom Season: Midsummer–fall

Habitat/Range: Occasional in moist to wet
areas, including wet depressions and low
thickets in prairies; found throughout the prairie
range, except for the southwestern portion.

Comments: *Doellingeria* is a genus of flowering
plants in the aster family. It contains species
formerly included in aster, but now considered
to be a distinct genus. It was formerly known as
Aster umbellatus.

HEATH ASTER
Symphyotrichum ericoides
Aster family (Asteraceae)

Description: A low, compact plant, up to 3' tall, with very leafy branches. The leaves are alternate, small, narrow, pointed, smooth along the edges, and less than 2" long and ¼" wide. The branches have numerous flower heads, with each flower head on a short stalk. The stalks have several small, leaf-like bracts. Flower heads are about ½" wide, with up to 20 white, petal-like ray flowers surrounding a small yellow disk.

Bloom Season: Late summer–fall

Habitat/Range: Scattered to common in prairies, hill prairies, pastures, old fields, and along roadsides; found throughout the prairie region.

Comments: Heath aster can commonly be found growing together in clumps, giving it a bushy appearance, with densely packed and overlapping flowers that resemble a heath or heather shrub.

TALL WHITE ASTER
Symphyotrichum lanceolatum
Aster family (Asteraceae)

Description: A plant usually appearing in colonies connected by long, slender, branched rhizomes. Stems are up to 5' tall, with sparse to moderate hairs toward the tips of branches. The leaves are alternate, up to 6" long and 1½" wide, narrow, tapering to a tip, and sometimes irregularly toothed along the leaf margin. The flower heads are in leafy clusters at the top of the plant. Each flower head is about 1" wide, with 20–45 white, petal-like ray flowers surrounding a yellow disk.

Bloom Season: Midsummer–fall

Habitat/Range: Moist depressions in upland prairies, wet prairies, and along streams; common throughout the prairie region.

Comments: The Zuni people used this plant to treat wounds and nosebleeds. The Iroquois used it to treat fever.

HAIRY ASTER
Symphyotrichum pilosum
Aster family (Asteraceae)

Description: A widely branched, spreading aster to a length of 4', with many thin, needle-like alternate leaves along the upper stems and flowering branches. The basal leaves are up to 4" long and usually die back before the flowers emerge. The stem leaves are alternate, thin, and needle-like. There are usually many flower heads scattered along the side branches and upper stems. The flower heads are numerous, about ½" wide, with 15–30 white, petal-like ray flowers and a central yellow disk with 20 or more disk flowers.

Bloom Season: Late summer–fall

Habitat/Range: Common in disturbed or overgrazed prairies, savannas, banks of streams and rivers, old fields, and roadsides; found throughout the prairie region.

Comments: Several Native American tribes thought the smoke from burning aster plants was helpful in reviving a person who had fainted. Some tribes brewed a tea of aster plants for headaches. A close relative, small-headed aster (*Symphyotrichum parviceps*), has shorter flower heads about ¼–⅜" across and fewer than 13 disk flowers. It occupies similar habitat and range with the hairy aster but is less common.

SPRING FORGET-ME-NOT
Myosotis verna
Borage family (Boraginaceae)

Description: An annual or sometimes biennial plant, ½–1½" tall, with stems and leaves densely covered with both spreading and appressed hairs. Leaves are alternate, stalkless, with the basal leaves withering away by flowering time. Each leaf is up to 2" long and ⅓" wide, with the margins and surfaces densely hairy. The flowers are at the tips of branching stems, stalked, with each cluster tightly curled at the tip, with flowers opening in succession as the tip unfurls and elongates. Each flower is about ⅛" wide, with 5 white, spreading lobes.

Bloom Season: Late spring–early summer

Habitat/Range: Common in wet, mesic, and dry prairies, sand prairies, savannas, and open, disturbed areas; found throughout the prairie region, but is less common in the northwestern part.

Comments: Also known as early scorpiongrass, which refers to the tight curling of the flower cluster similar to the tail of a scorpion.

MARBLESEED
Onosmodium molle
Borage family (Boraginaceae)

Description: A hairy-stemmed plant up to 4'
tall, with numerous leaves along the stem. The
leaves are alternate, hairy, and narrow, about
5" long and ½" wide. Both the upper and lower
leaf surfaces are densely hairy. The flowers are
tightly coiled at the ends of the upper branches,
with flowers opening in succession as the tip
unfurls and elongates. The tube-like flowers
are dull white to greenish white, each about ½"
long, with 5 lobes.

Bloom Season: Mid-spring to early summer

Habitat/Range: Occasional in mesic to dry
prairies, hill prairies, savannas, and pastures;
found throughout the prairie region.

Comments: Also known as *Onosmodium
bejariense*. Marbleseed is named for the hard,
white nutlet or seed. Another common name,
false gromwell (meaning "gritty meal"), refers
to its resemblance to nutlets of the genus
Lithospermum.

SPRING CRESS
Cardamine bulbosa
Mustard family (Brassicaceae)

Description: A smooth, sparingly branched
plant to 18" tall. The leaves at the base are
round, up to 2½" long, on long stalks, and
usually withered by flowering time. The stem
leaves are scattered, mostly without stalks, up
to 2" long and 1" wide, longer than broad, and
irregularly toothed. The flowers are small, about
½" wide when fully open, white, 4-petaled, and
appear in clusters at the end of a stalk.

Bloom Season: Spring–early summer

Habitat/Range: Occasional along banks of
prairie streams; found in the eastern two-thirds
of the prairie region.

Comments: Pioneers used the young shoots
and leaves of spring cress to give a peppery-
pungent taste to salads, and as cooked greens.
The base of the stem and the roots were used
as a mild horseradish.

HEDGE BINDWEED
Calystegia sepium
Morning glory family (Convolvulaceae)

Discussion: A twining vine that creeps along the ground or climbs, with smooth, branching stems up to 9' long. The long-stalked leaves, up to 4" long, are alternate along the stem and triangular, with 2 squarish lobes at the base. The long-stalked flowers arise singly from leaf axils. The flowers are funnel-shaped, large, up to 2½" across, and white to pink in color.

Bloom Season: Late spring–fall

Habitat/Range: Disturbed portions of upland prairies, margins of wet areas, pastures, fencerows, and roadsides; found throughout the prairie region.

Comments: On sunny days the flowers close by midday. The pulpy roots have historically been used as a purgative (a medicine stronger than a laxative); also used to treat jaundice and gallbladder ailments. A similar species, low bindweed (*Calystegia spithamaea*), differs by having shorter, finely hairy stems, up to 2' long, short leaf stalks, and heart-shaped leaf bases. Uncommon in prairies and open woods; found in the eastern part of the prairie range.

DODDER
Cuscuta spp. (several species)
Morning glory family (Convolvulaceae)

Description: Leafless annual plants, with stringy, orange stems that twine around and over other plants. Because dodder lacks green chlorophyll, which is needed to produce food from sunlight, these parasitic plants attach to a host plant with special roots called "haustoria" that penetrate the host plant's stem and absorb its nutrients. The flowers appear in dense clusters scattered along the stems. Each flower is small, about ¼" across, with 5 spreading white lobes.

Bloom Season: Summer–fall

Habitat/Range: Occasional in upland prairies, wet prairies, stream banks, fields, and along railroad tracks; occurs throughout the prairie region.

Comments: There are several species of dodder throughout the prairie region. All are very difficult to identify. Most dodder species have specific host plants, such as members of the aster family, including goldenrods, asters, sunflowers, ragweeds, and fleabanes; also milkweeds, penstemons, smartweeds, and others. A yellow dye can be made from dodders.

WILD POTATO VINE
Ipomoea pandurata
Morning glory family (Convolvulaceae)

Discussion: A trailing or climbing vine 10–15' long. The leaves are alternate, heart-shaped, smooth, and up to 6" long and nearly as wide. The leaf veins, margins, and leaf stalks are often purplish. There are 1–7 flowers on long stalks that emerge at the junction of the leaf and stem. The flowers are funnel-shaped, about 3" wide, with red or purple centers. The flowers close about midday.

Bloom Season: Late spring–summer

Habitat/Range: Occasional in mostly disturbed prairies, edges of prairies bordering woodlands, fencerows, and pastures; found throughout the prairie region, except for the northwestern portion.

Comments: The large root, which can weigh over 20 pounds, was used as a food source by Native Americans. The root was heated and applied to the skin to treat rheumatism and "hard tumors." Root tea was used by early settlers as a diuretic and a laxative and as a treatment for coughs, asthma, and the early stages of tuberculosis. Because the root is a strong laxative when eaten raw, it was often boiled like a potato to neutralize its effect before consuming. The taste is said to be somewhat bitter.

HOGWORT
Croton capitatus
Spurge family (Euphorbiaceae)

Description: Annual plants, up to 3' tall but much shorter on dry, thin soil, with a dense, white, woolly layer of tiny, star-shaped hairs on the stems and leaves. The leaves are alternate, stalked, up to 4" long and 1" wide, smooth along the margins, and with rounded bases. The flowers are in short, compact clusters near the ends of branches. Tiny male and female flowers are in each cluster. The female flowers lack petals, whereas the male flowers have 5 tiny, white petals.

Bloom Season: Summer–fall

Habitat/Range: Frequent in often disturbed upland prairies, sand prairies, and glades, as well as pastures, idle fields, and other disturbed areas; found in the southern part of the prairie region.

Comments: The oil in hogwort is toxic, and cattle have been poisoned from eating hay containing the plants.

PRAIRIE TEA
Croton monanthogynus
Spurge family (Euphorbiaceae)

Description: An annual plant, up to 2' tall and 3' wide, but much smaller on dry, thin soil, with a dense, white layer of tiny, star-shaped hairs on the stems and leaves. The leaves are alternate, stalked, up to 2" long and ¾" wide, smooth along the margins, and with rounded bases. The tiny flowers are in short, compact clusters in the axils of the upper leaves. There are both male and female flowers in each cluster. The female flowers lack petals, whereas the male flowers have 5 tiny, white petals.

Bloom Season: Summer–fall

Habitat/Range: Frequent in dry, often disturbed prairies, open woods, and glades, as well as pastures, idle fields, and other disturbed areas; found in the southern half of the prairie region.

Comments: As the common name implies, a leaf tea was made from various species of crotons by Native Americans. The Lakota, Kiowa, and Zuni made a tea to relieve stomach pains. Croton oil was rarely used in medicine in the United States, but it was used medicinally in Europe. Croton oil has now been reported to be a carcinogen. It can also cause skin dermatitis, and is no longer used in Europe. Twenty drops of the oil is considered lethal.

FLOWERING SPURGE
Euphorbia corollata
Spurge family (Euphorbiaceae)

Discussion: Slender, erect plants, with a pale bluish or yellowish-green cast, white, milky sap, and widely branching flower clusters. The narrow, smooth-edged leaves are alternate on the stem but sometimes opposite or whorled near the flower clusters. The flower heads are numerous, each about ½" across, with 5 chalky, white false petals surrounding a cup of tiny, yellow male flowers and a single female flower. The fruit is a 3-parted ball on a tiny stalk.

Bloom Season: Mid-spring–fall

Habitat/Range: Common in dry and mesic prairies, as well as in old fields, pastures, roadsides, and other disturbed sites; found throughout the prairie region, except for the northern part.

Comments: Native Americans used a leaf or root tea to treat chronic constipation, rheumatism, and diabetes. The root was mashed and applied to the skin to treat snakebite. The flowers, fruits, and leaves are eaten by wild turkeys. The seeds are eaten by greater prairie-chickens, bobwhite quail, and mourning doves. White-tailed deer feed upon the plants in spring and summer.

TOOTHED SPURGE
Euphorbia dentata
Spurge family (Euphorbiaceae)

Description: An annual plant, up to 2' tall, with hairy stems and milky sap. The leaves are opposite but sometimes alternate toward the upper nodes, stalked, ½–3" long and ¼–1½" wide, with toothed margins. Flowers are small cups emerging in clusters at the tops of stems, with numerous tiny male flowers, each with a single stamen and a single larger female flower, with a stalked pistil. There are 1–2 green, kidney-shaped glands around the lip of each cup. Sepals and petals are lacking, but leaves just below the flowers are light green to white at their base. The fruit is stalked and 3-lobed, with each lobe bearing a bumpy white, brown, or dark-gray seed.

Bloom Season: Summer–fall

Habitat/Range: Locally common in dry, rocky prairies, hill prairies, sand prairies, pastures, and open disturbed areas; found from Kansas to Illinois to Ohio, and southward; uncommon elsewhere in the prairie region.

Comments: Like other plants in the *Euphorbia* genus, the sap can be irritating to the skin and eyes. A related species, painted leaf—also known as fire-on-the-mountain (*Euphorbia cyathophora*)—differs by having alternate leaves and attractive red or yellow patches near the bases of the upper leaves; found in disturbed soils across the prairie region, except for North Dakota and northern Minnesota.

SNOW-ON-THE-PRAIRIE
Euphorbia bicolor
Spurge family (Euphorbiaceae)

Description: An annual plant from 1–4' tall, with white, milky sap. The leaves are alternate, stalkless, slender, 2–4" long, ½–1" wide, and are green and edged with a narrow band of white. The lower leaves are solid green, grow close to the stem, and are 1–1¼" long. The flower heads are numerous, each about ½" wide, with 5 white, petal-like structures surrounding a single female flower and several smaller male flowers.

Bloom Season: Late summer–fall

Habitat/Range: Common in dry prairies, open woods, pastures, and disturbed ground; found in the prairie region from Oklahoma and southwest, and Arkansas southward.

Comments: Similar to snow-on-the-mountain, when the stem is broken, it exudes a white, milky sap that can be irritating to the skin of some people. Snow-on-the-prairie can occur in dense stands that, from a distance, can appear as its namesake.

SNOW-ON-THE-MOUNTAIN
Euphorbia marginata
Spurge family (Euphorbiaceae)

Description: An annual plant with finely hairy stems up to 3' tall, with white, milky sap. The leaves are alternate and up to 4" long and 2½" wide, stalkless, with rounded bases and pointed tips. Toward the top of the stem, there is a whorl of leaves under 3–5 leafy branches, which are themselves branched. Leaves on the flower branches are often densely clustered and have broad white to sometimes pinkish bands along the margins. The flower heads are less than ½" wide, with 5 white petal-like structures surrounding a single female flower and several smaller male flowers.

Bloom Season: Summer–fall

Habitat/Range: Common in dry prairies, hill prairies, also pastures, railroads, and roadsides; mainly in the western part of the prairie region.

Comments: When the stem is broken, it exudes a white, milky sap that can be irritating to the skin of some people. This spurge can spread across large areas, often seeming to blanket the landscape with what appears from a distance to be snow; hence, the origin of the common name. The Lakota made a tea for mothers with insufficient breast milk. This may have been suggested by the plant's milky sap. The Lakota used crushed leaves as a liniment (a liquid or semi-liquid) for swellings.

CANADIAN MILK VETCH
Astragalus canadensis
Bean family (Fabaceae)

Description: Sturdy plants to 5' tall, with compound leaves alternating along the stem. The compound leaves are divided into 11–31 leaflets that are narrowly oval, smooth along the edges, and each 1–1½" long and ⅜–½" wide. The creamy white, ½" long flowers are crowded along a stalk that emerges above the leaves. Each flower has a hood-like upper petal over 2 smaller side petals flanking a lower lip. The pods are numerous, crowded, erect, and up to ¾" long.

Bloom Season: Summer

Habitat/Range: Occasional in prairies, hill prairies, sand prairies, prairie/woodland edges, moist thickets, and along streams; found throughout the prairie region.

Comments: Young Omaha-Ponca boys used the stalks with persistent dry pods as rattles in games where they imitated the tribal dances. Milk vetches, in general, had a reputation for increasing a cow's or goat's milk yield. A similar-looking but much smaller species, lotus milk vetch (*Astragalus lotiflorus*), is only 3–6" tall, but also has compound leaves and creamy white flowers. This plant is frequently occurring in hill prairies and sand prairies, and it is found on the western edge of the prairie region and westward.

41

WHITE WILD INDIGO
Baptisia alba var. *macrophylla*
Bean family (Fabaceae)

Description: A smooth, shrubby-looking plant up to 5' tall, often with a thin, white, waxy coating on the stems and leaves. The branched stems have alternate leaves that are each divided into 3 leaflets, 1–3" long, round at the tip and tapering at the base. Stems emerge above the leaves with showy white flowers, each about 1" long, having the structure of similar flowers in the bean family. The black seed pods are thick, pointed, and less than 2" long.

Bloom Season: Late spring–midsummer

Habitat/Range: Common in mesic and dry prairies, savannas, stream edges, fields, and roadsides; found throughout the prairie region.

Comments: These deep-rooted plants can persist in converted pastures and fields long after native prairie has been destroyed. Plants in the genus *Baptisia* have been used medicinally by Native Americans and early settlers as a tea for internal cleansing and externally for treating skin wounds. White wild indigo has been known to poison cattle if eaten in large quantities.

SESSILE-LEAVED TICK TREFOIL
Desmodium sessilifolium
Bean family (Fabaceae)

Description: Plants up to 4' tall, hairy, and typically unbranched below the flowers. Leaves are widely spaced along the stem, alternate, compound, with 3 narrow leaflets. Each leaf is stalkless, with the central leaflet 1–3" long and ¼–½" wide and slightly longer than the two side leaflets. Flowers are numerous, small, white to pinkish, about ¼" long, and having the structure of similar flowers in the bean family. The seed pods are flattened, hairy, about 1" long, and carrying 2–4 smooth brownish seeds.

Bloom Season: Summer

Habitat/Range: Common in upland prairies, sand prairies, savannas; also old fields, fencerows, and along roadsides; found across the prairie region but absent in the northern part.

Comments: Like other tick trefoils, the seeds are eaten by bobwhite quail, wild turkey, and mammals such as deer, rabbits, groundhogs, and white-footed mice. Also like other tick trefoils, the seed pods are covered with hooked hairs that easily stick to the fur of mammals and the clothing of humans, which helps their dispersal.

WHITE PRAIRIE CLOVER
Dalea candida
Bean family (Fabaceae)

Description: A finely leaved plant having a single or few stems arising from a common base, up to 2' tall. The leaves are smooth, divided into typically 7 narrow leaflets, each up to 1¼" long and less than ¼" wide. The flowers are crowded into cylindrical spikes 1–3" long at the tips of the stems. The small flowers, each about ¼" long, bloom first at the bottom and progress upward along the column, forming a skirt of white petals.

Bloom Season: Late May–summer

Habitat/Range: Found in high-quality mesic and dry prairies throughout the prairie range.

Comments: White prairie clover is sensitive to disturbance, especially grazing; its presence, in addition to that of other highly selective plants, is an indicator of high-quality habitat. Some Native Americans used the leaves for tea. The Ponca chewed the root for its pleasant taste. The Pawnee used the tough, elastic stems to make brooms. They also drank root tea to keep away disease. A similar species, round-headed prairie clover (*Dalea multiflora*), has round, white flower heads, about ½" in diameter; occurs on dry prairies and brushy hillsides; found in the very southwestern part of the prairie region and westward.

ILLINOIS BUNDLE FLOWER
Desmanthus illinoensis
Bean family (Fabaceae)

Description: Smooth, bushy plants up to 5' tall. The angled stem supports alternate, highly dissected leaves with numerous paired leaflets that appear fern-like. At the axil of the leaves, slender stalks emerge that support small, round flower clusters about ½" across, with each flower containing 5 small, white petals. The fine, long stamens projecting from each flower give the cluster a fuzzy appearance. The fruit is a round cluster up to 1½" across, with twisted or curved pods, each one containing 2–6 smooth seeds.

Bloom Season: Summer

Habitat/Range: Common and occasionally weedy in disturbed prairies, rocky prairies, along prairie edges, pastures, and roadsides; found in the western and central prairie region, becoming rare and local eastward.

Comments: The children of some Native American tribes used the dried seed pods as rattles. The boiled leaves were used by the Pawnee as a wash to relieve itching. The leaves and seeds are considered an important source of protein for wildlife and livestock.

ROUND-HEADED BUSH CLOVER
Lespedeza capitata
Bean family (Fabaceae)

Description: A slender, unbranched legume that grows to 5' tall and is covered with fine, silvery hairs. The leaves are alternate along the stem and divided into 3 narrow leaflets. The flowers occur in dense, rounded heads up to 1½" in diameter. The flowers are less than ½" long, creamy white, with a reddish to purplish spot at the base. Each flower has an upper petal, 2 side petals, and a lower lip.

Bloom Season: Midsummer–fall

Habitat/Range: Occasional to common on prairies, hill prairies, sand prairies, and savannas; found throughout the prairie region, except for the northern portion.

Comments: The Comanche used the leaves to make a tea. The Omaha and Ponca moistened one end of a short piece of the stem so it would stick to the skin, then lit the other end and allowed it to burn down to the skin. This was used to treat sharp pain associated with nerves and rheumatism. The leaves and seeds are eaten by wild turkeys. The seeds are eaten by a wide variety of wildlife. A related species, prairie bush clover (*Lespedeza leptostachya*), is federally listed as a threatened species and occurs in Minnesota, Illinois, Iowa, and Wisconsin. The plant has open flower clusters and much narrower leaflets.

BUFFALO CLOVER
Trifolium reflexum
Bean family (Fabaceae)

Description: Plants are annual but sometimes biennial, with low sprawling stems up to 1' long. The alternate leaves are on stalks, up to 2½" long, with 2 prominent stipules at the base of each stalk where it joins the stem. Leaves are divided into 3 oval leaflets, each ¾–1" long and ⅓–¾" wide, with minutely toothed edges. The flowers are clustered in a ball shape, about 1" across and on stalks ¾–2½" long. Each flower is creamy white to pale yellow and about ½" long, with a spreading upper petal, and 2 smaller side petals that surround a keel-like lower lip.

Bloom Season: Late spring–midsummer

Habitat/Range: Uncommon to rare in mesic to dry prairies, savannas, and open woodlands; found in the southern part of the prairie region.

Comments: Populations of buffalo clover seem to respond to disturbances such as fires and logging; they also appear along logging roads, foot trails, and, once, probably along bison trails—hence, the common name. Without continued disturbance, they usually disappear after a few years, although the seeds lay dormant in the soil until the next disturbance.

PRAIRIE BLUE-EYED GRASS
Sisyrinchium campestre
Iris family (Iridaceae)

Description: Small, clump-forming plants, with stems not branching at the top, up to 12" tall, with pointed, upright, grass-like leaves. The flower stems are flat, about ⅛" wide, with 2 narrow wings, and typically longer than the leaves. Several flowers, each on a slender stalk, emerge from a long-pointed, leaf-like bract at the top of the stem. Each flower is white or light to dark blue (see p. 211 for blue version), about ½" across, with a yellow center, and 3 sepals and 3 petals, which all look like petals. The tips of the sepals and petals vary, from rounded with a hair-like point, to notched, to shallowly toothed.

Bloom Season: Mid-spring–early summer

Habitat/Range: Common in dry upland prairies, savannas, glades, and rocky, open woods; found throughout the prairie region, but absent in North Dakota, and east of Illinois.

Comments: A similar species, eastern blue-eyed grass (*Sisyrinchium albidum*), has 3–4 leaf-like bracts surrounding a single flower cluster at the top of the stem. Flowers are white or pale violet. Habitat is similar to prairie blue-eyed grass; it is found in the eastern half of the prairie region.

AMERICAN BUGLEWEED
Lycopus americanus
Mint family (Lamiaceae)

Description: Plants up to 2' tall, with square stems. The leaves are opposite, up to 3½" long, with the leaf cut into coarse lobes or teeth along the margins. Flowers are in dense stands surrounding the stem at the bases of the leaves. Each flower is white, less than ¼" long, and with 4 lobes. This plant does not have the aromatic foliage often found with many other mints.

Bloom Season: Early summer–fall

Habitat/Range: Common in wet prairies, moist swales of upland prairies, margins of wet, marshy areas, fallow fields, and along roadsides; found throughout the prairie region.

Comments: The plant has been used as an astringent, mild sedative, and treatment for hyperthyroidism. It is also used in the treatment of coughs. Because the leaves are bitter-tasting, they are often not eaten by mammalian herbivores. The plant is also called common water horehound.

HAIRY MOUNTAIN MINT
Pycnanthemum pilosum
Mint family (Lamiaceae)

Description: Aromatic plants with square stems that are moderately to densely hairy and up to 4' tall. The numerous leaves are opposite, up to 3" long and ¾" wide, with bases rounded and stalkless. There are often small, leafy branches emerging from where the main leaves join the stem. The flowers are in dense clusters near the top of a branch. Each flower is less than ¼" long, tube-shaped, and with a 3-lobed lower lip and a single upper lip. The flowers are white to pale lavender, with small purple spots.

Bloom Season: Midsummer–fall

Habitat/Range: Occasional in mesic to dry prairies, savannas, old fields, pastures, and roadsides; found throughout the prairie region, except for the northwestern portion.

Comments: Like other mountain mints, the numerous flowers are good nectar sources for a variety of bees, wasps, flies, beetles, moths, and butterflies.

SLENDER MOUNTAIN MINT
Pycnanthemum tenuifolium
Mint family (Lamiaceae)

Description: Aromatic plants with smooth, square stems growing to a height of 3'. The stem, with numerous pairs of leaves, branches toward the top. The narrow, pointed leaves are up to 2" long and ¼" wide. Flower heads are densely packed, with each flower about ⅛" wide and a white to pale lavender upper lip, and a lower lip with 3 lobes. Both lips often have small purple spots.

Bloom Season: Late spring–summer

Habitat/Range: Common in mesic to dry prairies, savannas, old fields, pastures, and roadsides; found throughout the prairie region.

Comments: Native Americans used slender mountain mint, with its alluring scent, to bait mink traps and to make a tea for treating a run-down condition. The tea has been used as a seasoning in cooking.

COMMON MOUNTAIN MINT
Pycnanthemum virginianum
Mint family (Lamiaceae)

Description: Often bushy-looking plants up to 3' tall, with green or reddish square stems and scattered white hairs along the ridges. The leaves are opposite, stalkless, up to 2½" long and ½" wide, hairless, with smooth margins, a rounded base, and tapering to a pointed tip. The flowers are densely packed in flat clusters with each head about ¾" across and containing up to 50 flowers. The flowers in a head do not all flower at the same time. Each flower is about ⅛" long, tubular, with 2 lips. The upper lip has 2 lobes while the lower lip has 3 lobes. The lobes are white with purple spots. The outside of the tube is covered with fine hairs.

Bloom Season: Midsummer–fall

Habitat/Range: Frequent in mesic prairies, wet prairies, moist sand prairies, and moist open areas; found throughout the prairie region but less common in the southwestern part.

Comments: The genus *Pycnanthemum* is commonly known as mountain mint, but that is something of a misnomer because species in this group do not usually occur in mountainous habitats. Mountain mints attract many insects to its flowers, including various bees, wasps, flies, small butterflies, and beetles. The leaves are very fragrant; when crushed, they have a strong minty odor. The long bloom time, a month or more in the summer, makes it a great garden choice, especially for feeding pollinators.

COLIC ROOT
Aletris farinosa
Lily family (Liliaceae)

Description: A smooth, single-stemmed, wand-like plant, up to 2½" tall. The leaves are clustered at the base of the plant, with each strap-like leaf up to 8" long. The flowers are clustered at the top of a mostly bare stem. The white tubular flowers are about ¼" long, with 6 lobes, and covered with a rough surface.

Bloom Season: Summer

Habitat/Range: Occasional in moist, sandy prairies, sandy flats, open woods, marshes, and roadsides; found in the eastern and southern parts of the prairie region.

Comments: The outside of the flowers have an unusual rough texture, giving rise to the species name, *farinosa*, meaning "mealy." *Colic* is a Greek word meaning "relative to the colon." Colic (or cholic) is a form of pain that starts and stops abruptly. It occurs due to muscular contractions of the colon trying to relieve an obstruction by forcing content out. Native Americans used the root to treat stomach and bowel disorders, as well as rheumatism, jaundice, and lung disease. However, the fresh root is mildly poisonous.

FALSE GARLIC
Nothoscordum bivalve
Lily family (Liliaceae)

Description: A slender plant that grows from a bulb, producing leafless stems to 12" tall. The smooth, grass-like leaves that emerge from the base are long and narrow. The 5–12 fragrant flowers, each less than 1" wide, are on stalks that arise from a common point on top of the stem. There are 3 petals and 3 sepals, all about the same size, and they are white to slightly yellow in color. The 6 stamens are yellow.

Bloom Season: Spring; sometimes in fall

Habitat/Range: Common in mesic to dry prairies and open woodlands; found in the southern half of the prairie region.

Comments: Also called crow poison, the Cherokee harvested this plant to poison crows that were eating their corn. False garlic is a favorite nectar source for small butterflies, such as the falcate orangetip. This plant is related to the onion, which it resembles, but there is no characteristic onion odor.

PRAIRIE DOGTOOTH VIOLET
Erythronium mesochoreum
Lily family (Liliaceae)

Description: A single-flowering plant originating from a corm with stalks up to 4" tall. Flowering plants have a pair of flat basal leaves that are 3–6" long and 1¼" wide, with a slightly wider middle and narrowing at each end. The somewhat waxy leaves are folded along their lengths. Nonflowering plants produce only a single leaf. The white flowers are up to 1½" across, with 3 sepals and 3 petals that are similar in size and shape, and curve slightly backward when open. There are 6 large, yellow stamens.

Bloom Season: Early spring

Habitat/Range: Common in mesic to dry prairies; found in the prairie region from eastern Nebraska to Illinois and south to Texas.

Comments: The shape of the underground corm of the prairie dogtooth violet is said to resemble a dog's tooth. Native Americans used root tea for fevers, and a warm mass of leaves was applied to the skin for hard-to-heal ulcers. A similar species, white dogtooth violet (*Erythronium albidum*), has relatively flat leaves that are mottled with brown and resemble the pattern on a brown trout; hence, the other common name, white trout lily. The white sepals and petals bend strongly backward. They are mostly found in forests but sometimes occur in prairies.

STARRY FALSE SOLOMON'S SEAL
Maianthemum stellatum
Lily family (Liliaceae)

Description: The slightly zigzag stem stiffly arches to a length of up to 3'. The firm, spreading, somewhat curved leaves alternate along a smooth to finely hairy stem. Each slightly folded leaf is up to 6" long and 2" wide, with pointed tips and clasping bases, parallel veins along the length, and a slightly hairy underside. At the tip of the stem, up to 20 white, star-like flowers are arranged, each about ⅜" across, with 3 petals and 3 sepals that are similar in size and shape, and 6 yellow stamens. The fruit is a small berry, about ¼" across, that is initially green with purple stripes and ripens to a reddish-purple.

Bloom Season: Mid- to late spring

Habitat/Range: Locally frequent in open to partially shaded prairies and savannas; found across the northern two-thirds of the prairie region.

Comments: Formerly known as *Smilacena stellata*. The Paiute dried the root and pounded it into a powder; this was applied to a wound, causing blood to clot almost immediately. The roots were also used to treat stomach problems, menstrual disorders, and venereal disease. The fruit is bitter-tart but edible.

BUNCHFLOWER
Melanthium virginicum
Lily family (Liliaceae)

Description: Erect, stout plants, up to 5' tall, with long, grass-like leaves at the base, which alternate up the stem. The leaves are up to 20" long and up to 1" wide, with upper leaves being much shorter. The flowers occur along long branches at the top, up to 18" tall. Individual stalked flowers are ½–1" across, with 6 creamy white petals (3 petals and 3 sepals).

Bloom Season: Late spring–midsummer

Habitat/Range: Occasional in mesic to wet prairies and degraded remnant prairies along railroads and roadsides; found across the prairie region, except for the northwestern part.

Comments: Also known as *Veratrum virginicum*. The towering plums of white flowers are very conspicuous in open areas, making their identification from a distance very easy. The roots and stems contain alkaloids that are poisonous to livestock, and the root has been used to kill intestinal parasites. The flower turns black with age.

SOLOMON'S SEAL
Polygonatum biflorum var. *commutatum*
Lily family (Liliaceae)

Description: A gracefully arching plant with alternate leaves, it may reach to 5' in length. The stems are smooth, unbranched, and stout, supporting several leaves up to 7" long and 3" wide. The leaves are stalkless, almost clasping at the base, and have parallel veins and pale undersides. The tubular greenish-white flowers are about ¾" long, ending in 6 short lobes, and hang from slender stalks in clusters. The fruits are dark blue berries about ½" in diameter.

Bloom Season: Mid-spring–early summer

Habitat/Range: More of a woodland plant, but sometimes occurring in mesic prairies along thicket edges and streambanks; found throughout the prairie region, mostly in the eastern half.

Comments: Native Americans used the rhizome in a tea for treating internal pains. Externally, it was used as a wash for poison ivy, skin irritations, and hemorrhoids. Settlers used root tea for rheumatism, arthritis, and skin irritations. The young shoots, when boiled, are said to taste like asparagus, while the starchy rootstocks can serve as a substitute for potatoes. However, like many plants in the lily family, they are not common enough to be collected in the wild. Ruffed grouse, some songbirds, white-footed mice, and eastern wood rats are known to eat the berries.

WHITE CAMASS
Zigadenus elegans
Lily family (Liliaceae)

Description: The hairy stalk is up to 2½" tall, with grass-like leaves that are up to 12" long and less than ½" wide. The stems are often bluish-green from a white, waxy coating. Individual flowers are stalked and alternate along the upper stem. Each creamy white flower is about ½" across and composed of 6 petal-like segments. Each segment has a greenish, 2-lobed gland at the base.

Bloom Season: Early summer–midsummer

Habitat/Range: Occasional in prairies and open woods; found throughout the prairie region, except for the southern part.

Comments: All parts of white camass are poisonous, from alkaloids more toxic than strychnine. It is also known as death camass. Humans have been poisoned by mistakenly eating the bulbs, believing they were eating wild onions.

FALSE GAURA
Stenosiphon linifolius
Evening primrose family (Onagraceae)

Description: A biennial or short-lived perennial with stems up to 6' (sometimes 8') tall, with smooth and a somewhat waxy coating, at least toward the base. Basal leaves and stem leaves are stalkless, up to 3" long and ¾" wide, and smooth along the margins. The basal and lower stem leaves are usually absent at flowering time. The flowers are located on hairy, wand-like spikes. The white flowers are on stalks, with 4 reflexed sepals and 4 petals less than ¼" long.

Bloom season: Summer–fall

Habitat/Range: Occasional on prairies, especially dry rocky prairies, glades, and roadsides; found in the southwestern part of the prairie region.

Comments: Also known as *Oenothera glaucifolia*, false gaura is known to have a sweet fragrance that is especially noticeable in the evening, making it attractive to night-flying pollinators such as moths. False gaura drops its leaves during periods of drought and conducts photosynthesis in the stem. A rosette of leaves develops in the fall of the first year, and the stem arises in the second year.

WHITE LADY'S SLIPPER
Cypripedium candidum
Orchid family (Orchidaceae)

Description: Short plants, less than 1' tall, that can form large colonies. The 3–4 leaves along the stem are finely hairy, up to 6" long, 2" wide, and slightly pleated along their length. There is typically a single flower at the top of the stem in front of an erect, leaf-like bract. The flower has a broad, white "slipper" about 1" long, with two twisted greenish petals that slant downward and away from the slipper. Above and below the slipper are two greenish sepals. The petals and sepals are typically streaked purplish brown.

Bloom Season: Mid-spring–early summer

Habitat/Range: Rare in seepage areas in mesic prairies; found in the northern half of the prairie region.

Comments: With the destruction of most of its former habitat, finding the white lady's slipper is a special occasion. Fortunately, there are protected public lands where this delicate jewel of the wildflower world can still be admired.

RAGGED FRINGED ORCHID
Plantanthera lacera
Orchid family (Orchidaceae)

Description: A smooth, slender plant to about 2' tall, with 10–40 white to greenish-white flowers. The 2–5 leaves are alternating along the stem, from 3–10" long, lance-shaped, longest near the base of the stem and reduced in size upward. The flowers are less than 1" long and ½" wide, with a lip that has 3 lobes that are deeply divided into thread-like segments. The upper sepal and two upper petals are greenish and form a hood. The lateral sepals are also greenish, similar in shape, but spread outward. The spur is about ½" long.

Bloom Season: Late spring–midsummer

Habitat/Range: Occasional in mesic to dry prairies; found throughout the prairie region except for the northwestern part.

Comments: The species name, *lacera*, is Latin for "torn," in reference to the fringed lip of the flower. The fragrant flowers are pollinated primarily by moths, including noctuid moths and sphinx moths.

EASTERN PRAIRIE FRINGED ORCHID
Platanthera leucophaea
Orchid family (Orchidaceae)

Discussion: A smooth, single-stemmed orchid, growing to 2½' tall. The 3–6 leaves are alternate along the stem, up to 10" long, 1" wide, and clasp the stem. The 18–30 creamy-white flowers are located along the top of the stem. The lip of the flower is about ¾" long, with 3 lobes, each cut into narrow fringes. The upper sepal and two upper petals are creamy-white and form a hood. The lateral sepals are also creamy-white, similar in shape, but spread outward. The spur is ¾–1½" long.

Bloom Season: Early summer–midsummer

Habitat/Range: Very rare in mesic to wet prairies, sand prairies, and marshes; found in the eastern half of the prairie region.

Comments: Eastern prairie fringed orchid is listed as threatened by the US Fish and Wildlife Service under the federal Endangered Species Act. Unfortunately, this orchid has been eliminated throughout a large portion of its former range, due to plowing of many prairies and the heavy grazing of other sites by livestock. The plants emit a sweet fragrance, particularly around sunset, and are pollinated by hawk moths. The eastern prairie fringed orchid is similar to the western prairie fringed orchid, but the latter has a less-dense flower cluster, more flowers, and the flowers tend to be smaller.

WESTERN PRAIRIE FRINGED ORCHID
Platanthera praeclara
Orchid family (Orchidaceae)

Description: A smooth, single-stemmed orchid, growing to 2½' tall. The 3–6 leaves are alternate along the stem, up to 10" long, 1" wide, and clasp the stem. The flowers are in clusters along the tops of the stems, with 8–18 creamy-white flowers. The lip of the flower is about ¾–1¼" long, with 3 lobes, each cut into narrow fringes. The upper sepal and two upper petals are creamy-white and form a hood. The lateral sepals are also creamy-white, similar in shape, but spread outward. The spur is 1¼–2" long.

Bloom Season: Early summer–midsummer

Habitat/Range: Very rare in mesic to wet prairies; found in the western half of the prairie region.

Comments: Western prairie fringed orchid is listed as threatened by the US Fish and Wildlife Service under the federal Endangered Species Act. Unfortunately, this orchid has been eliminated throughout a large portion of its former range, due to plowing of many prairies and the heavy grazing of other sites by livestock. The plants emit a sweet fragrance, particularly around sunset, and are pollinated by hawk moths. The western prairie fringed orchid is similar to the eastern prairie fringed orchid, but the latter has a more-compact flower cluster, less flowers, and the flowers tend to be larger.

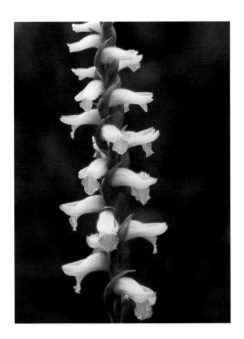 

NODDING LADIES' TRESSES
Spiranthes cernua
Orchid family (Orchidaceae)

Description: A slender orchid, up to 10" tall, with fine hairs on the stem and flowers. The 3–4 basal leaves are grass-like, up to 9" long, and often die back at the time of flowering. The upper stem leaves are reduced to scales. The white flowers are in a spiraled arrangement on the upper part of the stem. Each flower is up to ½" long, slightly nodding, with the sepals and petals forming a tube around the lip. The side sepals stay close to the flower and do not arch up and away. The mouth of the flower is sometimes light yellow. The flowers have a light vanilla-like scent.

Bloom Season: Midsummer–fall

Habitat/Range: Frequent in prairies, pastures, and old fields; found throughout the prairie region.

Comments: Important characteristics that separate nodding ladies' tresses from Great Plains Ladies' tresses are that the former has lateral sepals that do not spread upward and away from the rest of the flower. Also, the mouth of the orchid has a white to faint yellow center, and the flowers emit a weak, vanilla-like scent.

GREAT PLAINS LADY'S TRESSES
Spiranthes magnicamporum
Orchid family (Orchidaceae)

Description: A smooth, single-stemmed orchid, growing to 2½' tall. The 3–4 basal leaves are 5½" long and ½" wide, and usually die back before the flowering period. The upper stem leaves are reduced to scales. The white flowers are in a spiraled arrangement on the upper part of the stem. Each flower is up to ½" long, with the sepals and petals forming a tube around the lip. The side sepals are free to the base, spreading, the tips arching upward and angling away from the rest of the flower. The mouth of the flower is yellow to yellowish tan. The flowers have a strong vanilla-like scent.

Bloom Season: Midsummer–fall

Habitat/Range: Frequent in prairies, hill prairies, and glades; scattered throughout the prairie region.

Comments: Important characteristics that separate Great Plains lady's tresses from nodding lady's tresses are that the former has lateral sepals that spread upward and away from the rest of the flower. Also, the mouth of the orchid has a noticeable yellow center, and the flowers emit a strong vanilla-like scent.

SPRING LADY'S TRESSES
Spiranthes vernalis
Orchid family (Orchidaceae)

Description: The stem is finely hairy, up to 3' tall, with a single spiral of 30–40 flowers. The 4–6 leaves are basal, up to 10" long, and often withered at flowering time. The flowers are white, about ⅜–½" long, somewhat nodding, tubular, with 3 sepals and 3 petals. The larger lower petal has a yellowish throat.

Bloom Season: Late spring–midsummer

Habitat/Range: Uncommon in mesic to somewhat dry prairies; found throughout the prairie region, except for the northwestern part; also in old fields in the eastern part of the region.

Comments: Spring lady's tresses is the tallest and first to bloom of the lady's tresses in the prairie region. As with many other orchids, the frequency of flowering plants varies greatly from year to year. In general, often after flowering, orchids may not appear again for 2 or more years, mainly due to the large amount of energy it takes to produce flowers and fruits and the time it takes to replenish food reserves.

FOXGLOVE BEARDTONGUE
Penstemon digitalis
Plantain family (Plantaginaceae)

Description: A sturdy, somewhat glossy plant with unbranched stems to a height of 4'. The basal leaves are on long stalks and arranged in a rosette. The stem leaves are up to 4" long, opposite, without stalks, with their edges curved inward and toothed. The flowers are on spreading, branched stalks at the top of the stem. The white tubular flowers are ¾–1¼" long, often hairy on the outside, with 2 upper lobes and 3 lower lobes. There are purple lines running down the white throat of the flower.

Bloom Season: Mid-spring–midsummer

Habitat/Range: Common in mesic prairies, sand prairies, savannas, pastures, and roadsides; found throughout the prairie region.

Comments: The common name "foxglove" and the species name *digitalis* refer to the similarity of the flower to *Digitalis purpurea*, the foxglove from England used to treat ailments.

PALE BEARDTONGUE
Penstemon pallidus
Plantain family (Plantaginaceae)

Description: Slender, unbranched, hairy-stemmed plants to 2' tall, with opposite leaves that tend to point upward. The leaves are firm, pale, and velvety-hairy on both sides, with the margins randomly toothed. The leaves partly clasp the stem at the base and taper to a point on the end. The flowers are in branched clusters at the end of the stalk. Each tubular flower is about 1" long and marked inside with fine purple lines. The flower has a 2-lobed upper lip and 3-lobed lower lip. At the mouth of the flower is a large, sterile stamen with bright yellow hairs.

Bloom Season: Mid-spring–midsummer

Habitat/Range: Common in prairies, savannas, old fields, and roadsides; found throughout the prairie region, except for the western part.

Comments: The genus name *Penstemon* comes from the Greek words *penta*, meaning "5," and *stemon*, meaning "stamen," in reference to each flower having 5 stamens (4 are fertile, and 1 is sterile). The species name *pallida* comes from Latin meaning "pale," in reference to the pale white flowers and pale green leaves. Penstemons are called "beardtongue" because the unusual sterile stamen contained in the mouth of each flower has a tuft of small hairs.

WHITE WAND BEARDTONGUE
Penstemon tubaeflorus
Plantain family (Plantaginaceae)

Description: Smooth, single-stemmed plants to 3' tall, with narrow, opposite leaves. The stem leaves are up to 5" long and less than 1" wide, with broadly rounded bases, pointed tips, and lacking teeth along the margins. The flowers are clustered around the stem in tiers. Each tubular flower is up to 1" long, with sticky hairs on the inside, a relatively flat-faced opening, and a 2-lobed upper lip and a 3-lobed lower lip.

Bloom Season: Mid-spring–midsummer

Habitat/Range: Occasional in mesic to dry prairies, savannas, and roadsides; found throughout the prairie region, except for the northwestern part, and rare east of Missouri.

Comments: Native Americans used plants of this genus as a remedy for chills and fever. To treat toothache, they chewed the root pulp and placed it in the painful cavity.

CULVER'S ROOT
Veronicastrum virginicum
Plantain family (Plantaginaceae)

Description: A tall, graceful plant growing to a height of 6', with branching flower stems that resemble a candelabra. The leaves are in whorls of 3–8, with each up to 6" long and 1" wide. The leaf margins are finely toothed. The flowers are in dense clusters on spikes 3–9" long. Each tubular flower is about ¼" long, white, and with 4 lobes. The stamens have noticeable yellow to brownish-red tips.

Bloom Season: Summer

Habitat/Range: Occasional in mesic prairies, moist depressions in upland prairies, and savannas; found throughout the prairie region.

Comments: The Cherokee drank a root tea for treating backache, fever, hepatitis, and typhus. The Seneca made a root tea to use as a mild laxative. For the Menominee, Culver's root served as a strong physic, a reviver, and as a means of purification when they had been defiled by the touch of a bereaved person. Early doctors used the root to treat a variety of ailments, including liver disorders, pleurisy, and venereal diseases.

SENECA SNAKEROOT
Polygala senega
Milkwort family (Polygalaceae)

Description: Several unbranched stems emerge from one base, up to 20" tall. The leaves are alternate along the stem and up to 3½" long and less than 1" wide. The lower stem leaves are usually very small. The small, white flowers, about ¼" wide, are clustered along the upper part of the stem. Each flower has 3 small petals, with one of them usually fringed.

Bloom Season: Mid-spring–summer

Habitat/Range: Occasional in mesic to dry prairies, hill prairies, and open woodlands; found throughout the prairie region, except for Texas.

Comments: Seneca snakeroot was used by the Seneca Indians to treat snakebite. It was for this use that the colonists gave the plant its name. It was one of the first plants whose medicinal use was learned from the Indians. A root tea was used for respiratory ailments, rheumatism, heart troubles, convulsions, etc. A related species, whorled milkweed (*Polygala verticillata*), differs by being an annual, 6–12" tall, having leaves in whorls of 3–7, with each leaf about 1" long; occurring in prairies, loess hill prairies, sand prairies, savannas, and open disturbed sites; found throughout the prairie region.

SPRING BEAUTY
Claytonia virginica
Purslane family (Portulacaceae)

Description: Plants arise from tuberous roots, with flower stalks to 6" tall. One pair of opposite, grass-like leaves occurs about halfway up the stem. A single strap-like leaf up to 7" long is produced at the base. Not all plants flower in a year, but a single leaf identifies their presence. Flowers, usually less than ½" across, vary from white to pink, with distinctive darker pink veins running the length of the 5 petals. There is a pair of green sepals below the petals. The 5 anthers are typically pink.

Bloom Season: Late winter–late spring

Habitat/Range: Occasional to common in dry prairies, sand prairies, and savannas; found throughout the prairie region, except absent in the northwestern part.

Comments: Both Native Americans and early settlers dug the small, round, tuberous roots and ate them raw or boiled as a potato substitute. Their bland flavor has often been likened to that of chestnuts. The succulent leaves were used in salads. Deer are known to browse on the leaves when they first appear, and rodents eat the bulbs.

MEADOW ANEMONE
Anemone canadensis
Buttercup family (Ranunculaceae)

Description: Hairy leaves on long stalks are clustered at the base of the plant with a branching stem up to 2' tall supporting solitary flowers. Deeply cut leaves occur in whorls along the stem. The white flowers are up to 2" across, with 5 white, petal-like sepals and numerous yellow stamens. The seed head is a bur-like cluster of flattened fruits with beaks.

Bloom Season: Late spring–midsummer

Habitat/Range: Locally frequent in moist depressions in prairies, along streams, and roadsides; found in the northern half of the prairie region.

Comments: Also called Canada anemone, it can often be found occurring in large, matted colonies. Native Americans used a preparation of the roots and leaves to treat wounds, sores, and nosebleeds.

CAROLINA ANEMONE
Anemone caroliniana
Buttercup family (Ranunculaceae)

Description: A short-stemmed plant, 3–6" tall, with several basal leaves that are long-stalked and deeply divided. The leaves, up to 2" long, are divided into 3 divisions, which are further divided at the tip with 2–3 lobes. There is a whorl of 3 stalkless, lobed leaves on the stem below the flower. Flowers are solitary on the stem, about 1–1½" wide, with 8–20 white, to pink, to blue, to deep violet petal-like sepals, and numerous yellow stamens.

Bloom Season: Early spring–mid-spring

Habitat/Range: Infrequent in dry, often sandy, or rocky prairies and open rocky woods; found throughout the prairie region, but absent in the eastern one-third.

Comments: The flowers of Carolina anemone are highly variable throughout its range. They only bloom for a short period of time and close at night and on cloudy days. They are most easily located where vegetation is short and sparse.

THIMBLEWEED
Anemone cylindrica
Buttercup family (Ranunculaceae)

Description: Plants up to 2½' tall with hairy unbranched stems. There are basal leaves and 2 or 3 sets of opposite leaves (sometimes a whorl of 3) on the flowering stems. The leaves are stalked, divided into 3 leaflets, up to 4" long, hairy, and deeply lobed in 3–5 parts. Several tall flower stalks arise above the main whorl of leaves, with one flower on each stalk. Flowers are ¾" across, white, with 5 pointed, hairy, petal-like sepals and numerous yellow stamens around a greenish cone-shaped cylinder. The fruits develop on a cylinder up to 1½" tall and about ½" wide that resembles a thimble; hence, the common name.

Bloom Season: Summer

Habitat/Range: Frequent in mesic and dry prairies, loess hill prairies, sand savannas, and other sandy areas; found in the northern half of the prairie region.

Comments: The fruit develops into seeds with dense, woolly hairs that resemble small white tufts of cotton. Mammalian herbivores tend to avoid the leaves because they are toxic and cause a burning sensation in the mouth and irritation of the gastrointestinal tract. Thimbleweed is similar to tall thimbleweed but differs by having 3 or more leaves in the main whorl of stem leaves, while the latter usually has 2, and sometimes 3. Also, thimbleweed has a central head that is more than twice as long as wide, while tall thimbleweed has a shorter, central head that is less than twice as long as wide.

TALL THIMBLEWEED
Anemone virginiana
Buttercup family (Ranunculaceae)

Description: Plants up to 3' tall with hairy unbranched stems. There are basal leaves and a pair of 2, or sometimes 3 or more, compound leaves on the flowering stems. The leaves are stalked, divided into 3 leaflets, up to 4" long, hairy, and deeply lobed in 3–5 parts. Several tall flower stalks arise above the main whorl of leaves, with one flower on each stalk. Flowers are ¾" across, white, with 5 pointed, hairy, petal-like sepals and numerous yellow stamens around a greenish cone-shaped cylinder. The fruits develop on a cylinder ¾–1" tall and about ½" wide that resembles a thimble; hence, the common name.

Bloom Season: Summer

Habitat/Range: Occasionally in prairies, savannas, and open woods; found in prairies in the eastern part of the prairie region.

Comments: The fruit develops into seeds with dense, woolly hairs that resemble small, white tufts of cotton. Mammalian herbivores tend to avoid the leaves because they are toxic and cause a burning sensation in the mouth and irritation of the gastrointestinal tract. Tall thimbleweed is similar to thimbleweed but differs by having only 2, and sometimes 3, leaves in the main whorl of stem leaves, while the latter has 3 or more leaves. Also, tall thimbleweed has a central head that is shorter and less than twice as long as wide, while with thimbleweed, it is more than twice as long as wide.

PASQUEFLOWER
Pulsatilla patens
Buttercup family (Ranunculaceae)

Description: One of the first prairie wildflowers to bloom in the spring, often appearing while there is still snow on the ground. The plants are 2–16" tall, with basal leaves on long stalks that appear after the flowers bloom. The basal leaves have long, silky hairs and are deeply divided into several narrow, lobed, and toothed segments. The whorl of stem leaves below the flower is similar to the basal leaves but stalkless and smaller. A single flower emerges from a long stalk, with 5–8 showy, white, pale lavender, or purple petal-like sepals, each up to 1½" long, and with numerous parallel veins. Each seed has a long, feather-like plume.

Bloom Season: Early spring–mid-spring

Habitat/Range: Occasional in prairies, hill prairies, open slopes, and dry, rocky, or gravelly sites; found in the northwestern part of the prairie region and in a few sites in northern Illinois; also native to Europe, Russia, Mongolia, China, and Canada.

Comment: Also known as *Anemone patens*. Native Americans used crushed leaves to treat rheumatism, boils, burns, and sore eyes, and to promote the healing of wounds.

PURPLE MEADOW RUE
Thalictrum dasycarpum
Buttercup family (Ranunculaceae)

Description: A sometimes purplish, stout-stemmed plant to 5' tall, with compound leaves. The leaves are divided into numerous leaflets, each up to 2", with 3 pointed lobes at the tip. The small flowers are in branching clusters, with male and female flowers on separate plants. There are no petals, and the sepals drop early. The male flowers have many showy, white, thread-like stamens; the female flowers have a bur-like head of pistils.

Bloom Season: Late spring–early summer

Habitat/Range: Occasional in mesic prairies, wet prairies, wet meadows, and moist stream banks; found throughout the prairie region.

Comments: The Dakota broke off fruits when they were approaching maturity and stored them away for their pleasant odor, later rubbing and scattering them over their clothing. The hollow stems were used by small boys to make toy flutes. The Pawnee used this plant as a stimulant for horses by mixing plant material with a certain white clay and applying it as a snuff on the muzzle of horses. This was done when making forced marches of three or more days' duration in order to escape enemies. A closely related species, waxy meadow rue (*Thalictrum revolutum*), occurs in similar habitats. The leaves have a bad odor when crushed and have gland-tipped hairs on their undersides. Found throughout the prairie region, except for North Dakota, Nebraska, and Kansas.

NEW JERSEY TEA
Ceanothus americanus
Buckthorn family (Rhamnaceae)

Description: A small, wildflower-like shrub, up to 3' tall, with spreading branches. The stem is woody, with greenish-brown bark that becomes brown and flaky on older stems. The upper branches are mostly herbaceous, often dying back in winter. The leaves are alternate, stalked, up to 4" long and 2½" wide. The leaf margin is toothed, the surface hairy above and gray with velvety hairs below. The flowers are on branched clusters arising on long stalks from the bases of leaves of the current year's growth. The flowers are about ⅛" wide, with 5 white hooded petals, usually notched, each resembling a miniature ladle. There are 5 white stamens.

Bloom Season: Late spring–early summer

Habitat/Range: Common in prairies, savannas, and open woods; found throughout the prairie region, except for the Dakotas.

Comments: The leaves were used by Native Americans to make a tea. Tribes along the Atlantic Coast probably taught the colonists the use of New Jersey tea, used as a patriotic substitute for black tea during the American Revolution, after black tea was dumped into Boston Harbor. Native Americans also used a root tea for treating colds, fever, snakebite, stomach disorders, diarrhea, lung ailments, and constipation, and as a blood tonic. A similar species, prairie redroot (*Ceanothus herbaceous*), has narrower leaves and flatter flower clusters mostly at the ends of leafy branches of the current year's growth. Found in prairies and hill prairies throughout the prairie region.

WILD STRAWBERRY
Fragaria virginiana
Rose family (Rosaceae)

Description: This low, ground-hugging plant spreads by runners, often forming large colonies. Along the runners, hairy stalks up to 6" long support leaves, each of which is divided into 3 leaflets with teeth along the margins. The flowers, about 1" across, are in small clusters on leafless stalks and contain 5 white petals, 5 green sepals alternating with 5 leaf-like bracts, and numerous stamens. The fruit has an attractive scarlet color and grows to about ½" in length.

Bloom Season: Spring; sometimes in fall

Habitat/Range: Common in mesic to dry prairies, open woodlands, pastures, and old fields; found throughout the prairie region.

Comments: Some say wild strawberries are sweeter than the typical garden-variety strawberries, which are hybrids between the wild strawberry and the Chilean strawberry. Wild strawberries were greatly appreciated by Native Americans, and later, by early travelers and settlers. They are also nutritious, having more vitamin C than an equal weight of oranges.

AMERICAN BURNET
Sanguisorba canadensis
Rose family (Rosaceae)

Description: Plants with usually unbranched stems, smooth, to 5' tall, with alternate compound leaves up to 1½' long. The leaves are located mostly along the lower half of the stem and divided into 7–15 individually stalked leaflets, each up to 3" long. The leaflets are widest near the middle and toothed along the margins. The flowers are in dense, cylindrical clusters at the tops of the stem, with each white flower about ¼" wide, with 4 petal-like sepals and 4 long stamens, each about ½" long. Petals are absent.

Bloom Season: Mid- to late summer

Habitat/Range: Very rare in wet to mesic prairies in the prairie region, from northern Illinois and Michigan eastward.

Comments: The first part of genus name, *Sanguis*, originates from the Latin word for blood, and *sorba*, which translates as "to drink up," as many years ago, the plant sap was believed to be a remedy to stop bleeding.

NORTHERN BEDSTRAW
Galium boreale
Madder family (Rubiaceae)

Description: Plants 1–3' tall, with leaves whorled in groups of 4 along the stem. Leaves are ¾–2" long and about ¼" wide, broadest near the base and with a pointed tip. There are often smaller leaves at the nodes where the main leaves are attached. There are 3 distinct veins along the length of the leaves. The flowers are numerous in branching clusters at the top of the stems. Flowers are ⅛–¼" across, with 4 white lobes, pointed at the tip, and 4 white stamens.

Bloom Season: Late spring–summer

Habitat/Range: Frequent in mesic and dry prairies, moist depressions in prairies, open woods, and along roadsides; found in the prairie region from southeastern South Dakota and Iowa, eastward.

Comments: A similar species, wild madder (*Galium obtusum*), differs by having mostly spreading, matted stems instead of being erect, one distinct vein in the leaves instead of 3, and tiny flowers, up to ⅛" across. It occurs in wet prairies and wet depressions in upland prairies; found throughout the prairie region. Another species, stiff bedstraw (*Galium tinctorium*), also has spreading, matted stems but with even smaller flowers that have 3 lobes instead of 4. It also occurs in wet prairies and wet depressions in upland prairies; found throughout the prairie region.

LONG-LEAVED BLUETS
Houstonia longifolia
Madder family (Rubiaceae)

Description: Low, slender plants with several stems arising from the base to a height of 8". Leaves at the base of the stem are narrow, long, and present at flowering time; leaves along the stem are opposite, narrow, and smooth, ½–1" long and ¼" wide. The flowers are on stalks about ¼" long, white but sometimes tinged with pink, small, about ¼" across, and clustered at the tops of the leaf axils. The corolla is funnel-shaped, with 4 sharply pointed, hairless lobes, and 4 stamens that extend just beyond the lobes.

Bloom Season: Spring–midsummer

Habitat/Range: Occasional in dry prairies, hill prairies, glades, and rocky, open woods; found in the eastern two-thirds of the prairie region.

Comments: Long-leaved bluets were formerly known as *Houstonia longifolia.*

NARROW-LEAVED BLUETS
Houstonia nigricans
Madder family (Rubiaceae)

Description: Low, slender plants with several erect, stiff, often branched stems, arising from the base to a height of 8". The leaves at the base are usually absent at flowering time. Leaves are stalkless, opposite, up to 1½" long and ⅛" wide, mostly smooth, with pointed tips, and 1 vein along the length of the leaf. There is a pair of white, papery pointed stipules at the base of the opposite leaves. The flowers are numerous, stalkless, small, about ¼" across, funnel-shaped, with 4 pointed lobes that are white, pink, or sometimes pale violet. The surface of the lobes is hairy, and the 4 stamens extend just beyond the lobes.

Bloom Season: Late spring–fall

Habitat/Range: Occasional in dry, rocky prairies, hill prairies, and rocky, open woods; found in the southern half of the prairie region.

Comments: Narrow-leaved bluets are also known as *Stenaria nigricans* and formerly known as *Hedyotis nigricans.*

SMOOTH FALSE BUTTONWEED
Spermacoce glabra
Madder family (Rubiaceae)

Description: Annual plants with stems upright to loosely ascending or trailing, to 2' long. The stems are smooth and 4-angled. Leaves are opposite, stalkless, with short stipules, and 5–7 bristles at the leaf base. The leaves are up to 3" long and 1" wide, widest toward the middle, tapering at the base, pointed at the tip, and smooth along the margins. The flowers range from 3–30 in clusters around the stem at the base of the leaves. Each tiny, white flower is less than ¼" long and tube-shaped, with 4 lobes.

Bloom Season: Summer–fall

Range/Habitat: Common in wet prairies, moist depressions of sand prairies, banks of streams and rivers, and margins of ponds; found in the southern half of the prairie region.

Comments: Smooth false buttonweed is similar in appearance to American bugleweed but the former has leaves with smooth margins instead of toothed, and stipules and bristles at the junction where the leaves meet the stem.

FALSE TOADFLAX
Comandra umbellata
Sandalwood family (Santalaceae)

Description: A creeping underground rhizome sends up yellow-green plants to a height of 12". The smooth stems produce alternate narrow leaves up to 1½" long that lack stalks. Flattened clusters of flowers emerge at the top. Each flower is about ¼" long with 5 sepals; petals are absent. The fruit is urn-shaped, green, maturing to a chestnut brown or purplish brown. The flowers and fruits persist for some time.

Bloom Season: Late spring–early summer

Habitat/Range: Occasional in dry prairies, sandy sites, and savannas; found throughout the prairie region.

Comments: Like other species in the sandal-wood family, false toadflax is parasitic on other plants. However, it may be considered only partially parasitic, because the plant has its own green leaves that photosynthesize and provide energy for growth. Like mistletoe, false toadflax may need its host plant only for water. Native Americans ate the fruits, which are sweet, but consuming too many could produce nausea.

PRAIRIE ALUM ROOT
Heuchera richardsonii
Saxifrage family (Saxifragaceae)

Description: Hairy plants with tall, leafless flowering stalks, up to 2½' tall, arising from a base of long-stalked leaves. The leaves are round, up to 3½" across, with shallow lobes, toothed edges, and a heart-shaped leaf base. Small flowers are arranged along the top of a long, flowering stem. The flowers are somewhat bell-shaped and droop on individual short stalks that branch from the main flower stalks. Each flower is about ⅜" long, with 5 green sepals and 5 spatula-shaped petals that vary from white to pale green to lavender. The stamens are tipped with brilliant orange and extend just beyond the petals.

Bloom Season: Late spring–summer

Habitat/Range: Common in mesic to dry prairies, hill prairies, sand prairies, and open woods; found throughout the prairie region but absent in Arkansas and Texas.

Comments: Native Americans and early settlers used a root powder as an astringent to close wounds and to treat diarrhea and sore throat. The Meskwaki used the leaves as a dressing for open sores.

HORSE NETTLE
Solanum carolinense
Nightshade family (Solanaceae)

Description: An upright, branched plant, with spiny stems, up to 3' tall. The leaves, up to 6" long, are alternate, pointed at the tip, and tapering at the base. The leaf margins are wavy, with deep lobes. There are straw-colored spines along the veins on the underside of the leaf and along the leaf stalk. The flowers are few, loosely clustered at the end of stalks, and about ¾" across. The 5 white petals are united at the base. There are 5 large, bright yellow stamens. The fruit, about ¾" in diameter, is a smooth bright yellow berry, like a tiny tomato, which persists through the winter.

Bloom Season: Late spring–fall

Habitat/Range: Common in disturbed prairies, old fields, pastures, sandy ground, and roadsides; found throughout the prairie region.

Comments: Horse nettle and other nightshades are closely related to tomatoes and eggplant. However, the attractive bright yellow berries are toxic, and fatalities have been reported in children. Native Americans gargled wilted leaf tea for sore throat, applied wilted leaves to the skin for poison ivy rash, and drank tea for worms. The fruit is eaten by a variety of both birds and mammals.

YELLOW FLOWERS

Rudbeckia hirta

This section includes yellow, golden, and yellowish-orange to pale, creamy yellow flowers. Also, multiple-colored flowers that are predominantly yellow are included in this section.

WILD PARSLEY
Lomatium foeniculaceum
Parsley family (Apiaceae)

Description: A stemless plant, up to 1½' tall, with the leaves and flowers arising from a strong, deep taproot. The leaves are stalked, up to 8" long, and finely divided into numerous divisions. The flowers are arranged in flat-topped clusters about 4" across and joined on stout stalks generally arising above the leaves. Each flower is small, yellow to yellowish-green, and 5-parted.

Bloom Season: Spring

Habitat/Range: Locally frequent in dry prairies, rocky prairies, and open woods; found in the western third of the prairie region.

Comments: The seeds, foliage, and roots of wild parsley are edible and taste like parsley. Native Americans and early settlers dried and ground the root into a flour used to make biscuit-like cakes.

PRAIRIE PARSLEY
Polytaenia nuttallii
Parsley family (Apiaceae)

Description: A stout plant, to 3' tall, with thick, long-stalked, alternate, highly dissected leaves. The leaf stalks have wide, flat, clasping bases. The flowers are clustered in numerous branches that form a flat-topped head. Each cluster is on a long stalk and has 15–25 pale yellow flowers, each about ⅛" wide, with 5 tiny petals.

Bloom Season: Mid-spring–early summer

Habitat/Range: Occasional on upland prairies and savannas; found from western Indiana westward in the prairie region, but absent in the extreme northwestern part.

Comments: Prairie parsley is the tallest wild-flower blooming in the prairies in early spring, towering over Indian paintbrush, yellow star grass, hoary puccoon, shooting star, and others. The Meskwaki used tea made from the seeds to treat diarrhea.

YELLOW PIMPERNEL
Taenidia integerrima
Parsley family (Apiaceae)

Description: Slender, delicate plants with a whitish-powdered appearance, up to 3' tall. The leaves are alternate and divided into 2–3 segments, with 3–5 leaflets per segment. The leaflets are almost rounded, ½–1" long, and lack teeth along the margins. The flower heads form a loose, umbrella-shaped cluster to 3" across. The cluster contains 10–20 stalks, each tipped with its own small head of flowers. Each tiny flower has 5 yellow petals that curve inward at their tips.

Bloom Season: Mid-spring–early summer

Habitat/Range: Occasional in upland prairies and savannas; found throughout the prairie region, except for North Dakota and Kansas.

Comments: Both Native Americans and early settlers mixed the root of yellow pimpernel with other medicines to impart a pleasant aroma. The Meskwaki used it as a seasoning agent for some of their foods. In early folk medicine, a root tea was given for lung ailments.

GOLDEN ALEXANDERS
Zizia aurea
Parsley family (Apiaceae)

Description: A smooth, branched plant up to 3' tall, with alternate leaves divided into 3 leaflets. The leaflets can sometimes be divided again into another 1–3 leaflets. The lance-shaped leaflets are up to 3" long and 1" wide, with teeth along the margins. The flower heads are flat-topped and have several branches arising from a common point on the stem. Each yellow flower is less than ⅛" wide, with 5 tiny, incurved petals. The central flower within each cluster lacks a stalk.

Bloom Season: Mid-spring–early summer

Habitat/Range: Common in mesic prairies, savannas, wet thickets, and banks along streams; found throughout the prairie region.

Comments: The Meskwaki used the root to reduce fever. Early settlers considered the plant useful for treating syphilis and for healing wounds. A closely related species, heart-leaved meadow parsnip (*Zizia aptera*), also occurs in prairies. The leaves at the base of the stem are not divided into leaflets, and are heart-shaped at the base. Golden Alexanders is similar to meadow parsnip (*Thaspium trifoliatum*) (p. 76), but the latter's central flower in each flower cluster has a short stalk.

MEADOW PARSNIP
Thaspium trifoliatum
Parsley family (Apiaceae)

Description: A much-branched plant, up to 2½' tall and lacking hairs. The basal leaves are simple, heart-shaped, or sometimes divided into 3 leaflets. The leaves along the stem are on long stalks and divided into 3 leaflets, with a rounded base and small teeth along the margins. The flower heads are on stalks forming an umbrella-shaped cluster, with numerous, tiny flowers that are yellow but sometimes dark purple. The flowers are all on short stalks.

Bloom Season: Mid-spring–early summer

Habitat/Range: Occasional in upland prairies and savannas; found throughout the prairie region, except absent in the northwestern part.

Comments: Meadow parsnip can sometimes be confused with golden Alexanders (*Zizia aurea*), but it differs most noticeably by the latter having the central flower in a flower head lacking a stalk, so that the flower is slightly recessed.

PRAIRIE BROOMWEED
Amphiachyris dracunculoides
Aster family (Asteraceae)

Description: A wide spreading annual, up to 2' tall and 1½' wide, with a single, smooth, angled or grooved stem that branches mostly in the upper half of the stem. Leaves are alternate, narrow, tapering at the base, with a pointed tip, smooth margins, and up to 2" long. The leaf surface is smooth but with moderate to dense, indented, resinous dots, often somewhat sticky to the touch. Many flower heads appear on numerous spreading branches, forming a mound shape. Each yellow flower head has 7–10 ray flowers, each about ⅛" long, and 10–25 disk flowers.

Bloom Season: Midsummer–fall

Habitat/Range: Found in upland prairies, disturbed sites, and roadsides; common in the western part of the prairie region and in scattered locations elsewhere.

Comments: Formerly known as *Gutierrezia dracunculoides*. Native Americans and early settlers used these plants as brooms.

TEXAS GREENEYES
Berlandiera texana
Aster family (Asteraceae)

Description: Plants with a somewhat woody base, soft, loosely tangled hairs, and stems from 2–4' tall, with several branches toward the top. The leaves are alternate, up to 6" long, stalkless or with short petioles, broadly triangular, coarsely toothed along the margins, with the base heart-shaped, the tip pointed to blunt, and short, curved hairs on both sides. The flowers have 5–11 yellow ray flowers, each about ¾" long, and numerous maroon disk flowers.

Bloom Season: Summer

Habitat/Range: Common in dry prairies and rocky, open woods; found in the prairie region from Kansas and Missouri southward.

Comments: When the ray and disk flowers drop, the greenish center disks resemble green eyes; hence, the common name. The genus *Berlandiera* honors Jean-Louis Berlandier (1805–1851), a French-Swiss botanist and physician, who collected plants in Texas and Mexico in the early 1800s. The species *texana* refers to the State of Texas, where this plant was probably first observed and collected.

TICKSEED SUNFLOWER
Bidens aristosa
Aster family (Asteraceae)

Description: A smooth, much-branched annual, growing to up to 3' tall but sometimes to a height of 6' on rich soils. The leaves are opposite, stalked, and divided into 5–11 narrow, coarsely toothed leaflets. The flower heads are on individual stalks, with each head about 1½–2½" across, with 8 golden yellow, petal-like ray flowers surrounding a yellow central disk. The seeds resemble ticks and have 2 barbed, needle-like teeth that attach to clothing and hair.

Bloom Season: Late summer–fall

Habitat/Range: Common in wet prairies, edges of marshes, low depressions, ditches, and fallow fields; found throughout the prairie region, except for the northwestern part.

Comments: Tickseed sunflower is also known as beggar-ticks. The Cherokee used a similar species of *Bidens* in leaf tea to expel worms. The leaves were chewed for sore throat. The seeds are eaten by ducks, bobwhite quail, and some songbirds; the plants are eaten by cottontail rabbits.

LARGE-FLOWERED COREOPSIS
Coreopsis grandiflora
Aster family (Asteraceae)

Description: Slender, smooth plants, up to 2' tall, with opposite to sometimes alternate leaves. The leaves are about 3" long, 2" wide, and divided into slender, thread-like segments less than ¼" wide. Flower heads are on solitary stalks above the leaves. Each flower head has 6–12 golden yellow, petal-like ray flowers, each about 1" long, with 3–5 teeth or lobes at the tip. The numerous disk flowers are yellow to yellowish-orange.

Bloom Season: Mid-spring–midsummer

Habitat/Range: Locally frequent in dry prairies; found primarily in the southwestern portion of the prairie region.

Comments: The genus name, *Coreopsis*, comes from the Greek words *koris*, meaning "bug," and *opsis*, meaning "like," in reference to the shape of the seed, which resembles a tick. The species name, *grandiflora*, means "large-flowered." Through introduction and garden escapes, this coreopsis has become established in the eastern and central United States, well north of its native range.

LANCELEAF COREOPSIS
Coreopsis lanceolata
Aster family (Asteraceae)

Description: Branching plants with several smooth stems emerging from a clump to 2' tall. Leaves opposite, mainly near the base, up to 8" long, 1" wide, and lacking teeth along the margins. The showy, golden yellow flower heads are on long stalks. Each head has 8–10 fan-shaped ray flowers with jagged teeth at the tip and numerous yellow to yellowish-orange disk flowers.

Bloom Season: Mid-spring–midsummer

Habitat/Range: Locally common in dry, shallow, rocky to sandy soils; found in the southern half of the prairie region.

Comments: This showy, long-blooming perennial is easily grown from seed. Lanceleaf coreopsis closely resembles large-flowered coreopsis (*Coreopsis grandiflora*) (opposite), but the latter has thread-like leaves along the lower stem, smaller disk flowers, and 8 fan-shaped ray flowers with narrower, fringe-like teeth at the tip. The ranges of the two species overlap.

PRAIRIE COREOPSIS
Coreopsis palmata
Aster family (Asteraceae)

Description: Narrow, rigid-stemmed plants, usually 1–2½' tall. The leaves are opposite on the stem, with each leaf divided into 3 long, narrow segments. The middle segment can sometimes be divided again for another 1–2 segments. The flower heads are on individual stalks, with each head having 8 yellow, petal-like ray flowers, each up to 1" long, that surround a central yellow disk. The ends of the ray flowers are notched or toothed.

Bloom Season: Late spring–midsummer

Habitat/Range: Frequent in dry prairies and savannas; found throughout the prairie region, except for the northwestern part, and Texas.

Comments: The Meskwaki boiled the seeds and drank the brew. Some tribes applied the boiled seeds to painful areas of the body to relieve ailments such as rheumatism.

TALL COREOPSIS
Coreopsis tripteris
Aster family (Asteraceae)

Description: Tall, stout stems, sometimes with a whitish coating, up to 8' tall, but typically shorter. The leaves are opposite, with stalks, and divided into 3, and sometimes 5, narrow leaflets. Individual leaflets are up to 5" long and ¾" across. The flower heads are on several slender stalks at the top of the plant. Each head is about 1½" across, with 6–10 yellow, petal-like ray flowers surrounding a brown central disk. The flower heads have an anise scent.

Bloom Season: Summer–early fall

Habitat/Range: Occasional to common in mesic prairies and savannas; found throughout the prairie region, except for the northwestern part.

Comments: The Meskwaki boiled the plant to make a drink to treat internal pains and bleeding.

YELLOW CONEFLOWER
Echinacea paradoxa
Aster family (Asteraceae)

Description: Attractive, smooth, yellow-green plants with stout stems to 3' tall. The leaves lack hair and are smooth to the touch, up to 10" long and 1½" wide, tapering at each end, with several parallel veins running along the length of the leaf. The basal leaves are on long stalks, while the stems leaves are few. The flower heads are single on long stems, with several drooping, bright yellow ray flowers each up to 3½" long, surrounding a broad, purplish, conical central disk. The stamens are yellow.

Bloom Season: Late spring–summer

Habitat/Range: Localized in dry, often rocky upland prairies and dolomite glades; found in the prairie region from central Missouri to northern Arkansas.

Comments: The genus name, *Echinacea*, comes from the Greek word *echinos*, meaning "hedge-hog" or "sea urchin," in reference to the spiny center cone found in most flowers of this genus. The species name, *paradoxa*, refers to the paradox of why this species has yellow flowers instead of the usual purple flowers in this genus. A variety, *neglecta*, with pinkish to white ray flowers, occurs in south-central Oklahoma and one isolated population in Montgomery County, in eastern Texas.

NARROWLEAF GUMWEED
Grindelia lanceolata
Aster family (Asteraceae)

Description: This multibranched, reddish-stemmed plant grows to 3' tall, with sticky or gummy bracts resembling round burs below the flower heads. The leaves are upturned, alternate, smooth, up to 4" long and 1" wide, with the tip ending abruptly to a point, and scattered bristle-like teeth along the margins. The flower heads are about 1½" across, with 20–30 yellow, slender, petal-like ray flowers that are upturned, forming a cup. The yellow disk at the center of the flower head is flat.

Bloom Season: Late summer–fall

Habitat/Range: Common in dry, rocky upland prairies, glades, pastures, and roadsides; found mostly in the southern half of the prairie region.

Comments: Also known as spiny-toothed gumweed. Native Americans made a root tea for treating liver ailments. Crushed and soaked plants were applied to relieve the pain and swelling of rheumatic joints. An extraction has been used as a wash to relieve the skin rash of poison ivy.

SNEEZEWEED
Helenium autumnale
Aster family (Asteraceae)

Description: A very leafy-stemmed plant, up to 5' tall, with branching near the top. The stem has narrow wings of leafy tissue extending downward along the stem from the leaf bases. The leaves are alternate, up to 6" long and 1½" wide, broadest near the middle, and tapering at both ends. There are a few small, widely spaced teeth along the margins. The flower heads are about 2" in diameter, with 10–20 drooping, yellow, broadly fan-shaped, petal-like ray flowers surrounding a rounded, central, yellow disk. The ray flowers have 3 lobes at their tips.

Bloom Season: Midsummer–fall

Habitat/Range: Occasional in moist ground in prairies, wet prairies, meadows, and along streams; found throughout the prairie region.

Comments: The Meskwaki dried the flower heads and used them as an inhalant to treat head colds. To reduce fever, the Comanche soaked sneezeweed stems in water and bathed the patient's body. The dried flower heads were reportedly used as a snuff by early settlers. Sheep, cattle, and horses have been poisoned by eating large amounts of the plant, especially the seed heads.

PURPLE-HEADED SNEEZEWEED
Helenium flexuosum
Aster family (Asteraceae)

Description: A single-stemmed plant, up to 3' tall, with branching toward the top. The stem has leafy wings that originate at the base of the leaf and continue down the stem. The leaves are alternate, lacking stalks, up to 3" long, and less than 1" wide. The distinctive flower head, about 1½" across, has a round, brownish-purple central disk surrounded by 8–14 fan-shaped, yellow, petal-like ray flowers, each with 3 lobes.

Bloom Season: Summer–fall

Habitat/Range: Occasional in moist ground in prairies, wet prairies, meadows, and along streams; found in the southern half of the prairie region.

Comments: Sneezeweeds are considered poisonous to cattle if eaten in sufficient quantity. This is unlikely to happen, however, because of the plant's bitter taste. The plant is also poisonous to fishes and worms, as well as to insects. Research by the National Cancer Institute has demonstrated significant antitumor activity in this plant's chemistry.

COMMON SUNFLOWER
Helianthus annuus
Aster family (Asteraceae)

Description: A robust annual, with branching stems often up to 9' tall, the stems are stout and coarsely hairy. The leaves are alternate, on long stalks, up to 10" long, heart-shaped, notched at the base, with sandpapery surfaces, and coarse teeth along the margins. The flower heads are large, 4–10" across, with 20 or more yellow, petal-like ray flowers, each 1–2" long, that surround a reddish-brown central disk 1" or more in diameter.

Bloom Season: Midsummer–fall

Habitat/Range: Dry prairies, pastures, roadsides, and disturbed ground throughout the prairie region. Originally native to the western part of the region and introduced elsewhere.

Comment: Originally cultivated by Native Americans, the sunflower's seeds were used as food and a source for oil. Today, cultivated varieties with large seed heads and seeds are used to produce oil, food, and birdseed.

PLAINS SUNFLOWER
Helianthus petiolaris
Aster family (Asteraceae)

Description: An annual plant, 2–5' tall, with a taproot, single to branched stems, and a rough texture. The leaves are long-stalked, alternate, triangle- to narrow-shaped, 1½"–6" long and ½–3" wide, with a rough texture and somewhat wavy edges. Leaves are mostly toothless. Flowers are on stalks 1½–6" long. The flower heads are 1½–3" wide, with 12–25 yellow petal-like ray flowers and a center, ½–1" in diameter, with numerous dark brown to reddish-purple disk flowers. The center of the disk contains chaffy scales with white-hairy tips often appearing as a whitish spot.

Bloom Season: Summer–fall

Habitat/Range: Locally common in degraded upland prairies and sand prairies, roadsides, and other areas with disturbed rocky or sandy soil; found in the western part of the prairie region but introduced into other parts eastward where there are open, disturbed areas, often in sandy soil.

Comments: The plains sunflower resembles the common sunflower, but the latter has shorter, narrower leaves and smaller flowers. Both sunflowers occupy similar habitats. The Hopi mixed dried, ground petals with cornmeal to use as yellow face powder for ceremonial dances. The Navajo made a liquid from the plant that they sprinkled on their clothing to bring good luck when hunting.

SAWTOOTH SUNFLOWER
Helianthus grosseserratus
Aster family (Asteraceae)

Description: A tall, many-branched, colony-forming sunflower, up to 9' tall, often with several smooth stems emerging from a single base. The leaves are alternate, large, about 8" long and 2" wide, tapering at each end, with hairs on the underside. The margins are finely to coarsely toothed; hence, the common name. The flower heads are numerous, up to 3½" across, with 10–20 yellow, petal-like ray flowers surrounding a yellow disk.

Bloom Season: Midsummer–fall

Habitat/Range: Common in draws and thickets in wet to dry prairies and pastures, also along roadsides, ditches, streams, and often disturbed areas; found throughout the prairie region.

Comments: The Meskwaki mashed the flowers and applied them to burns. In the Southwest, Zuni medicine men cured rattlesnake bites by chewing the fresh or dried root and then sucking the snakebite wound. Various insects, birds, and mammals (including cattle) feed on either the plant or its seeds.

MAXIMILIAN SUNFLOWER
Helianthus maximilianii
Aster family (Asteraceae)

Description: Plants with densely hairy stems, up to 9' tall, with leaves alternate, narrow, and toothed along the margins. The leaves are up to 12" long, 2" wide, and curved and folded along the blade. The leaf surface is rough with minute, often flattened hairs, and the leaf margins have small, widely spaced teeth. Flower heads are on stout stalks along the upper part of the stem. Each head is up to 4" wide, with 10–25 yellow, petal-like ray flowers, each up to 1½" long, surrounding a yellow disk.

Bloom Season: Midsummer–fall

Habitat/Range: Frequent on dry prairies, hill prairies, and savannas; also old fields, roadsides, and open disturbed areas; found throughout the prairie region but populations east of Missouri are more recent introductions, or have escaped from cultivation.

Comments: Maximilian sunflower is named for Prince Maximilian of Wied-Neuwied (1782–1867), a German explorer, ethnologist, and naturalist, who encountered it on his travels in North America. The thick rhizome is edible and provided a food similar to the Jerusalem artichoke for Native American tribes, such as the Sioux. The showy, attractive plants are widely used in perennial gardens and are a popular nectar source for insects, while the seeds are eaten by a variety of songbirds.

WILLOW-LEAVED SUNFLOWER
Helianthus salicifolius
Aster family (Asteraceae)

Description: Plants with long-creeping, branched rhizomes, often occurring as colonies of stems, up to 10' tall. Stems are smooth, often with a whitish, waxy coating. Leaves numerous, alternate, often arching or drooping, narrow, 3–8" long and less than ¼" wide, with margins lacking teeth and the edges curled under. Flower heads numerous, 2–3" wide, on long, slender stalks, with 10–20, yellow, petal-like ray flowers, each about 1¼" long surrounding a reddish-brown to dark purple central disk.

Bloom Season: Late summer–fall

Habitat/Range: Locally common in dry upland prairies, rarely sand prairies, and also roadsides and disturbed areas; found in the southwestern prairie region, including Kansas, Missouri, Oklahoma, and Texas; introduced sporadically farther north and east.

Comments: The genus name comes from the Greek words *helios*, meaning "sun," and *anthos*, meaning "flower." The species name, *salicifolius*, means "with leaves," like *Salix* (willow). The attractive foliage and profuse late-summer to fall bloom make this an excellent choice for wildflower gardens.

ASHY SUNFLOWER
Helianthus mollis
Aster family (Asteraceae)

Description: Usually growing in colonies, these grayish-green plants reach a height of 4'. The stem and leaves have dense gray hairs that can be rubbed off. The leaves are opposite, stiff, up to 6" long and 3" wide, with rounded to notched, stalkless bases. The flower heads are on long stalks, with each head 2½–4" across. There are up to 30 yellow, petal-like ray flowers surrounding the yellow disk.

Bloom Season: Midsummer–fall

Habitat/Range: Common in upland prairies, savannas, thickets, and along roadsides; found throughout the prairie region, except for the northwestern part, and introduced in Wisconsin.

Comments: Ashy sunflower is sometimes mistaken for rosinweed (*Silphium integrifolium*), but the latter has leaves with a rough, sandpapery surface and lacks the dense gray hairs on the stems and leaves.

WESTERN SUNFLOWER
Helianthus occidentalis
Aster family (Asteraceae)

Description: A colony-forming sunflower, up to 3' tall, with spreading white hairs along the stem. There are up to 5 sets of opposite or 3-whorled leaves along the stem. The basal stem leaves are on long stalks and are 3–6" long and up to 2½" wide. The stem leaves are smaller, much fewer, and usually lack stalks. The flower heads are on short stalks at the top of plants. The flower heads are 1½–2" across, with 8–15 narrow, yellow, petal-like ray flowers surrounding a ½" central yellow disk.

Bloom Season: Midsummer–fall

Habitat/Range: Occasional in dry sandy or rocky prairies, and hill prairies; found throughout the prairie region, except for the northwestern part.

Comments: The species name, *occidentalis*, is Latin and means "western." The plant was first described in 1836, when the Great Lakes Region was considered the western part of the United States. Of the approximately 9 species of sunflowers in the prairie region, western sunflower is distinguished by its almost leafless stem.

STIFF SUNFLOWER
Helianthus pauciflorus
Aster family (Asteraceae)

Description: An often single-stemmed plant up to 6' tall, with widely spaced, opposite leaves that are progressively smaller toward the top. The leaves are thick, stiff, rough, long-pointed, broadest below the middle, and up to 12" long and 1–2½" wide. Flower heads are often solitary at the top of the stem, with the head 2½–4" wide, and 10–25 yellow petal-like ray flowers, each about 1½" long, surrounding a purplish-brown to sometimes yellow disk.

Bloom Season: Midsummer–fall

Habitat/Range: Widespread and locally frequent in dry prairies, hill prairies, gravel prairies, and sand prairies; found throughout the prairie region.

Comments: Formerly known as *Helianthus rigidus*, stiff sunflowers form colonies by spreading rhizomes, and are one of the earliest-blooming sunflowers.

JERUSALEM ARTICHOKE
Helianthus tuberosus
Aster family (Asteraceae)

Description: This stout, reddish-stemmed sunflower is up to 7' tall and covered with rough hairs. The leaves are opposite on the lower stem and usually alternate on the upper part. Rough, sandpapery hairs are also on the leaves, which are up to 10" long, lance-shaped, and stalked. The flower heads are on individual stalks at the tops of branches, with each head up to 4" across. There are 10–20 yellow, petal-like ray flowers surrounding a yellow central disk.

Bloom Season: Late summer–fall

Habitat/Range: Common in prairie draws, moist thickets, and along streams; found throughout the prairie region.

Comments: When the roots of this plant grow in good soil, they form edible tubers that have been grown and marketed commercially for centuries. The tubers are cooked like potatoes, diced, and added to salads, and even pickled.

OX-EYE SUNFLOWER
Heliopsis helianthoides
Aster family (Asteraceae)

Description: A spreading, branched plant up to 5' tall. The leaves are opposite, on stalks, shaped like arrowheads, up to 6" long and 3" wide. The margins have coarse teeth. The flower head is 2–4" across and on a long stalk. There are up to 20 pale to golden yellow ray flowers surrounding a cone-shaped yellow disk.

Bloom Season: Late spring–fall

Habitat/Range: Common in moist areas on prairies, sand prairies, and open thickets in prairies; found throughout the prairie region.

Comments: The genus name, *Heliopsis*, comes from the Greek words *helios*, for "sun," and *opsis*, for "appearance," in reference to the golden yellow ray flowers. The species name, *helianthoides*, means "resembling the genus *Helianthus*."

SOFT GOLDEN ASTER
Bradburia pilosa
Aster family (Asteraceae)

Description: A branched annual plant, up to 2' tall, with densely spreading hairs along the stem and leaves. The leaves are numerous, stalkless, narrow, less than 3" long and ½" wide, and toothed to mostly smooth along the margins. The flower heads are several, each less than 1" across, with 13–25 yellow ray flowers and 25–60 yellow disk flowers.

Bloom Season: Summer–fall

Habitat/Range: Locally frequent in dry prairies, sand prairies, dry open woodlands, glades, disturbed areas, and often in sandy soil; found in the prairie region from southeastern Kansas, southern Missouri, and southward.

Comments: Formerly known as *Chrysopsis pilosa* and *Heterotheca pilosa*.

GOLDEN ASTER
Heterotheca camporum
Aster family (Asteraceae)

Description: Plants with taproots and rhizomes, moderately hairy stems and branches, up to 3' tall. Leaves are stalkless, hairy, 1–3" long and about ½" wide, with smooth margins, and shortly tapering to a pointed tip. The flowers are 1½" wide, with 15–35 bright yellow ray flowers and 25–65 darker yellow disk flowers.

Bloom Season: Summer–fall

Habitat/Range: Common in sand prairies and disturbed areas, often in sandy soil; found in the prairie region from eastern Iowa, south to Arkansas, and eastward.

Comments: Formerly known as *Chrysopsis camporum*.

LONG-BEARDED HAWKWEED
Hieracium longipilum
Aster family (Asteraceae)

Description: Slender, mostly solitary stems, from 2–5' tall, with densely covered, stiff hairs, up to 1" long. The basal leaves are numerous, stalked, up to 10" long, about 1" wide, tapering at the base, pointed at the tip, densely hairy, and are often present at flowering time. The stem leaves are also densely hairy and gradu-ally reduced in size going up the stem. Flower heads are 8–20, in an open, cylindrical cluster at the top of the stem. Each flower is about ½" across on short, hairy stalks, with 8–20 yellow, petal-like ray flowers with notched tips. The bracts behind the flower are densely covered in short, dark, glandular hairs.

Bloom Season: Midsummer–late summer

Habitat/Range: Frequent in dry prairies, sand prairies, open woods, and sandy sites; found throughout the prairie region, but absent in the Dakotas.

Comments: A similar species, hairy hawkweed (*Hieracium gronovii*), differs by being less hairy, with hairs up to ¼" long and a more-open cluster of flowers. It occurs in sand prairies, sand savannas, and rocky, open woods; found throughout the prairie region, but absent in the northwestern part.

TWO-FLOWERED CYNTHIA
Krigia biflora
Aster family (Asteraceae)

Description: A dandelion-like plant with milky sap and a branching, smooth, bluish-green stem to 2' tall. The leaves at the base of the plant are spoon-shaped on a long stalk. The 1–3 stem leaves are much smaller and clasp the stem. There are 2–7 orange-yellow flower heads on each stem, with each head about 1½" across and containing 25–60 petal-like ray flowers.

Bloom Season: Mid-spring–late summer

Habitat/Range: Occasional in upland prairies, sandy areas, and rocky, open woodlands; found throughout the prairie region, except for the northwestern part, and Texas.

Comments: The species name, *biflora* ("with 2 flowers"), and common name are misleading, because the plant may have any number of flower heads.

POTATO DANDELION
Krigia dandelion
Aster family (Asteraceae)

Description: A dandelion-like plant with a bulbous underground tuber, a bare single stem each topped with a single flower, up to 15" tall, and with milky sap. The leaves are basal, with the margins wavy and widely toothed, up to 8" long and 1" wide. The flower heads are about 1½" across with 25–35 small, yellow-orange, petal-like ray flowers.

Bloom Season: Mid-spring–early summer

Habitat/Range: Occasional in upland prairies, sandy areas, and rocky, open woods; found in the southern part of the prairie region, from southeastern Kansas east to southern Indiana.

Comments: The genus name, *Krigia*, is in honor of David Krig (or Kreig), a German physician who was among the first to collect plants in Maryland. Potato dandelion flower heads open during the morning only under sunny conditions.

DWARF DANDELION
Krigia virginica
Aster family (Asteraceae)

Description: Small annuals with milky sap, up to 8" tall. Stems are mostly unbranched, with sparsely to moderately gland-tipped hairs. Leaves are all at the base or on the lower parts of stems, up to 4½" long and ½" wide. The margins are often wavy, with scattered pointed lobes. Flower heads are single at the tops of stems, with a yellow-orange head about ½" across, with 14–35 small, petal-like ray flowers.

Bloom Season: Mid-spring–summer

Habitat/Range: Occasional in depressions in upland prairies, sand prairies; also pastures, fields, and disturbed sites; found throughout the prairie region, except for the northwestern part.

Comments: A closely related species, western dwarf dandelion (*Krigia occidentalis*), differs by having 8 or fewer ribbed bracts at the base of each flower head, compared to 9 or more flat bracts in dwarf dandelion; locally common in upland prairies and sandy areas; found in the southwestern portion of the prairie region, and blooming in the spring.

WILD LETTUCE
Lactuca canadensis
Aster family (Asteraceae)

Description: Often multibranched at the tips, this smooth-stemmed biennial grows up to 8' tall and has milky-orange to tan sap. The leaves are alternate, stalkless, and up to 12" long and 6" wide (but usually smaller). The leaves vary from deeply lobed to rounded. The numerous flower heads are small, and occur in large branching clusters with 50–100 heads. Each head is less than ½" across, with 15–22 yellow, petal-like ray flowers. The flower and seed heads resemble miniature dandelions.

Bloom Season: Midsummer to early fall

Habitat/Range: Common in upland prairies, sand prairies, open thickets, woodland edges, and disturbed ground; found throughout the prairie region.

Comments: Native Americans used a root tea to treat diarrhea, heart and lung ailments, hemorrhaging, and nausea, and to relieve pain. The milky sap from the stems was used for treating skin eruptions. The bruised leaves were applied directly to insect stings. Both Native Americans and early settlers used a leaf tea to hasten milk flow after childbirth.

WESTERN WILD LETTUCE
Lactuca ludoviciana
Aster family (Asteraceae)

Description: A single-stemmed, smooth, biennial plant, up to 6' tall, with brownish sap. The leaves are alternate, stalkless, sometimes clasping, 8–12" long and 2–4" wide, with toothed margins, and often prickly along the midvein on the underside of the leaf. The flower heads are located on the tips of branches with 50–100 heads, each about ¾–1" across. There are 20–30 yellow to pale blue petal-like ray flowers. The flower and seed heads resemble miniature dandelions.

Bloom Season: Summer–fall

Habitat/Range: Found in prairies, hill prairies, roadsides, and disturbed ground; common in the western prairie region; infrequent to rare in the eastern prairie region.

Comments: The genus name, *Lactuca*, is Latin for "milk," referring to the plant's milky sap; the species name, *ludoviciana*, is the Latin version of the word "Louisiana." Native Americans used tea made from members of this genus as a nerve tonic, sedative, and pain reliever. The latex-like sap from the stem has been used for warts, pimples, poison ivy rash, and other skin irritations. Members of this genus may cause dermatitis or internal poisoning.

PRAIRIE DANDELION
Nothocalais cuspidata
Aster family (Asteraceae)

Description: A dandelion-like plant up to 8" tall, with milky sap. The leaves are clustered at the base, up to 12" long and 1" wide, with wavy margins along the blade. A leafless stalk supports a showy, single flower head up to 2" wide, with 35–80 bright yellow, petal-like ray flowers.

Bloom Season: Spring

Habitat/Range: Uncommon in dry, often rocky prairies and hill prairies with sparse vegetation; found from Illinois and Wisconsin westward in the prairie region.

Comments: Formerly known as *Agoseris cuspidata*. Prairie dandelion can be found growing with pasqueflower (see p. 65).

BUTTERWEED
Packera glabella
Aster family (Asteraceae)

Description: An annual arising from slender roots, with a smooth, unbranched stem, up to 3' tall. The leaves at the base of the stem are deeply divided with lobes and teeth, up to 8" long and 3" wide. The stem leaves are similar and gradually reduced in size upward. The flowers are in a terminal cluster, with numerous flower heads. Each flower head is ¾–1" across, with 12–20 yellow, petal-like ray flowers surrounding a yellow disk.

Bloom Season: Spring–early summer

Habitat/Range: Locally common in wet prairies, moist depressions in upland prairies, and sand prairies, and moist, open disturbed ground; found in the prairie region from Missouri south to Texas and eastward.

Comments: Formerly known as *Senecio glabellus*. The genus is from the Latin *senex*, meaning "old man," an allusion to the gray-haired tufts of filaments attached to the seeds. The name *Packera* is a New World genus composed of 75 taxa, separated from the Old World genus *Senecio*, based on molecular, morphological, and palynological data (the study of pollen grains). Butterweed is in reference to the color of the flowers.

93

PRAIRIE RAGWORT
Packera plattensis
Aster family (Asteraceae)

Description: A biennial or short-lived perennial with stems single or rarely 2–3 in a cluster, up to 2' tall, with dense, white, cobwebby hairs on the stem and leaves, but less so when mature. The basal leaves are up to 3" long and 1½" wide, long-stalked, toothed along the margins, and usually divided into lobes. The stem leaves are smaller and stalkless, with the margins usually divided into lobes. Up to 10 (rarely 20) flower heads occur in a flattened cluster at the top of the stem. Each head is ½–1" wide, with 8–13 yellow, petal-like ray flowers, each about ¼" long, surrounding a small, yellow-orange disk.

Bloom Season: Mid-spring–early summer

Habitat/Range: Frequent in dry upland prairies, hill prairies, and in sandy, gravelly, rocky soils; found throughout the prairie region, but less common eastward.

Comments: Formerly known as *Senecio plattensis*. Prairie ragwort foliage is toxic to humans and cattle. It contains pyrrolizidine alkaloids that can damage the liver and cause other health problems. A closely related species, balsam ragwort (*Packera paupercula*), differs by having basal leaves more than 3 times as long as they are wide, and few if any cobwebby hairs on the leaves and stem; occurs in mesic prairies, and wet meadows; found throughout the prairie region, except for the southwestern part from Nebraska, south to Texas.

GRAY-HEADED CONEFLOWER
Ratibida pinnata
Aster family (Asteraceae)

Description: A slender, hairy-stemmed plant, up to 5' tall, often branching toward the top. The leaves are divided into 3–7 slender leaflets, with a few teeth or small side lobes along the margins. The leaves at the base of the stem are on long stalks, with the leaf blade up to 7" long. The leaves on the stem are alternate and smaller. Each flower head has its own long stalk. The 5–10 yellow ray flowers droop downward, each about 2" long and less than ½" wide. They surround a conical disk about ¾" tall. Prior to opening, the small disk flowers are ashy gray, but they turn brown as the flowers open. The crushed heads have a distinct anise scent.

Bloom Season: Mid-spring–early fall

Habitat/Range: Common in mesic to dry prairies and savannas, especially in areas that have had some past disturbance; found throughout the prairie region, except for North Dakota and Texas.

Comments: Native Americans made a tea from the flower cones and leaves. The Meskwaki used the root to cure toothache.

PRAIRIE CONEFLOWER
Ratibida columnifera
Aster family (Asteraceae)

Description: A single-stemmed plant, but often in clusters, up to 2' tall. The leaves are up to 6" long and 2½" wide, divided into 5–13 narrow leaflets. There are from 4–11 drooping ray flowers that are yellow or red to reddish-brown, with varying degrees of yellow along the edges and toward the tip. The flower column is cylindrical and contains numerous disk flowers that vary from yellow to red to purple.

Bloom Season: Summer–fall

Habitat/Range: Occasional in upland prairies, pastures, roadsides, and often disturbed areas; found in the western part of the prairie region and introduced elsewhere.

Comments: Also known as Mexican hat. The Cheyenne made a tea from the leaves and stems and rubbed it on a rattlesnake bite to relieve the pain; they also used it to treat areas affected by poison ivy rash. Prairie coneflower is sometimes used in garden and wildflower plantings.

BLACK-EYED SUSAN
Rudbeckia hirta
Aster family (Asteraceae)

Description: This short-lived perennial grows 1–3' tall, with rough and hairy leaves and stems. The basal leaves are up to 5" long and 1" wide. Along the stem, the leaves are alternate, up to 4" long, ½–2" wide, widest in the middle, and tapering toward the tip. Flower heads are single at the top of each stem branch, with showy heads about 2–3" across. There are 20–30 yellow to orangish-yellow flowers that surround a dark brown to purple-brown dome-shaped disk about ½" long.

Bloom Season: Mid-spring–fall

Habitat/Range: Common in mesic to dry prairies, old fields, pastures, and roadsides; found throughout the prairie region.

Comments: The Potawatomi prepared a root tea for curing colds. Early settlers used the plant as a stimulant and a diuretic. A yellow dye is made from this plant. A closely related species, rough coneflower (*Rudbeckia grandiflora*), is from 3–5' tall, with upright leaves, 8–12 ray flowers, each 1" long, and a dome-shaped disk, ¾–1¼" long; summer blooming; found in prairies; occurs in the southwestern part of the prairie region, and introduced elsewhere.

SWEET CONEFLOWER
Rudbeckia subtomentosa
Aster family (Asteraceae)

Description: Plants up to 6' tall, branched near the top, often with dense, short hairs along the upper stem. The stem leaves are alternate, with short stalks or stalkless, have large teeth along the margins, and are often covered with soft, dense hairs. The leaves, at least on the lower part of the stem, are divided into 3 deep lobes, and up to 8" long and 4½" wide. The upper leaves usually lack lobes; they are up to 3" long and 1" across. The flower heads are on long, individual stalks, with each head up to 3" wide. The heads have 6–20, yellow, petal-like ray flowers, surrounding a dome-shaped, brown central disk.

Bloom Season: Summer

Habitat/Range: Locally frequent in mesic prairies, depressions in upland prairies, and banks of streams; found throughout the prairie region, except for the northwestern part.

Comments: The common name, sweet coneflower, comes from the flower's anise scent. This plant is also known as sweet black-eyed Susan.

BROWN-EYED SUSAN
Rudbeckia triloba
Aster family (Asteraceae)

Description: A biennial to short-lived perennial with several branches, up to 5' tall, and with spreading hairs on the stems. The leaves are alternate and hairy, with the lower ones 3-lobed and often shed at the time of flowering. The upper stem leaves are narrow, stalkless, about 4" long, and with toothed edges. The flower heads are numerous, with each head up to 1¾" across. Each head has 6–12 yellow, petal-like ray flowers surrounding a dome-shaped brown disk. The ray flowers are grooved along their lengths and narrowly notched at the tips.

Bloom Season: Summer–fall

Habitat/Range: Occasional along prairie/forest borders, moist thickets, low woods, and along streams; found throughout the prairie region, except for the Dakotas.

Comments: The flower heads of brown-eyed Susan are smaller and much more numerous than those of black-eyed Susan. The plants are also significantly taller and more widely branched, which also helps to differentiate them from black-eyed Susan.

ROSINWEED
Silphium integrifolium
Aster family (Asteraceae)

Description: Often occurring in colonies, these stout, single-stemmed plants grow to 6' tall. The leaves are opposite but may be slightly alternate, or even whorled. The leaves lack stalks, are up to 6" long and 2½" wide, with a rough, sandpapery texture, and vary in shape from narrow and long to broad and round; teeth may be present along the margins. The flower heads are about 3" wide, with 15–35 yellow, petal-like ray flowers, each 1–2" long, surrounding a yellow central disk of small, sterile flowers.

Bloom Season: Summer–fall

Habitat/Range: Common in mesic prairies, hill prairies, savannas, and roadsides; found throughout the prairie region, except for the Dakotas, Minnesota, and Texas.

Comments: Rosinweed is named for its sticky resin that exudes from the stem when cut or bruised. Plants in the genus *Silphium* resemble sunflowers (*Helianthus* species), but unlike the latter, their ray flowers produce the seeds, whereas in sunflowers, the disk flowers produce the seeds. Native Americans used the root of rosinweed for pain relief.

COMPASS PLANT
Silphium laciniatum
Aster family (Asteraceae)

Description: A tall, stout plant up to 8' in height, with very large basal leaves, sometimes over 1' long. The deeply cut basal leaves are commonly oriented in a north–south direction, in order to take maximum advantage of the sun's rays; hence, the common name. The stem leaves are smaller, alternate, and clasping at the base. The flower heads are along the upper part of a single, long, hairy stalk. Each head is up to 4½" across, with 20–30 yellow petal-like ray flowers that surround a yellow center, with many sterile disk flowers.

Bloom Season: Summer–fall

Habitat/Range: Common in mesic and dry prairies, sand prairies, savannas, and roadsides; found throughout the prairie region, except for North Dakota.

Comments: The Omaha and Ponca avoided camping wherever compass plant grew abundantly, because they believed the plants attracted lightning. They sometimes burned the dried root during an electrical storm to act as a charm against a lightning strike. The root was used by Native Americans and early settlers to alleviate head colds or pains. The dried leaves were used for treating dry, obstinate coughs and intermittent fevers. Many Native American children chewed the resin that exudes from the stem as a chewing gum.

CUP PLANT
Silphium perfoliatum
Aster family (Asteraceae)

Description: Large plants up to 8' tall, branching near the top, with stout, square stems. The large upper leaves are cupped around the stem tight enough to hold rainwater. The opposite leaves, up to 8" long and 5" across, have wavy margins, large teeth, and are rough to the touch on both sides. The flower heads are at the tops of branches, numerous, and up to 3" across. Each head has 20–30 yellow, petal-like ray flowers that surround a yellow center with sterile disk flowers.

Bloom Season: Summer–fall

Habitat/Range: Common in moist areas in prairies and along prairie streams, low thickets, and low-lying woodland edges; found throughout the prairie region, except for Texas.

Comments: The Omaha and Ponca used the root as a smoke treatment, inhaling the fumes for head colds, nerve pains, and rheumatism. Also, the resinous sap that exudes from the stem was chewed as a gum to help prevent vomiting. This plant is also known as carpenter's weed because of its straight, square stem.

PRAIRIE DOCK
Silphium terebinthinaceum
Aster family (Asteraceae)

Description: A tall, wand-like stem rises 3–10' above a cluster of large, spade-shaped basal leaves. The leaves are up to 16" long, very rough in texture, with a heart-shaped base and coarse teeth along the margins. The flower heads occur at the top of a smooth, shiny, nearly leafless stalk. The heads are 2–3" across, with 12–20 yellow, petal-like ray flowers that surround a yellow center with sterile disk flowers.

Bloom Season: Summer–fall

Habitat/Range: Common in mesic prairies, savannas, and rocky and sandy sites; also along railroads and roadsides; found in the eastern prairie region, but absent in the western part.

Comments: Native Americans made a root tea to alleviate feebleness and to expel intestinal worms. Leaf tea was used for coughs, lung ailments, and asthma. Like compass plant, prairie dock is also known to align its leaves on a north–south axis in order to take maximum advantage of the sun's rays.

GRASS-LEAVED GOLDENROD
Euthamia graminifolia
Aster family (Asteraceae)

Description: Plants up to 3' tall, with hairy stems and leaves, and the upper half of the stem branched. The leaves are alternate, up to 5" long and ⅜" wide, with 3 distinct parallel veins along the length of the blade and with minute, resinous spots on the underside. The yellow flowers are in a branched, flat-topped cluster at the top of the stem. Each flower head is about ¼" across, with 15–25 petal-like ray flowers and 5–10 central disk flowers.

Bloom Season: Late summer–fall

Habitat/Range: Occasional in prairies, sandy fields, and edges of marshes; found throughout much of the prairie region, but is somewhat rare in the southern part.

Comments: Formerly known as *Solidago graminifolia*.

PLAINS GRASS-LEAVED GOLDENROD
Euthamia gymnospermoides
Aster family (Asteraceae)

Description: Rather spindly plants, up to 3' tall, branching in the upper half of the stem. The leaves are alternate along the hairless stem, with leaf blades up to 4" long and less than ⅛" wide, hairless, with minute, resinous spots on the underside. A prominent vein runs down the center of the leaf. Small flower heads are about ¼" wide and are found in small, flattened clusters at the tips of the stem branches. Each head typically has 7–11, yellow, petal-like ray flowers surrounding 4–6 small, yellow, disk flowers.

Bloom Season: Late summer–fall

Habitat/Range: Occasional in upland prairies, sand prairies, savannas, meadows along rivers, and sandy fields; found throughout the prairie region, but rare north of Iowa.

Comments: Formerly known as *Solidago gymnospermoides*.

RIDDELL'S GOLDENROD
Oligoneuron riddellii
Aster family (Asteraceae)

Description: A showy plant with somewhat shiny stems and several fine ridges or grooves along its length, up to 3' tall. The leaves, up to 3" long and ½" wide, are loosely alternate along the stem, toothless along the margins, shiny, somewhat folded along the blade, sheathing at the base, and tending to curve away from the stem. Flowers are in a short, dense, domed cluster at the top of the stem, with numerous heads on all sides of the branches. Each small head is up to ⅜" across, with 7–9 yellow, petal-like ray flowers, surrounding 6–10 yellow disk flowers.

Bloom Season: Late summer–fall

Habitat/Range: Occasional in wet to mesic prairies and calcareous wetland seeps; found across the prairie region, except for the southwestern part.

Comments: Formerly known as *Solidago riddellii*. The rounded, flat cluster of flowers is unique from other goldenrods, except for stiff goldenrod (*Oligoneuron rigidum*). However, the latter prefers dry sandy habitats, and its stem leaves are noticeably rounder, with rough, hairy surfaces.

STIFF GOLDENROD
Oligoneuron rigidum
Aster family (Asteraceae)

Description: A coarse, stout plant, with stems up to 5' tall, usually hairy, giving the plant a pale to gray-green cast. The large basal leaves are on long stalks and up to 10" long and 5" wide. The stem leaves are alternate, stalkless, and progressively smaller upward. All the leaves are rough and leathery. The flower heads are in a flat-topped to somewhat rounded, densely packed cluster. Each head is about ½" across, with 7–14 yellow, petal-like ray flowers surrounding a yellow central disk.

Bloom Season: Late summer–fall

Habitat/Range: Common in upland prairies, hill prairies, savannas, old fields, roadsides, and open disturbed areas; found throughout the prairie region.

Comments: Formerly known as *Solidago rigida*. Bee stings were once treated with a lotion made from the flowers of stiff goldenrod. Leaf tea was used to treat swollen throats. The rounded, flat cluster of flowers is unique from other goldenrods, except for Riddell's goldenrod (*Oligoneuron riddellii*). However, the latter prefers wet to mesic prairies and calcareous wetland seeps, and its stem leaves are shiny, somewhat folded along the blade, sheathing at the base, and tending to curve away from the stem.

TALL GOLDENROD
Solidago altissima
Aster family (Asteraceae)

Description: A large, hairy-stemmed golden-rod, up to 7' tall, with many alternate leaves, the largest of which occur along the middle part of the stem. The leaves are up to 6" long and 1¼" wide, with some teeth along the margins, especially toward the tip. The upper side of the leaf is rough, while the underside is hairy, with 3 prominent veins. The flower heads are arranged in a pyramidal cluster, with the heads all occurring on the upper side of the branches. Each head is about ¼" across, with 10–16 yellow, petal-like ray flowers. The green bracts under the flower heads are more than ⅛" tall.

Bloom Season: Midsummer–fall

Habitat/Range: Common in upland prairies, hill prairies, sand prairies, and savannas; also in old fields, pastures, roadsides, and open disturbed areas; found throughout the prairie region.

Comments: Native Americans made a tea from this plant to treat kidney problems; they also chewed crushed flowers for sore throat. Of the goldenrods, this species is the most commonly infected by the goldenrod gall. This round swell-ing along the stem is caused by certain moths and flies that lay an egg in the stem. The larva hatches and secretes a chemical that causes the plant tissue to swell around it; the larva then eats the tissue and overwinters in its protected home, emerging in the spring as an adult.

CANADA GOLDENROD
Solidago canadensis
Aster family (Asteraceae)

Description: Plants with 1 to several unbranched, hairy stems, up to 6' tall, that arise from creeping rhizomes. The leaves are alternate, narrow, short-stalked to stalkless, 1–6" long and ¼–¾" wide, with 3 parallel veins running the length of each leaf, and shallow teeth along the margins. The flower heads are arranged in a pyramidal cluster, with the heads all occurring on the upper side of the branches. Each head is less than ¼" across, with 6–12 yellow, petal-like ray flowers. The green bracts under the flower heads are less than ⅛" tall.

Bloom Season: Summer–fall

Habitat/Range: Common in upland prairies and savannas; also in old fields, pastures, roadsides, and open disturbed areas; found throughout the prairie region.

Comments: Native Americans used the flowers to make a medicinal tea used to treat fever, diarrhea, insomnia, and snakebite. The roots were used for burns. A similar species, late goldenrod (*Solidago gigantea*), has smooth stems, sometimes with a white, waxy coating; occurs in moist sites, including wet and mesic prairies, banks of streams and rivers, and disturbed areas; found throughout the prairie region.

EARLY GOLDENROD
Solidago juncea
Aster family (Asteraceae)

Description: An upright plant to 3' tall, with a smooth stem and fine lines or grooves along its length. The basal leaves are up to 8" long and 1" wide. The stem leaves are alternate, smaller, tapering at the base and tip, with some small teeth along the margins. A single prominent vein runs the length of the leaves. The flower heads are crowded together on the tops of arching side branches. Each head has about 7–12 very small, yellow, petal-like ray flowers and 8–15 tiny disc flowers.

Bloom Season: Summer–fall

Habitat/Range: Common in upland prairies, sand prairies, gravel prairies, savannas, old fields, and roadsides; found throughout the prairie region, except for the western part, from North Dakota south to Texas.

Comments: Early goldenrod is one of the first goldenrods to flower, doing so in early summer. It is often grown in gardens as an ornamental.

MISSOURI GOLDENROD
Solidago missouriensis
Aster family (Asteraceae)

Description: Smooth-stemmed plants to 3' tall, with several fine lines or grooves along its length. Basal and lowermost leaves up to 6" long and less than ½" wide are often absent at flowering time. The stem leaves are alternate, smooth, unstalked, 2–6" long and less than ½" wide, pointed at the tips, with 3 veins running the length of the blades, and with small clusters of leaves at the axils of the main leaves. The flower heads are crowded together on the tops of branches. Each head has about 7–13, yellow, petal-like ray flowers and 6–15 disc flowers.

Bloom Season: Summer fall

Habitat/Range: Common in dry upland prairies, hill prairies, rocky open areas, savannas, old fields, and roadsides; found throughout the prairie region.

Comments: Missouri goldenrod is known to colonize disturbed soils. During the Dust Bowl era, it flourished in the dry, cleared soil. As the drought ended and the grasses returned, it became less common, disappearing in many areas. Missouri goldenrod increases in overgrazed pastures, and can be found in soils turned over by burrowing animals and on roadsides and western mining sites.

OLD-FIELD GOLDENROD
Solidago nemoralis
Aster family (Asteraceae)

Description: The stems vary from arching to upright, growing up to 2½' tall, with dense, short, gray hairs on the stems, and leaves that give the plant a gray-green appearance. The basal leaves are present at flowering time, up to 4" long and ¾" wide, with 1 main vein running the length of the blade. The stem leaves are progressively smaller toward the top of the stem. The flower heads are densely packed on the tops of short branches. Each head is less than ¼" across, with 5–9 yellow, petal-like ray flowers and 3–9 disc flowers.

Bloom Season: Summer–fall

Habitat/Range: Common in prairies, old fields, pastures, and roadsides; found throughout the prairie region.

Comments: The upright form of old-field goldenrod is easy to identify at a distance by its slightly bent tip. Native American tribes like the Houma used it medicinally to treat jaundice. The Goshute used the seeds for food, and the Navajo used the seeds for incense.

SHOWY GOLDENROD
Solidago speciosa
Aster family (Asteraceae)

Description: Sturdy, sometimes red, unbranched stems, up to 4' tall, with alternate, smooth leaves. The lower leaves are large, about 12" long and 4" wide, and wither around flowering time. The upper leaves decrease in size going up the stem. The flowers are densely arranged on branches in an elongate, cylindrical cluster at the top of the stem. Each flower head is about ½" across, with 6–8 yellow, petal-like ray flowers and 4–5 small disk flowers.

Bloom Season: Late summer–fall

Habitat/Range: Occasional in upland prairies, hill prairies, savannas, and roadsides; found throughout the prairie region.

Comments: This is one of the showiest of about 125 species of goldenrod that occur in the United States. It is popular as an ornamental in gardens and wildflower plantings. The Chippewa used an extract from the roots and stems to treat hemorrhages, sprains, and skin problems, and as a tonic.

STIFF GREENTHREAD
Thelesperma filifolium
Aster family (Asteraceae)

Description: An annual or short-lived perennial plant, 1–3' tall, with several stems arising from a central rootstock. The leaves are numerous, opposite, 2–4½" long, and deeply divided into 2–3 narrow, thread-like segments. Flower heads are on long stalks, urn-shaped, 1–1½" wide, with 8 golden yellow, petal-like ray flowers that are sometimes reddish-tinged at the base, and with the tips 3-lobed. The disk flowers are numerous and orangish-yellow, with reddish-brown veins.

Bloom Season: Late spring–summer

Habitat/Range: Locally frequent in sandy or rocky prairies, roadsides, and disturbed sites; found in the prairie region from Kansas southward, including southwestern Arkansas.

Comments: The flower buds are known to droop before flowering and become upright when open. A similar species, Colorado greenthread (*Thelesperma megapotamicum*), also known as *Thelesperma ambiguum*, differs by being a perennial and having petal-like ray flowers absent, so only the disk flowers are present; occurs infrequently in prairies, pastures, and roadsides; found on the western edge of the prairie region and westward.

YELLOW CROWNBEARD
Verbesina helianthoides
Aster family (Asteraceae)

Description: Flaps of leafy tissue or "wings" run down the length of the hairy stem that can reach a height of 3½'. The leaves are alternate, up to 6" long, tapering at the base, with pointed tips and teeth along the margins. There are coarse hairs on the upper surface, while the lower surface is soft-hairy. The flower heads are large, with 8–15 yellow, petal-like ray flowers surrounding a yellow disk.

Bloom Season: Late spring–fall

Habitat/Range: Common in dry prairies, savannas, and rocky, open woods; found throughout the southern half of the prairie region.

Comments: The plant is also known as wingstem. Primarily, long-tongued bees visit the flowers for pollen and nectar. Bobwhite quail, songbirds, and small mammals eat the seeds.

HOARY PUCCOON
Lithospermum canescens
Borage family (Boraginaceae)

Description: Single stems, with several emerging from the base of older plants, 6–18" tall, with dense, soft hairs on the stems and leaves that give the plant a gray-green color. The leaves are alternate, stalkless, about 2½" long and less than ½" wide, and lack teeth along the margins. The deep golden flowers are in a flattened cluster at the top of the plant. Each flower is about ½" wide, about ½" long, tubular-shaped, with 5 spreading, rounded lobes.

Bloom Season: Spring–early summer

Habitat/Range: Common in mesic to dry prairies, hill prairies, and savannas, but seldom in sandy sites; found throughout the prairie region.

Comments: Native Americans used leaf tea as a wash for fevers accompanied by spasms, and as a wash rubbed on persons thought to be near convulsions. To the Menominee, the white, ripened seed of this plant was a type of sacred bead used in special ceremonies. A red dye was extracted from the roots.

CAROLINA PUCCOON
Lithospermum caroliniense
Borage family (Boraginaceae)

Description: Single-stemmed plants, 1–2½'
tall, with short, bristly hairs. The leaves are
stalkless, up to 1½" long and ⅜" wide, linear,
with pointed tips and covered with short, stiff
hairs. The flowers are single on short stalks
arising from the axils of arching branches at the
top of the stems. Each flower is about 1" across,
¾" long, and tubular, with 5 orange-yellow,
petal-like lobes. The stamens are hidden inside
the tube.

Bloom Season: Spring–early summer

Habitat/Range: Occasional in sandy soils
of prairies, hill prairies, savannas, and open
woods; found throughout the prairie region,
except for North Dakota.

Comments: The orange-yellow flowers are very
showy and can be seen from a considerable
distance. Carolina puccoon is easily mistaken
for hoary puccoon (*Lithospermum canescens*),
which has smaller flowers and longer, softer
hairs on the stems.

FRINGED PUCCOON
Lithospermum incisum
Borage family (Boraginaceae)

Description: Densely hairy plants to 15" tall,
with narrow, alternate leaves up to 3" long and
less than ¼" wide. Flowers are in clusters at
the tops of stems, with each lemon yellow to
bright yellow flower up to 1½" long, 1" wide,
tubular-shaped, and with 5 spreading lobes that
are unevenly toothed to nearly fringed along the
margins.

Bloom Season: Mid-spring–early summer

Habitat/Range: Occasional in dry upland
prairies, hill prairies, and rocky, open areas;
found throughout the prairie region, except for
Michigan and Ohio.

Comments: The first flowers are large and
sterile, while later in the season the flowers are
much smaller, and self-pollinated; they could
easily be mistaken for a different species. The
Blackfeet made an incense from the dried tops,
which they burned during ceremonial events.
The Cheyenne ground the dried leaves, roots,
and stems and applied them to a limb to treat
paralysis.

PRICKLY PEAR
Opuntia humifusa
Cactus family (Cactaceae)

Description: A low-growing cactus with enlarged, fleshy, spiny, green stems that often grows in colonies. The stem segments or pads are narrow, up to 5" long and 3" wide. The upper one-third of the pad may have 1–2 needle-like spines, spreading, which emerge from clusters of small bristles. These clusters or tufts are scattered across the surface of the pad. The showy flowers are up to 4" across and open from single buds along the edge of the pad (new pads also emerge along the edge). The 8–12 large, bright yellow petals have a waxy surface, often with a reddish center. Numerous yellow stamens surround a stout central style. The fruit is cylindrical, up to 2" long, and red when ripe.

Bloom Season: Late spring–midsummer

Habitat/Range: Frequent in dry rocky or sandy sites, including prairies, savannas, fields, and pastures; found throughout the prairie region, except for the northwestern part.

Comment: The spines and bristles are covered with microscopic reflexed barbs at their tips, making them difficult to extract. Native Americans ate the ripe fruit, pads, buds, and flowers raw, cooked, or dried. A closely related species, plains prickly pear (*Opuntia macrorhiza*), differs by having more than 2 spines per cluster that are turned backward (reflexed), and the spines are found along the upper two-thirds of the pad. Another cactus, fragile prickly pear (*Opuntia fragilis*), is short and sprawling, with a more-cylindrical pad, up to 2" long and ½–1" wide; yellow flowers are 1½–2" wide; occurs in dry rocky or sandy prairies; found in northern Illinois to Wisconsin and westward.

NITS AND LICE
Hypericum drummondii
St. John's wort family (Clusiaceae)

Description: Slender annuals, less than 1' tall, with lower stems reddish-brown and many pairs of tiny, pointed, opposite leaves. The stem and leaves are covered with minute yellowish-brown to dark brown or black resinous dots, whose appearance inspired the common name of the plant. Each leaf is up to ¾" long and ⅛" wide, needle-like, sharply pointed, and narrowing at the base. The flowers are mostly solitary in the leaf axils, sometimes with small, loose clusters of 3 or 5 flowers at the branch tips. Each flower is up to ⅓" wide, with 5 pointed, green sepals that are slightly longer than the 5 orange-yellow petals.

Bloom Season: Summer

Habitat/Range: Occasional in dry open areas in sand or clay soils in prairies, glades, pastures, and old fields; found in the southern half of the prairie region.

Comments: The species name, *drummondii*, is named for Thomas Drummond (1790–1835), a naturalist, born in Scotland, who collected plants and birds primarily in the New Orleans vicinity and in Texas.

SPOTTED ST. JOHN'S WORT
Hypericum pseudomaculatum
St. John's wort family (Clusiaceae)

Description: The sturdy stem of this plant is somewhat branched at the top and up to 3½' tall. The undersides of the leaves, sepals, and petals are covered with numerous tiny black dots. The leaves are opposite, lacking stalks, up to 2½" long and ¾" wide, oval to somewhat triangular-shaped, and mostly pointed at the tip. The flowers are clustered at the top of the stem and in short side branches. Each flower has 5 yellow petals, each ⅜–½" long, and numerous stamens.

Bloom Season: Summer

Habitat/Range: Locally frequent in prairies, savannas, and dry, open woods; found in the prairie region from Illinois, Missouri, and eastern Kansas southward.

Comments: *Hypericum pseudomaculatum* was formerly known as *Hypericum punctatum* var. *pseudomaculatum*, and it has been elevated to species level.

SPOTTED ST. JOHN'S WORT
Hypericum punctatum
St. John's wort family (Clusiaceae)

Description: The sturdy stem of this plant is somewhat branched at the top and up to 3' tall. The undersides of the leaves, sepals, and petals are covered with numerous tiny black dots. The leaves are opposite, lacking stalks, up to 2½" long and ¼" wide, oval, and rounded at the tip. The flowers are clustered at the top of the stem and in short side branches. Each flower has 5 yellow petals, each ¼–⅜" long, and numerous stamens.

Bloom Season: Summer

Habitat/Range: Common in low areas in prairies, savannas, along streams, fields, and pastures; found throughout the prairie region, except for the northwestern part.

Comments: A similar species, common St. John's wort (*Hypericum perforatum*), differs by having smaller leaves, ⅛–¾" long and ⅛–¼" wide. Also, the stems are much more branched, and there are fewer black dots on the petals, sepals, and stems. Native to Europe, it has been popularized by its use in the treatment of depression. Found in degraded prairies, pastures, old fields, roadsides, and other disturbed areas.

GREAT ST. JOHN'S WORT
Hypericum pyramidatum
St. John's wort family (Clusiaceae)

Description: A tall St. John's wort, 3–5' in height, with a somewhat woody rootstock and stem base. The main stem is 4-angled and slightly winged on the angles of young plants, becoming 4-lined with maturity. The leaves are opposite, stalkless, up to 3" long and 1" wide, with smooth margins, rounded at the base, and tapering to a pointed tip. The flowers are bright to golden yellow, 2–2½" across, with 5 petals, numerous yellow stamens, and a pistil with 5 styles.

Bloom Season: Summer

Habitat/Range: Occasional in mesic prairies, wet prairies, and moist open areas; found in the prairie region from Minnesota to northern Missouri and eastward.

Comments: Also known as *Hypericum ascyron*. The size of the plants and flowers sets apart great St. John's wort from other herbaceous St. John's worts. It is sometimes cultivated in gardens.

ROUND-FRUITED ST. JOHN'S WORT
Hypericum sphaerocarpum
St. John's wort family (Clusiaceae)

Description: The stem is somewhat woody and often branched at the base, up to 30" tall. The leaves are opposite, linear, of equal width throughout, up to 3" long, about ½" wide, and smooth along the edges. The flowers are compact and much branched at the top, with 5 yellow petals, each about ⅜" long, with many yellow stamens.

Bloom Season: Mid-spring–summer

Habitat/Range: Common in dry rocky prairies, glades, and pastures; found throughout the prairie region, but absent in the northwestern part.

Comments: Unlike most members of the St. John's wort family, round-fruited St. John's wort lacks black dots on the leaves and flowers. St. John's wort is said to have gotten its common name from the red resin that is contained in small, black glands in the flower petals and leaves of some of the species. In the Middle Ages, it was said that this was the blood shed by St. John the Baptist when he was beheaded. The word *wort* is an Old English word for "plant."

GROUND PLUM
Astragalus crassicarpus var. *trichocalyx*
Bean family (Fabaceae)

Description: Plants usually with several trailing stems, up to 2' long, connected to a thick woody taproot. The leaves are hairy, up to 6" long, and alternating along the stem on short stalks. Each leaf has 7–13 pairs of slightly folded leaflets, each ¾" long and ⅓" wide. The flowers are in small clusters at the ends of branches, with 5–25 flowers in each cluster. Each flower is about ¾–1" long and creamy white to greenish-yellow. The upper petal is larger and flaring at the tip, below which are two side petals and a lower lip.

Bloom Season: Mid-spring–late spring

Habitat/Range: Locally frequent in dry prairies, loess hill prairies, and rocky woods; found throughout the prairie region, but absent in Wisconsin and Illinois eastward.

Comments: The fruits are succulent, shiny pods, about 1" in diameter, that become dry and hard when they age. They contain numerous small seeds. When ripe, the fruit has a reddish cast; it was widely used for food by Native Americans and early settlers. They are said to taste like raw pea pods. A blue variety of ground plum, *Astragalus crassicarpus* var. *crassicarpus*, can be found on page 198.

CREAM WILD INDIGO
Baptisia bracteata var. *leucophaea*

Description: A coarse, hairy, bush-like plant with spreading branches up to 2' tall. The leaves are alternate on the stem and divided into 3 leaflets, each up to 3½" long. The bracts at the base of the leaflets are large and give the appearance of 5 leaflets instead of 3. The flower spike, up to 1' long, droops with numerous creamy yellow flowers, each about 1" long and having the arrangement typical of members of the bean family. The seed pods are black, pointed at the tip, and up to 2" long.

Bloom Season: Mid-spring–late spring

Habitat/Range: Common in mesic to dry prairies, sand prairies, sand savannas, and pastures; found throughout the prairie region except for the Dakotas and Ohio.

YELLOW WILD INDIGO
Baptisia sphaerocarpa
Bean family (Fabaceae)

Description: A smooth, branched, shrub-like plant, up to 4' tall. The leaves are alternate, divided into 3 leaflets, each less than 2" long. The flowers are on stalks well above the leaves. Each bright yellow flower is about ½" long, with an upper petal, 2 smaller side petals, and a middle keel-shaped lip. The seed pods are inflated to ¾" long and ½" wide, and turn tan to brown when ripe.

Bloom Season: Late spring–early summer

Habitat/Range: Occasional in prairies, sandy soils, and roadsides; found in the southwestern part of the prairie region.

Comments: Similar to blue wild indigo in appearance, yellow wild indigo is a sturdy, drought-resistant plant that does well in a backyard garden setting.

PARTRIDGE PEA
Chamaecrista fasciculata
Bean family (Fabaceae)

Description: An annual plant, up to 2' tall, with alternate leaves, each divided into about 20 pairs of leaflets. The leaflets are narrow, less than 1" long, about ⅛" wide, and rounded at both ends, with a small bristle at the tip. Near the middle of each leaf stalk there is a small, saucer-shaped gland. The leaflets fold up at night, and sometimes when touched. There are 1–4 flowers, up to 1½" wide, on slender stalks that emerge at the axil of the leaf and stem. There are 5 yellow petals, with 3 slightly smaller than the other 2, and with a tinge of red at the base of each petal. There are 10 yellow to dark red stamens.

Bloom Season: Summer–fall

Habitat/Range: Common in upland prairies, savannas, pastures, fields, and often in disturbed sandy soils; found throughout the prairie region, except for North Dakota.

Comments: Cherokee and early settlers used the root for treating fever, cramps, heart ailments, and constipation. A related species, small-flowered partridge pea (*Chamaecrista nictitans*), can be found in the same range and habitat as partridge pea, but differs by having smaller flowers (less than ¾" wide) and 5 stamens.

RATTLEBOX
Crotalaria sagittalis
Bean family (Fabaceae)

Description: Annual plants up to 1' tall, with soft, densely hairy stems and leaves. The leaves are alternate, narrow, and up to 3" long and ¾" wide, with a blunt or pointed tip. Flowers occur from 1–4 at the ends of short side branches. Each flower is on a slender stalk with small leaf-like bracts. There are 5 long-pointed, green, hairy sepals at the base of the flower. Each flower is yellow, about ⅜" long, with the shape and arrangement typical of members of the bean family. The fruit is an inflated pod to 1¼" long, initially light green, ripening to a purplish-black.

Bloom Season: Late spring–early fall

Habitat/Range: Occasional in upland prairies, sand prairies, savannas, old fields, pastures, and open disturbed ground; found throughout the prairie region, except for North Dakota.

Comments: When the pod ripens, the seeds rattle freely within the pod; hence, the common name. The kidney-shaped seeds have been used as a substitute for coffee, but are poisonous to pigs and horses.

YELLOW-PUFF
Neptunia lutea
Bean family (Fabaceae)

Description: Hairy plants with creeping stems that can grow to 4' in length. The leaves are compound and divided into 8–18 pairs of small leaflets. The solitary flower heads are on long stalks and composed of 30–60 small, yellow flowers, each with 5 miniature petals, and 10 yellow stamens.

Bloom Season: Summer–early fall

Habitat/Range: Common in dry prairies, open woodlands, and roadsides; found in the southwestern part of the prairie region.

Comments: The leaves close upon touch, as well as at night and during periods of cloudy weather.

WILD SENNA
Senna marilandica
Bean family (Fabaceae)

Description: One to several smooth stems, up to 6' tall, with large, alternate leaves. The leaves are on stalks up to 2" long with a small gland near the base. The leaves are up to 8" long and divided into 8–12 pairs of leaflets, each about 2" long and 1" wide, with small, bristle-like points at the tips. The flowers vary from numerous on branched clusters to only 1–4 on stalks emerging from the junction of a leaf and stem. Each flower is about 1" across, with 5 narrow, yellow petals that are often curled and 10 brownish-red stamens. The hanging, flattened pods are up to 4" long and ½" wide.

Bloom Season: Summer

Habitat/Range: Occasional along moist open areas along prairie streams; found throughout the prairie region, except for the northwestern part.

Comments: Also known as Maryland senna. The Meskwaki ate the seeds, softened by soaking, as a mucilaginous medicine for sore throat. The Cherokee used the bruised root moistened with water for dressing sores. They also used the root in a tea as a cure for fever, and as a laxative.

PENCIL FLOWER
Stylosanthes biflora
Bean family (Fabaceae)

Description: A small, wiry-stemmed plant, often branched at the base, hairy, up to 8" tall. The leaves are alternate, divided into 3 leaflets, each up to 2" long and ½" wide. There are widely scattered bristles along the leaf margins. The flowers are nested in leafy clusters at the tops of branches and are arranged in the style typical of the bean family. The orange-yellow flowers are about ¼" long.

Bloom Season: Late spring–summer

Habitat/Range: Common in dry prairies, sand prairies, glades, and rocky, open woods; found in the prairie region from Kansas eastward to Ohio, and south.

Comments: Pencil flower is named for the similarity of the flower's orange-yellow color to the paint on a #2 wood pencil.

SPOTTED BEEBALM
Monarda punctata
Mint family (Lamiaceae)

Description: The often showy, pinkish-purple bracts obscure the dull yellow flowers of this plant. This annual or short-lived perennial reaches a height to 3', with a finely hairy stem and toothed, opposite leaves on short stalks. The leaves are about 3½" long and up to 1" wide. The flowers are arranged in whorls, with 1–5 whorls stacked one above the other, separated by a whorl of pinkish-purple, leaf-like bracts. Each pale yellow, tubular flower is about 1" long and dotted with dark spots. The lower lip has 3 lobes.

Bloom Season: Summer–fall

Habitat/Range: Occasional in sand prairies, sand savannas, and pastures and fields in sandy areas; found throughout the prairie region, but absent in the Dakotas.

Comments: Also known as horsemint. Native Americans used leaf tea for colds, fever, flu, stomach cramps, coughs, and bowel ailments. Historically, doctors used this mint as a stimulant and diuretic.

YELLOW STAR GRASS
Hypoxis hirsuta
Lily family (Liliaceae)

Description: Small, hairy plants producing yellow, star-like flowers with grassy leaves; hence, the common name. When flowering begins, the plants are about 5" tall; as they mature, they may reach up to 1' in height. The long, grass-like leaves are about 8" long and ¼" wide. The flower stalks are shorter than the leaves, with 2–7 flowers appearing in succession. The flowers are about ½" wide, with 6 yellow petals and 6 yellow stamens.

Bloom Season: Spring; rarely reblooming through summer and fall

Habitat/Range: Common in mesic to dry prairies, savannas, open woodlands, and glades; found throughout the prairie region.

Comments: The Cherokee made an infusion of the leaves as a heart medicine, and the corm (a bulb-like underground structure) was used to treat ulcers. Various species of bees, flies, and beetles visit the flower to feed on its pollen, and small rodents feed on the corms. The seeds are eaten by bobwhite quail.

GROOVED YELLOW FLAX
Linum sulcatum
Flax family (Linaceae)

Description: A pale green annual plant, up to 2½' tall, with a stiff stem that branches near the top. The branches have conspicuous grooves or ridges. The tiny leaves are alternate on the stem, about 1" long and only ⅛" wide, pointed at the tip, stalkless, with tiny, round glands at the base of the leaf. The flowers are scattered among the branches on short stalks. The flowers are about ¾" across, with 5 pale yellow petals that drop off shortly after flowering.

Bloom Season: Mid-spring–early fall

Habitat/Range: Occasional in dry upland prairies, hill prairies, sand prairies, and glades; found throughout the prairie region.

Comments: A related species, small yellow flax (*Linum medium* var. *texanum*), differs by being a perennial, lacking the small round glands at the base of the leaf, and lacking grooves or furrows on the branches. The habitat and range is similar to grooved yellow flax, but it is absent in the northwestern part of the prairie range. Various species of flax have been cultivated since before recorded history for the fibers in their stems, used to make linen, and the oil in their seeds, used to make linseed oil. The seeds were also used for a variety of medicinal remedies. The most widely used, common flax (*Linum usitatissimum*), has blue flowers and originated in Europe.

STICKLEAF
Mentzelia oligosperma
Stickleaf family (Loasaceae)

Description: A spreading to erect plant with much-branched, whitish, rough, brittle stems, ½–3' tall, with hooked hairs on the stem and leaves. The leaves are alternate, stalkless, and broadest below the middle, up to 2½" long and 1" wide, with margins coarsely toothed to lobed, blunt or pointed tips. Flowers arise from leaf axils toward the tips of branches. Each flower is about ¾" wide and open in the morning. The 5 pale yellow to orange petals are about ¼" long, with tips pointed, and 5–40 stamens about as long as the petals.

Bloom Season: Summer

Habitat/Range: Occasional in dry, rocky prairies, glades, and rocky pastures; found in the central and western part of the prairie region.

Comments: The common name refers to the determined manner in which the leaves stick to clothing and fur. When entwined in sheep's wool, the leaves can lower the wool's market value. The *Mentzelia* genus is native to the New World. There are about 80 species of annual (and some perennial) herbs and some shrubs in this genus, 68 of which are found growing in greater North America.

TOOTHED EVENING PRIMROSE
Calylophus serrulatus
Evening primrose family (Onagraceae)

Description: Often woody at the base, with 1 to many smooth to densely hairy branches, up to 1½" tall. The leaves are alternate, stalkless, hairy, narrow, up to 2" long and ⅛" wide, and usually toothed or wavy along the edges. The flowers are solitary and stalkless and arise at the bases of upper leaves. Each flower is bright yellow, fading to dark yellow to orange, about 1" across. There are 4 petals, each shallow notched at the tip, and 8 stamens.

Bloom Season: Late spring–summer

Habitat/Range: Occasional in rocky or gravelly prairies, hill prairies, and sand prairies; found in the western part of the prairie region, and rare to absent in the eastern part.

Comments: Also known as *Oenothera serrulata*. The flowers open in the morning and close in the afternoon, unlike many species in this family that open in the evening and are pollinated by night-flying insects; hence, the name evening primrose.

SEEDBOX
Ludwigia alternifolia
Evening primrose family (Onagraceae)

Description: A widely branching plant, up to 4' tall. The leaves are alternate, up to 4" long and less than 1" wide, broadest at the middle and tapering to the tip and base. The flowers are single, on short stalks, and arise at the junction of the leaf and stem. Each flower is about ¾" across, with 4 reddish to green, triangular sepals, 4 yellow petals, which fall shortly after flowering, and 4 stamens. The seed capsules are more or less square, up to ¼" across, angled or narrowly winged, and contain numerous small seeds.

Bloom Season: Summer

Habitat/Range: Common in wet open areas in prairies, wet prairies, along streams and marshes, and roadsides; found throughout the prairie region, except for the northwestern part.

Comments: Also called rattlebox, in reference to the unusual box-like seed capsules, which, when mature, will rattle when shaken. The genus name, *Ludwigia*, is in honor of Christian Ludwig, professor of botany at Leipzig, Germany, in the late 18th century, and the species name, *alternifolia*, refers to how the leaves are arranged on the stem.

COMMON EVENING PRIMROSE
Oenothera biennis
Evening primrose family (Onagraceae)

Description: A biennial with a stout, some-times hairy stem tinged with red, as are parts of the older leaves, up to 7' tall. The basal leaves are stalked, 4–12" long and 1–2" wide, and irregularly toothed along the margins. The stem leaves are alternate, lance-shaped, pointed at the tip, hairy on both sides, toothed along the margins, and up to 6" long and 2" wide. The flowers are numerous along a long column, with yellow petals that open to 2½" across. The 4 yellow petals have a shallow notch at the end. There are 8 yellow stamens.

Bloom Season: Summer–fall

Habitat/Range: Common to abundant in disturbed areas in prairies, pastures, and fields, and along streams and roadsides; found throughout the prairie region.

Comments: The flowers open in the evening and close by midmorning on sunny days. The flowers emit a creosote smell that particularly attracts night-flying sphinx moths. Native Americans ate the seeds and the first-year roots (the second-year roots are too woody). After this plant was introduced to Europe from North America in the early 1600s, Europeans ate its roots and put the young shoots into salads. The entire plant was prepared and used to treat whooping cough, hiccups, and asthma.

CUT-LEAVED EVENING PRIMROSE
Oenothera laciniata
Evening primrose family (Onagraceae)

Description: Generally small plants that often sprawl across the ground to a length of ½–2'. The leaves are alternate along the stem, 1–4" long and up to 1" across, with the lower leaves stalked, the upper stalkless. The leaves are shallowly to deeply lobed along the edges, with sparsely hairy upper surfaces and undersides densely hairy. The flowers are single in the mid- and upper leaf axils, each about 1" across, with 4 heart-shaped, yellow petals. There are 8 yellow stamens surrounding a yellow, cross-shaped style. The 4 narrow sepals hang down below the petals along the long floral tube (ovary), which is characteristic of evening primroses.

Bloom Season: Late spring–summer

Habitat/Range: Common in sand prairies and sandy disturbed ground; found throughout the prairie region, but rare in the northwestern part.

Comments: As with many evening primroses, cut-leaved evening primrose blooms during the night and closes usually by mid-morning the next day. Although native to the United States, this plant can be found in many other places as an introduced species, and sometimes as a noxious weed. It has been reported in Hawaii, Australia, Britain, France, Korea, Japan, and other areas. Many plants from other countries have certainly caused problems in the United States when they were intentionally or accidentally introduced. Unfortunately, this same process can be extended to other parts of the world by way of transport of plants native to the United States.

FOURPOINT EVENING PRIMROSE
Oenothera rhombipetala
Evening primrose family (Onagraceae)

Discussion: A hairy annual or biennial plant, 1–4' tall, with stems erect and often branched from the base. First-year plants have a basal rosette of stalked leaves that is up to 6" in diameter. The leaves on the stem are alternate, stalkless, crowded, gradually reduced up the stem, ½–4" long and less than ¾" wide, with the margins entire or toothed and often wavy. The flowers are densely arranged along a spike about 1' long. The flowers have 4 yellow petals each ¾–1¼" long and ½–1¼" wide at the end of a 1–2" long floral tube, with 8 stamens.

Bloom Season: Summer–fall

Habitat/Range: Occasional in sand prairies, banks of rivers, roadsides, and disturbed sandy ground; found in the western part of the prairie region from Nebraska south; also eastern Iowa, western Illinois, and Wisconsin.

Comments: The showy flowers open around sunset and close during the morning. The flowers are pollinated by night-flying moths.

THREAD-LEAVED SUNDROPS
Oenothera linifolia
Evening primrose family (Onagraceae)

Description: A thin, branching annual, up to 1' tall, with many narrow, alternate, thread-like leaves. The leaves are ⅓–¾" long and about ⅛" wide, with smooth margins and a pointed tip. There are smaller leaves clustered at the leaf axils. The flowers are less than ½" across, with 4 yellow petals, 8 stamens, and a 4-lobed stigma.

Bloom Season: Mid-spring–midsummer

Habitat/Range: Locally frequent in rocky or sandy prairies, open woods, and glades; found in the southern half of the prairie region.

Comments: The flowers of thread-leaved sundrops open in the evening and usually stay open through the following midday.

MISSOURI EVENING PRIMROSE
Oenothera macrocarpa
Evening primrose family (Onagraceae)

Description: A low, sprawling to erect plant, up to 15" long. The alternate narrow leaves are several on a stem and up to 5" long and 1" wide. The leaves are long-pointed at the tip, with a tapering base and small, silky hairs. The base of the leaves and the stem are often red. The showy flowers emerge from leaf axils on the upper part of the stem. They are up to 5" across, with 4 large, yellow to bright yellow petals that turn orange when fading. The fruit is a brown, papery capsule 3–4" long with 4 broad wings.

Bloom Season: Mid-spring–midsummer

Habitat/Range: Locally frequent in limestone or dolomite dry rocky prairies and glades; found in the southwestern part of the prairie region from southeastern Nebraska to Missouri and south.

Comments: Formerly known as *Oenothera missouriensis*. The flowers open in the late evening and close the next day by mid-morning. The flowers are pollinated primarily by night-flying sphinx moths.

PRAIRIE SUNDROPS
Oenothera pilosella
Evening primrose family (Onagraceae)

Description: Unbranched, alternate-leaved plants, up to 2½' tall, with soft hairy stems and leaves. The basal leaves, up to 3" long and 2" wide, overwinter and usually wither at flowering time. The stem leaves are alternate, widest at the middle, up to 4" long and 1" wide. The yellow to deep yellow flowers arise singly at the axils of the leaves. Flowers are about 2" across, with 4 broadly rounded petals with shallow notching at the tips.

Bloom Season: Late spring–summer

Habitat/Range: Occasional in mesic to wet prairies and wet depressions in upland prairies; found in the eastern half of the prairie range, but absent in the western part, including Minnesota.

Comments: Prairie sundrop flowers bloom once during the day, unlike most others in the primrose family, which are one-time night bloomers. The flowers are pollinated primarily by long-tongued bees, butterflies, and skippers.

STEMLESS EVENING PRIMROSE
Oenothera triloba
Evening primrose family (Onagraceae)

Description: A winter annual, with the seeds germinating in the fall and the basal leaves overwintering. Stems are usually absent or inconspicuous. Leaves are basal, numerous, up to 4" long, with short stalks and several deep lobes along the margins, with the end lobe being the largest. The solitary flowers are stalked, about 1¼" wide, with 4 yellow to pale yellow petals. The petals are broadly rounded to occasionally notched at the tip, with a small sharp point in the notch.

Bloom Season: Spring–early summer

Habitat/Range: Common in dry prairies, glades, rocky open woods, and disturbed ground; found in the prairie region from Kansas and southwest, and Missouri southward.

Comments: Like many other evening primroses, stemless evening primrose flowers open in the evening and close by late morning the following day. Among the Zuni people, the plant is used as an ingredient for "schumaakwe cakes," and also used externally for rheumatism and swelling. They also grind the roots and use them as food.

LARGE YELLOW LADY'S SLIPPER
Cypripedium parviflorum var. *pubescens*
Orchid family (Orchidaceae)

Description: Stout, unbranched stems, often forming clumps from a single rhizome, up to 30" tall. The stems and leaves are finely hairy, with the base of the 3–5 alternate leaves forming a sheath around the stem. The leaves are pleated with parallel veins and vary from narrow to round, with pointed tips, and are up to 9" long and 5" wide. There are 1–2 flowers per stem. Each flower has 2 twisted narrow petals, 2–3½" long on either side of an inflated petal, called a "slipper," and 1¼–2¼" long. Above and below the slipper are 2 broad sepals. The sepals and lateral petals are yellowish-green to greenish-brown.

Bloom Season: Mid-spring–early summer

Habitat/Range: An uncommon plant usually occurring in woodlands and wetlands, but occasionally in prairies and some eastern hill prairies); found in the prairie region from Minnesota south to northern Arkansas and eastward.

Comments: Native Americans used the powdered root as a sedative, tranquilizer, and a pain reliever.

DOWNY PAINTED CUP
Castilleja sessilifolia
Broomrape family (Orobanchaceae)

Description: Several hairy, unbranched stems arising from a single base up to 15" tall. The leaves are alternate, stalkless, up to 2" long, narrow with rounded tips or narrowly lobed in 3 segments. The leaves near the base of the stem are often long, narrow, and undivided. Flowers are in a dense, leafy cluster at the top of the stems. The pale yellow flowers are tubular, 1½–2¼" long, with a long slender upper lip and a shorter lower lip, lobed in 3 parts.

Bloom Season: Mid-spring–early summer

Habitat/Range: Occasional in dry prairies, hill prairies, rocky hillsides, and sandy soil; found in the prairie region from northern Illinois west to eastern Kansas and northward.

Comments: The genus *Castilleja* was formerly in the snapdragon family (Scrophulariaceae). Downey painted cup is partially parasitic, obtaining water and nutrients from other plants by tapping their roots. Host plants include other wildflowers and also various native grasses, such as hairy grama and junegrass, as well as eastern red cedar.

SMALL YELLOW LADY'S SLIPPER
Cypripedium parviflorum var. *parviflorum*
Orchid family (Orchidaceae)

Discussion: Stout, unbranched stems, often forming clumps from a single rhizome, up to 22" tall. The stems and leaves are finely hairy, with the base of the 4–6 alternate leaves forming a sheath around the stem. The leaves are pleated with parallel veins and vary from narrow to round, with pointed tips, and are up to 6" long and 3" wide. Each stem has at least 1 flower, but occasionally 2. The flower has 2 twisted, narrow petals, 1½–2" long, on either side of an inflated petal, called a "slipper," ¾–1¼" long. Above and below the slipper are 2 broad sepals. The sepals and lateral petals are reddish-purple to brown.

Bloom Season: Mid-spring–early summer

Habitat/Range: Infrequent in mesic prairies, wet sand prairies, and seepage areas in prairie wetlands; found in the prairie region from Minnesota south to northern Arkansas and eastward.

Comments: Both large and small yellow lady's slippers were widely used in 19th-century America as a sedative for nervous headaches, hysteria, insomnia, and nervous irritability.

WOOD BETONY
Pedicularis canadensis
Broomrape family (Orobanchaceae)

Description: Several hairy stems emerge from a clump of fern-like basal leaves. The stems are about 6–10" tall when in flower and grow to about 18" tall as they mature. The basal leaves are narrow, deeply divided, and about 6" long. In the spring, they start out as a beautiful wine color before they turn green. Leaves along the stem are scattered and alternate. The flowers are nearly 1" long and densely clustered at the top of the stem. There are 2 lips, with the upper lip yellow or purple, flattened, and curved in a long arch to form a hood. The lower lip has 3 rounded lobes.

Bloom Season: Spring

Habitat/Range: Common in mesic to dry prairies, savannas, glades, and pastures; found throughout the prairie region.

Comments: Wood betony is also called "lousewort," from the belief that cattle and sheep grazing in pastures with this plant were once expected to become infested with lice. The Meskwaki and Potawatomi boiled the whole plant to make a tea for reducing internal swelling, tumors, and some types of external swelling. The Ojibwa used the plant as a love charm. The chopped-up root was put into food that was cooking without the knowledge of the couple who were to eat it. If they had been quarrelsome, they would once again become lovers.

YELLOW WOOD SORREL
Oxalis dillenii
Wood sorrel family (Oxalidaceae)

Description: Small hairs lying flat along the stem give the plant a grayish appearance. The stems are up to 6–12" tall. The leaves have 3 leaflets on long stalks. Individual flowers are also on long stalks and arranged in a loose cluster at the tips of branches. Each flower is about ½" across, with 5 yellow petals. The fruit is upright, hairy, and attached to stalks that are at right angles to the stem.

Bloom Season: Late spring–fall

Habitat/Range: Common in upland prairies, savannas, pastures, fields, and roadsides; found throughout the prairie region.

Comments: The leaves and flowers were eaten by Native Americans of various tribes. The powdered leaves were boiled in water and used to expel intestinal worms, to reduce fever, and to increase urine flow. The distinctive sour taste, which comes from oxalic acid, has been used to flavor salads. A similar species, which shares the same common name of yellow wood sorrel, is *Oxalis stricta*. It differs by having the fruit stalk upright and hairs that are spreading, and not with a grayish cast. It has a similar habitat and range.

LANCE-LEAVED LOOSESTRIFE
Lysimachia lanceolata
Primrose family (Primulaceae)

Description: A single-stemmed plant, up to 2' tall, with very short side branches. The stem sends out stolons (runners) at the base to produce more plants. The leaves are opposite, closely spaced, and vary in shape, from rounded and stalked on the lower stem to narrow and tapering on the middle and upper parts. The stem leaves are up to 6" long, less than ¾" wide, pointed at the tip, and tapering to the base. The flowers dangle on long, individual stalks, with each flower about ¾" wide. The 5 yellow petals have ragged lobes and finely pointed tips.

Bloom Season: Late spring–summer

Habitat/Range: Occasional in mesic to dry prairies, savannas, pastures, and woodlands; found throughout the prairie region, except for Kansas, north to the Dakotas, and Minnesota.

Comments: A closely related species, fringed loosestrife (*Lysimachia ciliata*), has leaves over 1" wide and a fringe of short hairs along the base of the leaves. It grows primarily in moist, shaded areas but can also occur in prairies; found throughout the prairie region, except for Texas.

NARROW-LEAVED LOOSESTRIFE
Lysimachia quadrifolia
Primrose family (Primulaceae)

Description: Slender stems up to 2' tall, with very narrow, stalkless leaves that are opposite on the stem. The leaves are 3" long, less than ¼" wide, with smooth edges that are slightly turned down. The flowers are on long, slender stalks that bend, causing the flower to droop. There are 5 broad, yellow petals each about ⅝" long, with margins that are somewhat uneven and often with an extended point.

Bloom Season: Summer

Habitat/Range: Occasional in mesic prairies, low areas in upland prairies, and in sandy soils; found in the eastern prairie region, and absent from the Dakotas southward.

Comments: Native Americans made tea from loosestrife plants for kidney trouble, bowel complaints, and other problems. Tea from the root was used to induce vomiting. The flowers of the loosestrifes are unusual in that they produce a flora oil, rather than nectar. Insects like the melittid bee gather the floral oil and pollen, form a ball, and feed it to its developing larvae. The flowers attract few insects otherwise.

EARLY BUTTERCUP
Ranunculus fascicularis
Buttercup family (Ranunculaceae)

Description: Small, hairy plants with distinctive, shiny yellow flowers. Leaves are mostly basal, emerging on hairy stalks up to 4" long. The hairy leaves are divided into 3 segments, which are again divided into smaller lobes. Flowers are about 1" across, with 5 shiny yellow petals that are rounded at the tip and usually streaked with green at the base. Numerous yellow stamens surround the yellowish center that turns green with maturity.

Bloom Season: Late winter–early spring

Habitat/Range: Frequent in dry prairies, savannas, and open woods; found throughout the prairie region, but absent in the western part.

Comments: The common name early buttercup is appropriate, because it is typically the first yellow buttercup to bloom in late winter to early spring. As in many buttercups, early buttercup is considered to be a toxic plant that can cause minor skin irritation lasting minutes if touched. If eaten, symptoms include burning of the mouth, abdominal pain, vomiting, and bloody diarrhea. The sap can cause skin redness, burning sensation, and blisters.

PRAIRIE BUTTERCUP
Ranunculus rhomboideus
Buttercup family (Ranunculaceae)

Description: Plants less than 10" tall, with long, soft hairs on the leaves and stems. The basal leaves are on long stalks about 2" long, with leaves about 1½" long, ¾" wide, and with coarse, rounded teeth along the margins as the leaves mature. The stem leaves are usually stalkless and divided into 3 narrow lobes. A single flower is attached to a hairy stalk that arises from the axil of a leaf. The stems and flowers may be only 2–3" tall when they start to flower, but the stems eventually elongate. Each flower is about ¾" across with 5 small, hairy sepals, 5 yellow, glossy petals, and many yellow stamens surrounding a bulbous green center.

Bloom Season: Spring

Habitat/Range: Occurs in dry prairies, hill prairies, and open woodlands; found in the northern half of the prairie region.

Comments: Prairie buttercup is among the first prairie plants to bloom in the spring. As in many buttercups, prairie buttercup is considered to be a toxic plant. Refer to comments under early buttercup (above) for more details.

SWAMP AGRIMONY
Agrimonia parviflora
Rose family (Rosaceae)

Description: Stout, hairy stems with wand-like branches, up to 6' tall. The leaves are alternate, stalked, up to 12" long, and divided into 11–23 leaflets, with the larger leaflets interspersed with many small ones. The leaflets are hairy, with many teeth along the margins. The flowers are arranged alternately along the stem, small, about ¼" across, with 5 yellow petals. The flowers develop into bur-like fruits, with hooked bristles that easily cling to clothing and fur.

Bloom Season: Midsummer–early fall

Habitat/Range: Common in wet ground in prairies, wet prairies, savannas, moist woods, marshes, thickets, and along streams; found in the prairie region from southeast Nebraska east to southern Michigan, and south.

Comments: An herbal tea made from the whole plant has been used to stop internal bleeding; also used for diarrhea, inflammation of the gallbladder, jaundice, and gout.

PRAIRIE CINQUEFOIL
Drymocallis arguta
Rose family (Rosaceae)

Description: Stout, single-stemmed plants below the flower clusters, up to 3' tall, with spreading hairs on the stems and leaves. The leaves are alternate, with each leaf composed of 3–11 toothed leaflets. The lower leaves are long-stalked, with the stalks and leaves becoming progressively smaller upward along the stem. The end leaflet is the longest, up to 3". The flowers, each about ¾" across, appear on branched stems, each with 5 pointed, hairy green sepals about as long as the petals and 5 creamy white to pale yellow, rounded petals. There are 25 yellow stamens surrounding a yellow, cone-shaped center.

Bloom Season: Late spring–summer

Habitat/Range: Occasional in mesic and dry prairies, hill prairies, sand prairies, and savannas; found throughout the prairie region, but less common in the southern half, and absent from Texas.

Comments: Formerly known as *Potentilla arguta*. Prairie cinquefoil's root system is a taproot with short rhizomes at the surface, which allow the plant to form tight clumps. The whole plant, including the root, has been used in tea or as a poultice (moist, warm plant material applied to the skin); to stop bleeding (as an astringent to capillaries); on cuts and wounds; and to treat diarrhea and dysentery.

COMMON CINQUEFOIL
Potentilla simplex
Rose family (Rosaceae)

Description: A trailing plant, often rooting at the nodes, with a stiff, hairy stem up to 3' long. The leaves are alternate along the stem, with long stalks. The leaves each have 5 leaflets that are fan-shaped, up to 3" long, with teeth along the margins. The flowers are on long stalks emerging at the axil of the stem and leaf. Each flower is about ½" across, with 5 pointed, green sepals alternating with 5 rounded, often notched, bright yellow petals and 25–30 stamens.

Bloom Season: Mid-spring–summer

Habitat/Range: Common in upland prairies, hill prairies, glades, and savannas; also old fields and pastures; found throughout the prairie region, but less common in the western part, and absent in the Dakotas and Texas.

Comments: In folk medicine, a tea made from various species of cinquefoil was used for a variety of inflammations, for throat and stomach ulcers, and for fever and diarrhea. As a mouthwash and gargle, the tea was used to treat throat, tonsil, and gum inflammations.

GROUND CHERRY
Physalis longifolia
Nightshade family (Solanaceae)

Description: An upright, branched plant up to 2' tall. The smooth stems have ridges along their length. The leaves are thin, alternate, long-stalked, lance-shaped, and smooth to sparsely hairy. The flowers are single on stalks arising from the axil of the leaf and stem. The bell-shaped flowers are about 1½" long and attached to a dangling stalk. The 5-angled, united, pale yellow petals have purple near the base and 5 yellow stamens. The fruit is enclosed in an inflated papery husk.

Bloom Season: Late spring–fall

Habitat/Range: Frequent in wet prairies, wet depressions in prairies, savannas, fields, pastures, and roadsides; found throughout the prairie region, but less frequent in the north-western part.

Comments: Although Native Americans and early settlers ate ground cherries either raw or cooked, today the unripe fruits are considered poisonous. Ground cherries were sometimes used to treat snakebite, and a tea brewed from the plant was said to cure dropsy (edema). Insects, birds, and rodents eat the fruits in late autumn. A closely related species, lance-leaved ground cherry (*Physalis virginiana*), differs by having moderate to densely hairy stems and leaves. It is found frequently in dry prairies, hill prairies, old fields, and pastures throughout the prairie region.

BUFFALO BUR
Solanum rostratum
Nightshade family (Solanaceae)

Description: An annual, multibranched plant, up to 2½' tall, with star-shaped hairs and abundant yellowish prickles that are purplish at the base. The leaves are alternate, stalked, up to 6" long and 4" wide, with irregular and deeply rounded lobes. There are long, sharply pointed, yellow prickles along the leaf stalk and the major veins on both sides of the leaf. Flowers are stalked, with 5–15 arising from near the ends of branches. Each flower is about ½–1" across, shallowly funnel-shaped, with 5 bright yellow fused petals that have crinkled or wavy edges. There are 5 large stamens. The fruit is a round berry covered with many prickles and contains many dark seeds.

Bloom Season: Summer–fall

Habitat/Range: Locally common on disturbed portions of dry prairies, hill prairies, pastures, roadsides, and waste areas; found in the western part of the prairie region, but introduced eastward.

Comments: Buffalo bur, although native to the Central States, has spread both east and west. It has also made its way to Eurasia, Australia, and South Africa, where it is regarded as a troublesome weed. The spiny fruit contains alkaloids that are toxic to mammalian herbivores, and its spines can injure their gastrointestinal tracts and mouthparts. The spiny fruits can also cling to the fur of bison, sheep, and other woolly animals, which aids in their dispersal.

RED AND ORANGE FLOWERS

Castilleja coccinea

This section includes red and orange flowers. Because red flowers grade into both pink flowers and purple flowers, those sections should also be checked.

BUTTERFLY WEED
Asclepias tuberosa
Milkweed family (Asclepiadaceae)

Description: Several stout stems may arise from a common base, giving the plant a bushy appearance, up to 2½' tall. The stems are covered with coarse, spreading hairs and lack the milky latex sap that is typical of the milkweed family. The mostly alternate leaves are stalkless, about 4" long and 1" wide, widest in the middle and tapering at both ends, very hairy, and dark green. The flowers are in clusters at the tops of stems and vary from deep red to brilliant orange to yellow. Each flower is less than ¾" long, with 5 reflexed petals below 5 erect hoods. The seed pods are about 6" long and ¾" thick, with fine hairs.

Bloom Season: Late spring–summer

Habitat/Range: Common in upland prairies, glades, savannas, sandy sites, and roadsides; found throughout the prairie region.

Comments: Also called pleurisy root, because it was considered to be a cure for pleurisy, an inflammation of the covering of the lungs. Several tribes revered this plant as a healer. They used the leaves to induce vomiting and the roots to treat dysentery, diarrhea, constipation, lung inflammations, rheumatism, fever, and pneumonia. The roots were also mashed and applied externally to bruises, swellings, and wounds. Butterfly weed is appropriately named for its popularity with butterflies, especially the monarch butterfly. The larvae consume the leaves, while the adults feed on the nectar.

BLANKET FLOWER
Gaillardia pulchella
Aster family (Asteraceae)

Description: An annual or short-lived perennial, up to 2' tall, with freely branching, hairy stems. The leaves are alternate, 1–4" long and ¼–1" wide, and either lacking teeth along the margins, or toothed, or lobed. The showy flower heads are 1–2" across on long stalks, with the 6–16 petal-like ray flowers red or reddish-purple, with yellow tips that are 3-lobed. The tubular disk flowers are purple.

Bloom Season: Late spring–early fall

Habitat/Range: Occasional to common in the southwestern part of the prairie region in prairies, especially with sandy soils, and commonly cultivated and escaped elsewhere.

Comments: Also known as firewheel and Indian blanket, this showy wildflower is often planted as an ornamental in gardens. The common name suggests its resemblance to the rich and warm colors and patterns of the blankets woven by Native Americans. However, some authorities suggest this common name originally referred to the habit of wild populations of these plants to form colonies and blanket the ground. A similar species, prairie blanket flower (*Gaillardia aestivalis*), has yellow ray and disk flowers, with the ray flowers narrow at the base. There are also small, soft bristles scattered among the disk flowers. Found in dry prairies, sandy areas, and disturbed ground in the southwestern part of the prairie region from Kansas southward.

CARDINAL FLOWER
Lobelia cardinalis
Bellflower family (Campanulaceae)

Description: The leafy stem is usually unbranched, up to 4' tall, with milky sap. The basal leaves have short stalks and are up to 6" long and about 2" wide. The stem leaves are alternate, stalkless, narrow, and less than 2" long. The leaves are widest in the middle and taper at both ends, with fine teeth along the margins. The crimson flowers are alternately arranged on individual stalks along a dense spike at the top of the plant. Each flower is about 1½" long with 2 lips: the upper lip has 2 small, narrow lobes, and the lower lip has 3 lobes. The 5 stamens and style extend from a red central column.

Bloom Season: Midsummer–early fall

Habitat/Range: Locally frequent in wet sites, including marshy depressions in prairies and borders of prairie streams, as well as ditches and wet roadsides. Found throughout the prairie region, but absent in the Dakotas.

Comments: The crimson, tubular flowers are a favorite with hummingbirds. The Meskwaki crushed and dried the plant and threw it to the winds to ward off approaching storms. It was also scattered over a grave as the final ceremonial rite. Other tribes used a root tea as treatment for stomachache and intestinal worms, and as an ingredient in a love potion. Leaf tea was used for colds, nosebleeds, fever, headache, and rheumatism.

ROYAL CATCHFLY
Silene regia
Pink family (Caryophyllaceae)

Description: Slender plants, up to 5' tall, with generally smooth stems on the lower part but with sticky hairs near the top. The leaves are opposite and stalkless, with 10–20 pairs along the stem. Each leaf is about 5" long and 3" wide, smooth along the margins, slightly clasping at the base, and blunt to slightly pointed at the tip. The flowers are crimson, tubular, about 1" long, with sticky hairs along the 5-toothed calyx, and 5 narrow petals with small teeth along the tips. There are 10 stamens extending beyond the petals.

Bloom Season: Late spring–summer

Habitat/Range: Uncommon to rare in mesic to dry upland prairies, savannas, woodlands, borders of glades, and along fencerows in former prairie habitat. Found mostly in the southern half of Missouri and rare to endangered, due to the destruction of habitat, in the southern and eastern parts of the prairie region.

Comments: Royal catchfly is a very showy plant that is becoming rare or eliminated from loss of habitat throughout its range. The bright, tubular flowers attract larger butterflies like the black swallowtail; also ruby-throated hummingbirds. The plant's showy color and long flowering period makes it an excellent butterfly and wildflower garden addition. Plants and seeds are often available from nurseries and companies that sell wildflowers rather than collecting from the wild. The sticky calyx with its gland-tipped hairs traps small insects, giving the plant its common name of "catchfly."

MICHIGAN LILY
Lilium michiganese
Lily family (Liliaceae)

Description: A stately plant arising from a bulb, with a smooth, stout stem to 6' tall. The lower leaves are in whorls around the stem, while the upper leaves are alternate. The leaves are waxy and thick, up to 5" long and less than 1" wide, broadest near the middle, and tapering at both ends. The flowers hang down from long stalks at the top of the stem. There are 1–12 flowers, depending upon the age of the plant. Each flower is up to 3" wide, with 3 petal-like sepals and 3 petals that strongly curve back. The orange-yellow to orange-red sepals and petals sometimes fade to yellow on the underside and have many dark purple spots. The 6 reddish-brown stamens and the stigma show prominently.

Bloom Season: Early summer–midsummer

Habitat/Range: Occasional in mesic prairies, depressions in prairies, moist thickets at prairie edges, and moist savannas; found throughout the prairie region.

Comments: Also called turk's cap lily. Some tribes of Native Americans used the roots to thicken soups, and others used a tea made from the bulbs to treat snakebite. When chewed to a paste, the flower was a treatment for spider bites.

PRAIRIE LILY
Lilium philadelphicum
Lily family (Liliaceae)

Description: Stems arise from a small bulb and vary from ½–3' tall, with alternate or opposite leaves on the lower stem and whorls of 4–7 leaves on the upper part of the stem. The leaves are pointed and 2–4" long. The 1–3 showy reddish-orange to red flowers are 3–4" across, upright, with 3 petal-like sepals and 3 petals. Inside the flower, on the lower parts of the sepals and petals, there are purplish spots with patches of yellow. Six prominent stamens and stigma extend beyond the flower.

Bloom Season: Early summer–midsummer

Habitat/Range: Uncommon in mesic prairies, moist sand prairies, and woodlands; found in the northern half of the prairie region.

Comments: Also known as wood lily, this showy wildflower is more commonly found in prairies than woods in the prairie region. Sensitive to disturbance, the presence of prairie lily is an indicator of a high-quality prairie.

ORANGE FRINGED ORCHID
Platanthera ciliaris
Orchid family (Orchidaceae)

Description: A stem from 1½–3' tall with a column of showy yellow to orange flowers. The leaves are alternate, with 2–5 leaves up to 12" long that are reduced in size progressively upward along the stem. The flowers are clustered at the top of the stem with 30–60 yellow to orange flowers, each about 1" long. There are 3 rounded sepals, with the top sepal forming a hood; 2 small, narrow, slightly fringed upper petals; and a lower lip that is narrow and deeply fringed along the margin. There is a slender spur that protrudes from the base of the flower.

Bloom Season: Summer–early fall

Habitat/Range: Uncommon in moist sand prairies, sand flats, acid seeps, and bogs; found in the southern and eastern prairie region states, absent from Kansas on a line to Wisconsin and northwestward.

Comments: Also known as yellow fringed orchid. The Cherokee made a tea of the plant parts for treating headaches. The Seminole used the root for treating snakebite. The pollinators are primarily swallowtail butterflies.

INDIAN PAINTBRUSH
Castilleja coccinea
Broomrape family (Orobanchaceae)

Description: A biennial plant, with single, hairy stems, typically about 12" tall. The leaves are alternate, stalkless, yellowish-green, hairy, ¾–3" long, and divided into 3 lobes. The flowers are concentrated in a dense cluster at the top of the stem that elongates as the flowers open. The brilliant red color does not come from the flower but from leafy bracts that arise from under each flower. The inconspicuous flower is greenish-yellow and tubular. Although typically red, Indian paintbrush is sometimes yellow.

Bloom Season: Spring–early summer

Habitat/Range: Common in mesic and dry prairies, sand prairies, savannas, glades, and fens; found throughout the prairie region.

Comments: Typical of many members of this family, Indian paintbrush is a partial parasite, sometimes attaching to roots of other plants to obtain nourishment. Native Americans used weak flower tea as a treatment for rheumatism and as a contraceptive; they also used it as a secret love charm in food and as a poison "to destroy your enemies."

142

PINK FLOWERS

Sabatia angularis

This section includes flowers ranging from pale pinkish-white to vivid electric pink to pinkish-magenta. Because pink flowers grade into purple flowers or white flowers, those sections should also be checked.

CLASPING MILKWEED
Asclepias amplexicaulis
Milkweed family (Asclepiadaceae)

Description: Single, unbranched stems, with milky sap, up to 30" long, often curve upward instead of being totally erect. The plants are smooth, with up to 5 pairs of leaves. The leaves are up to 6" long and 3" wide, with leaf bases frequently overlapping that of the opposite leaf, and with wavy or curly margins. There is typically 1 flower cluster on each plant (sometimes 2), each with 20 to 40 flowers on long stalks. Each flower is up to ¾" long, with reflexed green to pink petals flanking 5 pink, cup-like hoods. The seed pods are 4–6" long.

Bloom Season: Mid-spring–early summer

Habitat/Range: Occasional in dry upland prairies, sand prairies, and dry open woodlands; found throughout the prairie region, but absent in the Dakotas.

Comments: The loose cluster of flowers on long stalks gives the resemblance to a starburst fireworks display.

SWAMP MILKWEED
Asclepias incarnata
Milkweed family (Asclepiadaceae)

Description: This smooth-stemmed, branching plant, up to 5' tall, has milky sap and narrow, opposite leaves. The leaves are up to 6" long and 1" wide, pointed at the tip, and narrowed at the base, with short stalks. The flowers are clustered at the tops of branches. Each flower is about ¼" across, with 5 reflexed, pink petals surrounding 5 light pink to whitish hoods. The seed pods are paired, slender, up to 4" long, and tapering at both ends.

Bloom Season: Summer

Habitat/Range: Common in wet prairies, marshes, sloughs, and along streams and shores; found throughout the prairie region.

Comments: Swamp milkweed is the only milkweed found growing in saturated soils. Swamp milkweed is gaining in popularity as a garden ornamental, especially in rain gardens. The flowers are also very popular with many kinds of insects, including bumblebees, honeybees, and butterflies, including monarch butterflies. New England colonists used swamp milkweed to treat asthma, rheumatism, syphilis, and intestinal worms, and as a heart tonic.

PRAIRIE MILKWEED
Asclepias sullivantii
Milkweed family (Asclepiadaceae)

Description: Sturdy, thick-stemmed, hairless plants, up to 3' tall, with milky sap. The oval leaves are stalkless, opposite, up to 7" long and 3½" wide, with pointed tips and broad bases. The midrib of the leaf is typically reddish-pink. There are from one to several flower clusters near the top of the stem, with each cluster having up to 40 flowers. Each flower is about ½" across with 5 reddish-pink petals that are reflexed, and 5 erect, pink hoods. The fruiting pods are about 4" long, 1½" wide, and typically have soft, pointed projections on the upper half.

Bloom Season: Early summer–midsummer

Habitat/Range: Occasional in mesic to wet prairies; found across the middle part of the prairie region, rare in the northern part, and absent in Arkansas and Texas.

Comments: Also known as Sullivant's milkweed, it is found in high-quality mesic and wet prairies. The species *sullivantii* was named for William Starling Sullivant (1803–1873), a botanist from Columbus, Ohio, who was the leading American bryologist of his time. His studies of bryophytes (mosses and liverworts) formed the basis for further investigations of these plants in the United States.

COMMON MILKWEED
Asclepias syriaca
Milkweed family (Asclepiadaceae)

Description: A robust plant, up to 5' tall, with a stout stem, large leaves, and large flower clusters. The stem is unbranched, with fine hairs and milky sap. The leaves are opposite, thick, leathery, oval, hairy, on short stalks, up to 8" long and 4" wide, and with pinkish veins. The pink flowers are about ¼" across, with 5 reflexed petals surrounding 5 spreading hoods, each about ⅛–¼" long, and with 5 tiny, pointed horns arising from them. The fruits are pods up to 4" long, with soft spines on the surface, and filled with numerous seeds, each with silky hairs at one end.

Bloom Season: Late spring–summer

Habitat/Range: Common to abundant in open disturbed areas, including pastures, fields, and roadsides; occasional in prairies, especially degraded prairies; found throughout the prairie region, except for Texas.

Comments: Native Americans used root tea as a laxative and as a diuretic to expel kidney stones and treat dropsy (edema). The milky latex sap was applied to warts, moles, and ringworm. Common milkweed was also used by early American physicians for treating asthma and rheumatism. A similar species, showy milkweed (*Asclepias speciosa*), differs by having larger flowers and exceptionally long hoods, each about ½" long, that make the flower heads showy; also, its horns are long and slender. Common in moist, sandy, or rocky prairies and along prairie streams; found in Minnesota and along the western edge of the prairie region, and westward.

AMERICAN BASKETFLOWER
Centaurea americana
Aster family (Asteraceae)

Description: A somewhat coarse annual plant, up to 5' tall, often with one branching stem. The basal leaves are toothed and up to 8" long, while the stem leaves have margins that are sparsely toothed to smooth and 2–4" long. Leaves are stalkless, sharply pointed at the tip, tapering at the base, and covered with minute, yellow to brown resin glands. Flower heads are up to 4" wide with an outer ring of sterile light pink to magenta florets and inner creamy white fertile florets with blue tips.

Bloom Season: Late spring–midsummer

Habitat/Range: Locally frequent in often-disturbed dry prairies, roadsides, and open ground; found in the prairie region from southeastern Kansas southward.

Comments: Also known as American star-thistle, and the synonym *Plectocephalus americanus*. "Basketflower" refers to the basket-like weave pattern that the inflorescence has underneath the flower head, which gives the appearance that the bloom is setting in a ready-made basket.

SPOTTED JOE-PYE WEED
Eutrochium maculatum
Aster family (Asteraceae)

Description: Stems unbranched, up to 6' tall, green with purple spots or sometimes purple throughout, with widely spaced whorls of 4–6 coarsely toothed leaves. Each leaf is broadest near the middle, up to 9" long and 2" wide and tapering to a pointed tip. The numerous flowers heads are in flat to shallowly rounded clusters at the top of the plant. Flower heads lack petal-like ray flowers and are made up of 8–20 pink to purplish disk flowers, each about ⅓" long. Conspicuous thread-like, purple styles extend from the flower heads.

Bloom Season: Late spring–early fall

Habitat/Range: Locally common in moist, often sandy soils, wet prairies, wet sand prairies, marshes, and fens; found in the northern half of the region.

Comments: Formerly known as *Eupatorium maculatum*. Native Americans used tea from the plant as a diuretic for dropsy (edema), painful urination, gout, and kidney infections. Root tea was used for fever, colds, chills, diarrhea, and liver and kidney ailments.

SKELETON PLANT
Lygodesmia juncea
Aster family (Asteraceae)

Description: Stiff, hairless, much-branched plants, 6–18" tall, with milky to yellowish sap. The lower leaves are small, narrow, alternate, ½–2" long, while the upper leaves are inconspicuous and scale-like. The flower heads are single at the tops of branches, with each head ½–¾" across and consisting of 5 pink, petal-like ray flowers with 5 small teeth at the tips.

Bloom Season: Summer

Habitat/Range: Common in dry upland prairies, hill prairies, pastures, and roadsides; found in the western prairie region.

Comments: The stems appear leafless, which inspired the name skeleton plant. Spherical galls are often seen on the stems, and they are caused by the gall wasp. Native Americans used the plant to treat diarrhea, coughs, heartburn, and kidney ailments. Skeleton plant is unpalatable to livestock because of its bitterness.

BARBARA'S BUTTONS
Marshallia caespitosa
Aster family (Asteraceae)

Description: Somewhat spindly plants, about 10" tall, sparsely to densely hairy, with fine ridges and grooves along the stem. Leaves are basal, grass-like, up to 6" long and ½" wide, with small, yellowish dots along the leaf. Numerous parallel veins run along their length. Flowers are in dense, button-like heads up to 1½" across, with 40–90 pink to white disk flowers. Each flower has 5 narrow, strap-shaped lobes.

Bloom Season: Mid-spring–early summer

Habitat/Range: Uncommon in dry upland prairies, open woodlands, rocky slopes, and glades; found in the southwestern prairie region from southeastern Kansas and southwestern Missouri southward.

Comments: The origin of the name "Barbara's buttons" is unknown, but the first printed use of the common name is in Small's *Manual of the Southeastern Flora* (1933).

SHOWY TICK TREFOIL
Desmodium canadense
Bean family (Fabaceae)

Description: Plants up to 6' tall, branched above, with long, soft hairs on the stem. Leaves are alternate along the stem and divided into 3 leaflets. The leaflets are 2–3 times longer than broad, on short stalks. The flowers are in elongated clusters, with each flower about ½" long. The bright pink to purple petals have a large, flaring upper petal, and 2 small side petals flanking a keel-like lower lip. The fruit pods are in 3–5 segments with hooked hairs along the margins that enable the pods to easily attach to fur and clothing.

Bloom Season: Midsummer–late summer

Habitat/Range: Frequent in mesic to dry prairies, savannas, and pastures; found throughout the prairie region, but rare in Texas.

Comments: In general reference to tick trefoils: "There is something witch-like about them; though so rare and remote, yet evidently, from those bur-like pods, expecting to come in contact with some traveling man or beast without their knowledge, to be transported to new hillsides; lying in wait, as it were, to catch by the hem of the berry-picker's garments and so get a lift to new quarters" (Henry David Thoreau, 1856).

ILLINOIS TICK TREFOIL
Desmodium illinoense
Bean family (Fabaceae)

Description: Plants 3–6' tall, hairy, typically unbranched, with alternate, stalked leaves. The leaves are divided into 3 leaflets, with the middle leaflet up to 4" long and 2" wide, and the two side leaflets smaller, about 2½" long and 1½" wide. The flowers are loosely clustered along the upper part of unbranched stems. The pink to purple flowers are about ⅓" across, with a large, flaring upper petal and two small side petals flanking a keel-like lower lip. The fruit pods are in 3–6 flattened, hairy segments.

Bloom Season: Summer–early fall

Habitat/Range: Common in dry upland prairies, sand prairies, sandy open woodlands, pastures and roadsides; found in the prairie region from southeastern South Dakota south and eastward to Ohio.

Comments: This tall tick trefoil can surprisingly withstand close roadside mowing and yet emerge with very tall stems between mowings. The stem, leaves, and fruit pods are covered with hooked hairs that easily attach to fur and clothing.

PERPLEXING TICK TREFOIL
Desmodium perplexum
Bean family (Fabaceae)

Description: A slender-stemmed, hairy plant, up to 3½' tall, with several branches arising from the base. The leaves are alternate, with 3 leaflets. The middle leaflet is stalked and from 1½–2½ times longer than broad. There are fine hairs flattened on the lower leaf surface. The flowers are small, pink, in loose branches, about ¼" long, and having the shape and arrangement typical of members of the bean family. The light brown seed pods easily attach to clothing and fur.

Bloom Season: Late summer–fall

Habitat/Range: Common in dry upland prairies, savannas, rocky open woods, old fields, and pastures; found throughout the prairie region, but absent in the northwestern part, and Texas.

Comments: Formerly called *Desmodium paniculatum* var. *dillenii*. Unfortunately, it has been reclassified by taxonomists on several occasions, which may be the reason for the *perplexum* in its scientific name. The Cherokee chewed the roots of perplexing tick trefoil to treat sore gums.

SENSITIVE BRIAR
Mimosa nuttallii
Bean family (Fabaceae)

Description: A trailing or sprawling plant, up to 4' long, with angled stems and abundant hooked prickles. The leaves are alternate, stalked, and divided twice, with the numerous individual leaflets less than ½" long. The flowers are densely packed in round clusters, each about ¾–1" across, on individual stalks arising from the leaf axils. The overall pink color and shape come from 8–10 stamens in each flower. The fruit is a very prickly pod up to 3½" long.

Bloom Season: Late spring–summer

Habitat/Range: Common in dry upland prairies, savannas, openings in dry upland forests, and roadsides; found in the southwestern part of the prairie region, rare to absent in the northern and eastern parts.

Comments: Formerly known as *Schrankia uncinata*. The leaflets have sensitive hairs that trigger them to close when touched. Seeds from this plant contain a purgative and have been used in laxatives. Bobwhite quail are known to eat the seeds, and wild turkey feed on the leaves. This plant is also appropriately named "devil's shoestrings" by rural children running barefoot through the prickly stems.

TRAILING WILD BEAN
Strophostyles helvula
Bean family (Fabaceae)

Description: A trailing or twining annual vine, up to 5' long, often branching above. The lowest leaves are usually opposite, the rest, alternate. The leaves are on stalks and divided into 3 rounded leaflets, up to 2½" long, sparsely hairy, usually with a large lobe along one of the margins or on both sides. The pink flowers are few to several, clustered along the vine, and up to ½" long. The pods are narrow and up to 4" long.

Bloom Season: Late spring–fall

Habitat/Range: Occasional in upland prairies, wet prairies, sand prairies, savannas, pastures, old fields, and roadsides; found in the prairie region, but rare in South Dakota and absent in North Dakota.

Comments: The closely related small wild bean (*Strophostyles leiosperma*) has silky-gray stems and leaflets; its leaflets are narrow, unlobed, and up to 2" long. The only perennial wild bean (*Strophostyles umbellata*) has somewhat leathery leaflets, and lacks lobes and hairs. All three of these wild beans occupy similar habitats, but the latter is absent in the northwestern part of the prairie region. The seeds of these plants are eaten by mourning dove, bobwhite quail, and wild turkey; the stems and foliage, by white-tailed deer.

GOAT'S RUE
Tephrosia virginiana
Bean family (Fabaceae)

Description: A small plant, up to 2' tall, with 1 to several hairy stems emerging from the same base. The leaves are alternate, hairy, and divided into as many as 15 pairs of leaflets, with a single leaflet at the tip. Each leaflet is up to 1¼" long and ⅜" wide, with a small bristle at the tip. The dense hairs give the plant a gray cast. The flowers are in dense clusters at the tops of stems, with each flower about ¾" long and consisting of a spreading, pale yellow upper petal and 2 pink side petals that flank a keel-like lip. The fruits are narrow, whitish, hairy, and about 2" long.

Bloom Season: Late spring–midsummer

Habitat/Range: Common in upland prairies, sand prairies, savannas, dry rocky woodlands, and glades; found throughout the prairie region, but rare or absent in the northwestern part.

Comments: Native Americans and early settlers made a tea from the roots to treat intestinal parasites. Cherokee women washed their hair in it, believing the toughness of the roots would transfer to their hair and prevent it from falling out. Some early ball players rubbed their hands, arms, and legs with goat's rue to toughen them. Native Americans used the root, which contains rotenone, to stun fish.

COMMON ROSE GENTIAN
Sabatia angularis
Gentian family (Gentianaceae)

Description: Annual or biennial plants up to 2' tall, with smooth, square stems and opposite branches, giving it a candelabra-like appearance. The leaves are opposite, stalkless, up to 1½" long and 1" wide, smooth, and lacking teeth along the margins. The flowers are on individual stalks, up to 1½" across, with 5–6 rose-pink (rarely white) petals, with a yellow inner ring at the base.

Bloom Season: Summer

Habitat/Range: Locally frequent in moist depressions of upland prairies, wet prairies, open woods, and old fields; found in the prairie region from southeastern Kansas to Illinois to Ohio and southward.

Comments: A closely related species, prairie rose gentian (*Sabatia campestris*), differs by being somewhat smaller in stature, with alternate, fewer branches and less flowers overall; locally frequent in somewhat drier prairies, sand prairies, and open disturbed sites; found in the prairie region from southeastern Kansas, to Missouri, and Illinois, southward.

LEMON MINT
Monarda citriodora
Mint family (Lamiaceae)

Description: Annuals with finely hairy square stems up to 3' tall. The leaves are opposite, somewhat hairy, stalked, toothed along the margins, up to 3" long and ¾" wide, and broadest at or below the middle, with a sharply pointed tip. The leaves along the upper stem are often in whorls. The flowers are in 2–6 dense clusters, one above the other along the upper stem. Each flower head is surrounded at the base by hairy, leaf-like bracts that are whitish to pinkish and with pointed tips. Each white to pink to pinkish-purple flower is ⅝–1" long, with 2 lips: The lower lip is 3-lobed, and often with purple spots or lines, while the upper lip is strongly arched downward.

Bloom Season: Late spring–midsummer

Habitat/Range: Occasional to frequent in sandy or rocky upland prairies, woodlands, glades, and pastures; found in the southwestern part of the prairie region from eastern Kansas and Missouri southward.

Comments: The leaves of lemon mint have a distinctive lemony aroma when rubbed. Teas made from the leaves have been used to treat colds, coughs, fever, and respiratory problems.

FALSE DRAGONHEAD
Physostegia virginiana
Mint family (Lamiaceae)

Description: Single or sparingly branched stems, up to 5' tall. The leaves are opposite, stalkless, narrow, up to 5" long and 1½" wide, with teeth along the margins. The pink flowers are tightly clustered in long spikes at the tops of stems. Each tubular flower is about 1" long, with 2 lips, the upper lip resembling a hood, the lower lip, divided into 3 lobes.

Bloom Season: Late spring–summer

Habitat/Range: Occasional in wet prairies, moist areas in upland prairies, savannas, and moist soil along streams; found throughout the prairie region.

Comments: Also called obedient plant, because the flowers, when moved to one side, remain in that position. The closely related *Physostegia angustifolia*, which has the same common name, differs by having narrower leaves (less than ½" wide) that are also rather thick and stiff; in addition, the flowers along the spike are more loosely spaced. Found mainly in the southwestern part of the prairie region in similar habitats.

SMOOTH HEDGE NETTLE
Stachys tenuifolia
Mint family (Lamiaceae)

Description: Square-stemmed plants that are hairy along the ridges, usually unbranched, and up to 3' tall. Leaves are 2–6" long, about 1" wide, with toothed edges along the margins. Flowers are in several whorls of 6 along the upper stem. Flowers are about ½" long, with 2 pink lips; the lower lip is broad, spreading, and 3-lobed.

Bloom Season: Summer

Habitat/Range: Occasional in wet prairies, moist depressions in upland prairies, and sand prairies; found throughout the prairie region.

Comment: Also known as germander. Native Americans used leaf tea to induce menstruation, urination, and sweating. The plant was also used to treat lung ailments, intestinal worms, piles, and, externally, as a gargle and antiseptic dressing. A closely related species—wound-wort, or hedge nettle (*Stachys pilosa*)—has stems that are hairy on the sides as well as the ridges. Occurring in wet prairies, moist soils in upland prairies, and sand prairies; found in the northern half of the prairie region.

WOOD SAGE
Teucrium canadense
Mint family (Lamiaceae)

Description: Usually unbranched plants, up to 4' tall, with fine, downy hair on square stems. The leaves are opposite, stalked, up to 6" long and 2½" wide, widest near the base, tapering to a pointed tip, and with coarse teeth along the margins. The flowers are clustered along a narrow column, with each flower on a short stalk about ⅛" long. Each pink flower is about ¾" long, with the upper lip absent; the lower lip has 2 upper lobes and 3 lower lobes. The central lower lobe is broad, with two smaller side lobes all marked with dark red to purple blotches.

Bloom Season: Late spring–late summer

Habitat/Range: Common in wet prairies, moist thickets, low disturbed open ground, moist areas in pastures, and roadsides; found throughout the prairie region.

Comments: Also known as germander. Leaf tea was used to induce menstruation, urination, and sweating. The plant was also used to treat lung ailments, intestinal worms, piles, and, externally, as a gargle and antiseptic dressing.

WILD GARLIC
Allium canadense var. *canadense*
Lily family (Liliaceae)

Description: A plant up to 2' tall, arising from a bulb. The leaves, which emerge mostly from the base of the plant, are long, narrow, flat, and up to 12" long and about ⅛" wide. A single, long stem contains a rounded cluster at the top on individual stalks. Each pink flower has 3 sepals and 3 petals, all identical in size, and 6 stamens. All or some of the flowers are replaced by small, hard, stalkless bulblets that fall to the ground to produce new plants.

Bloom Season: Late spring–early summer

Habitat/Range: Common in often-degraded prairies, openings in forests; also old fields, pastures, roadsides, and other disturbed areas. Found throughout the prairie region.

Comments: Wild garlic has strong antiseptic properties. Native Americans and early settlers often applied the plant juices to wounds and burns. The Dakota and Winnebago used the plant to treat bee stings and snakebite. Settlers used the plant for fever, blood disorders, lung troubles, internal parasites, skin problems, hemorrhoids, earaches, rheumatism, and arthritis. When Father Marquette made his famous journey from Green Bay to the present site of Chicago, wild garlic was an important part of his food supply.

WILD ONION
Allium canadense var. *lavendulare*
Lily family (Liliaceae)

Description: A plant up to 20" tall, arising from a bulb. The grass-like leaves are at the base, with long, narrow, flat leaves, up to 12" long and ⅛" wide. A single, long stem contains a rounded cluster of pink flowers at the top on individual stalks that are 3–5 times as long as the flower. Each pink flower has 3 sepals and 3 petals, all identical in size, with 6 stamens that do not extend beyond the petals.

Bloom Season: Mid-spring–early summer

Habitat/Range: Common in upland prairies, glades, rocky open woodlands, and roadsides; found from Iowa to South Dakota to the south-western part of the prairie region.

Comments: Formerly known as *Allium mutabile*. Another wild onion variety, *Allium canadense* var. *mobilense*, differs by having a shorter stem; it is up to 12" tall, also with pink flowers, but with individual stalks that are 2–4 times as long as the flower. Found in the southwestern part of the prairie region in similar habitat.

NODDING WILD ONION
Allium cernuum
Lily family (Liliaceae)

Description: A smooth, leafless, thin-stemmed plant, up to 1½' tall, with several shorter, flat, grass-like leaves at the base, up to 16" long. The stem bends at the top, causing the cluster of flowers to nod downward. Each flower is on about a 1"-long stalk. The pink to white flowers are small, about ¼" long, with 3 sepals and 3 petals, all identical in size.

Bloom Season: Summer

Habitat/Range: Occasional on dry prairies, hill prairies, glades, and rocky roadsides; found in scattered locations across the prairie region, but absent in the western part.

Comments: Cherokee used this plant's slender bulbs for colds, colic, croup, and fever. After a dose of spotted beebalm (*Monarda punctata*) tea, the juice of this wild onion was taken for "gravel" (kidney stones) and dropsy (edema).

AUTUMN ONION
Allium stellatum
Lily family (Liliaceae)

Description: This plant is very similar to nodding wild onion (*Allium cernuum*) (p. 156), except the upper stem is straight, not bent, and the flowers are upright and not hanging down. The leaves are basal but typically wither and disappear at the time of flowering. The flowers of autumn onion are a deep reddish-pink, compared to the pale pink flowers of nodding wild onion.

Bloom Season: Midsummer–fall

Habitat/Range: Frequent in dry prairies, hill prairies, dry, rocky sites associated with limestone, and along rocky roadsides; found mainly in the western half of the prairie region.

Comments: Also known as prairie onion and cliff onion, this is the characteristic late-summer/early-fall blooming wild onion in the prairie region. The flowers attract small flying insects, primarily flower flies and small bees.

PINK POPPY MALLOW
Callirhoe alcaeoides
Mallow family (Malvaceae)

Description: A spreading plant, ½–2' tall, with a thick turnip-like rootstock. Stems are few to several and branched from the base. Leaves are alternate, stalked, 1½–4" long and 1–3" wide, with 5–7 lobes. Flowers are single or in small clusters on stalks up to 4" long. Each flower is ¾–1¾" wide, with 5 pale pink to white to pale lavender lobes that are often fringed at the tip. The stamens are numerous and united into a column.

Bloom Season: Late spring–summer

Habitat/Range: Occasional on rocky or sandy prairies and open woods; found in the west-central part of the prairie region.

Comments: The flowers have a fragrant odor, and the roots of poppy mallows have been used as a substitute for sweet potatoes. The Osage dug the roots of poppy mallows in late summer or fall and stored them in caches to eat during the winter. The leaves are also edible and have been used to thicken soups.

LARGE-FLOWERED GAURA
Oenothera filiformis
Evening primrose family (Onagraceae)

Description: A tall annual or biennial plant reaching a height of 7' tall, branching toward the top, with moderate to densely curved hairs lying flat along the stems. The leaves are alternate on the stem up to 6" long and ⅜" wide, with widely spaced teeth along the margins, and silky hairs along the surface. The flowers are about 1" long and scattered along the upper stem, with 4 pinkish petals that are arranged in an upward-pointing, semicircular fan shape. Below are 8 downward-pointing stamens and a thread-like style, with 4 narrow lobes at the tip.

Bloom Season: Summer–early fall

Habitat/Range: Locally frequent in dry and rocky prairies, sand prairies, old fields, pastures, disturbed sites, and roadsides; found in the prairie region from Illinois west to Nebraska, and southward.

Comments: Formerly known as *Gaura longiflora*. A closely related species, biennial gaura (*Oenothera biennis*, formerly known as *Gaura biennis*), is usually shorter, less than 6' tall, with straight hairs spreading away from the stem, instead of lying flat along the stem, like large-flowered gaura. Found in the prairie region mostly in the same habitat and range as large-flowered gaura, but less common westward. The name *gaura* comes from the Greek *gauros*, meaning "superb," in reference to its beautiful flowers.

SHOWY EVENING PRIMROSE
Oenothera speciosa
Evening primrose family (Onagraceae)

Description: A low-growing, either trailing or somewhat upright plant, with stems up to 2' long. The leaves are alternate, narrow, up to 3½" long and 1" wide, with wavy to weakly toothed margins. The flowers emerge on long stalks from the leaf axils. A showy pink to white flower, up to 3" across, with 4 broad petals that are cleft at the tip. The petals are tinged with yellow at the base and marked with thin, dark pink lines. There are 8 stamens and a longer style with a narrowly 4-lobed tip.

Bloom Season: Mid-spring–midsummer

Habitat/Range: Locally common in rocky prairies, pastures, roadsides, and disturbed areas with sparse vegetation; found in the southern half of the prairie region, from Missouri and Kansas southward, and introduced elsewhere.

Comments: Showy evening primrose is a popular addition to wildflower gardens, but it can spread aggressively by runners and seeds.

PRAIRIE GRASS PINK
Calopogon oklahomensis
Orchid family (Orchidaceae)

Description: A slender, smooth, single-stemmed plant less than 2' tall, with a single grass-like leaf that emerges from the base and somewhat exceeds the height of the stem. Up to 8 fragrant flowers occur at the top of the stem. The flowers range from vivid electric pink to pale pink or even white, with 3 petal-like sepals, each about ¾" long. There are 3 petals—2 narrower and shorter than the sepals, and 1 upper petal that is flared into a rounded triangular lobe at the end, with dense yellow to purple hairs along its length.

Bloom Season: Mid-spring–midsummer

Habitat/Range: Occasional in mesic to dry upland prairies and open woods; found in the prairie region from southeastern Kansas and Missouri southward, and rare in the north-central part.

Comments: A closely related species, grass pink (*Calopogon tuberosus*), has brighter magenta flowers that extend well above the grass-like leaf; this orchid blooms in midsummer, and is found in wetter habitats, such as bogs, fens, and swamps scattered across the prairie region, but it is more common in the northern part.

VIOLET WOOD SORREL
Oxalis violacea
Wood sorrel family (Oxalidaceae)

Description: Small plants up to 6" tall, with numerous 3-parted leaves arising from the base on stalks. The leaflets are slightly to deeply folded with small notches at the tip, often with spots or blotches of purple on the upper surface, and often solid purple underneath. The flower stems extend past the leaves, with several individually stalked flowers at the top. Each flower is about ½" wide, with 5 pink to violet petals.

Bloom Season: Mid-spring–early summer, and sometimes in the fall

Habitat/Range: Common in mesic to dry prairies, savannas, and open, rocky woodlands; found throughout the prairie region.

Comments: The plant parts contain a sour, watery juice from which the name "sorrel" is derived. Native Americans used powdered leaves boiled in water to help expel intestinal worms. The plant was also used to reduce fevers and to increase urine flow. All parts of the plant are edible and have been added to salads for the sour taste; however, using it in moderation is advisable, due to a high concentration of oxalic acid, which can be poisonous.

SMOOTH PHLOX
Phlox glaberrima
Phlox family (Polemoniaceae)

Description: Smooth, hairless plants, up to 3' tall, but usually less than 2' in height. The leaves are stalkless, smooth, opposite on the stem, up to 5" long and ⅝" wide, broadest at the base, and gradually tapering to a pointed tip. The deep-pink to magenta flowers are in a rounded cluster at the top of the stem, each about ½" wide and tubular, opening into 5 broad lobes.

Bloom Season: Late spring–summer

Habitat/Range: Occasional to common in moist to mesic prairies, moist sand prairies, bottomland forests, seeps, and fens; found throughout the prairie region, except for Kansas and Iowa northward, and also Texas.

Comments: The genus name *Phlox* is derived from the Greek word *Phlox*, meaning "flame," in reference to the intense flower colors of some varieties. The species name *glaberrima* means "completely glabrous" (without hairs). Smooth phlox is an excellent spring-blooming phlox for the perennial border, wildflower meadow, or native plant garden.

DOWNY PHLOX
Phlox pilosa
Phlox family (Polemoniaceae)

Description: Hairy, usually single-stemmed plants to 2' tall, with widely spaced pairs of opposite, stalkless leaves. The leaves are hairy, up to 3" long and ½" wide, broadest at the base, and gradually tapering to pointed tips. The pink to purplish flowers are grouped into loosely branched clusters. Each flower is about ¾" across, with a long tube and 5 rounded lobes. The base of each lobe often has darker-pink markings.

Bloom Season: Mid-spring–midsummer

Habitat/Range: Common in mesic to dry prairies, often rocky or sandy, savannas, and glades; found throughout the prairie region.

Comments: Sometimes specimens of downy phlox with white flowers and pink centers are found. The Meskwaki made a tea of the leaves and used it as a wash for treating eczema. They also used the root mixed with several unspecified plants as part of a love potion.

PINK MILKWORT
Polygala incarnata
Milkwort family (Polygalaceae)

Description: Annual plants with a bluish-green or grayish-green stem, about 1' tall, but sometimes up to 2' tall, with widely spaced pairs of stalked, opposite leaves. The leaves are tiny, alternate, very narrow, and less than ½" long. Flowers are in dense clusters at the tops of stems. Each pink to purple (or rarely white) flower is about ⅛" wide and ¼" long, with tiny green sepals, 2 larger petal-like sepals, and 3 petals united into a tube that ends in 6 lobes that are fringed and cleft.

Bloom Season: Mid-spring–fall

Habitat/Range: Occasional in dry upland prairies, savannas, and glades; from Iowa to southern Wisconsin southward in the prairie region.

Comments: Pink milkwort produces seeds with fleshy appendages that are a mechanism for dispersal. The fleshy appendages (or *arils*) attract ants to carry off the seeds for their nutritious value, thus providing an effective way to disperse these annual plants.

FIELD MILKWORT
Polygala sanguinea
Milkwort family (Polygalaceae)

Description: Small annual plants less than 1' tall, usually with a single, angled stem. The leaves are alternate, widely spaced, narrow, and up to 1¾" long and ⅛" wide. The flowers are in a dense, cylindrical cluster at the tops of branches. The flowers vary from pink to white or greenish and are less than ¼" long. The flowers have 5 sepals, with the upper 1 and lower 2 small and green. The 2 side sepals are larger and pink to white, like the 3 small petals that are united into a small tube in the center, with 8 tiny, yellow-tipped stamens.

Bloom Season: Late spring–fall

Habitat/Range: Frequent in upland prairies, sand prairies, savannas, sand savannas, woodland edges, glades, and abandoned fields; found throughout the prairie region, but absent in the Dakotas.

Comments: Field milkwort has been used to treat respiratory maladies.

SHOOTING STAR
Dodecatheon meadia
Primrose family (Primulaceae)

Description: The leaves spread out from the base of the plant that sends up a flower stalk to 2' tall. The basal leaves are stalked, smooth, up to 8" long and 3" wide, and tapering to rounded tips. The flowers are clustered at the top of a smooth stem on numerous arching stalks, each ending in a single flower. The stalks bend over, causing the flowers to droop. The flowers have 5 petals, each about 1" long, that bend back, resembling a fanciful tail of a shooting star. The petals vary in color from white to dark pink, and are joined at their bases by a small yellowish tube. The 5 stamens, with their dark-brown bases, are held together to form a beak-like cone. The flower stalks become upright as fruits develop.

Bloom Season: Mid- to late spring

Habitat/Range: Common in mesic to dry prairies, savannas, rocky hill prairies, and hillsides; found throughout the prairie region, but rare in Michigan and Minnesota.

Comments: Also known as *Primula meadia*. Flowers of the shooting star have a fragrance similar to the odor of grape juice. Pollination of the flower is by bumblebees, which are strong enough to pry open the beak-like cone.

QUEEN OF THE PRAIRIE
Filipendula rubra
Rose family (Rosaceae)

Description: A smooth, hollow-stemmed plant with longitudinal ridges, ranging from 4–7' tall. The leaves are alternate, compound, and large, with toothed stipules at the base that clasp the leaf stalks. The leaves are sometimes more than 2' long and divided into several narrow, irregularly toothed segments of varying size on the same leaf. The end leaflet is large and deeply divided into 7–9 leaf-like lobes up to 4" long, which themselves are sometimes again further lobed and divided. The flowers are in branching, spray-like clusters at the tops of the stems. The deep-pink flowers are about ⅜" across, with 5 small, blunt reflexed sepals and 5 pink petals surrounding from 15 to numerous stamens.

Bloom Season: Early summer–midsummer

Habitat/Range: Rare and local in moist to wet prairies, prairie seeps, and fens; found in the prairie region from Minnesota south to Missouri, and eastward.

Comments: Native Americans and early settlers used this plant for a variety of medicinal applications, including treatment of arthritis, fever, and skin ailments.

PRAIRIE SMOKE
Geum triflorum
Rose family (Rosaceae)

Description: Hairy-stemmed plants, less than 1' tall, with many basal leaves. The basal leaves are hairy, up to 7" long, and divided into as many as 19 toothed segments. A pair of smaller, opposite, deeply divided leaves occur along the middle of the stem. Each stem has 3–6 individually stalked, nodding flowers less than ¾" across, with 5 triangular, pink to reddish-purple sepals surrounding 5 smaller, pinkish petals. The showy fruits have long, feathery plumes, up to 2" long.

Bloom Season: Mid- to late spring

Habitat/Range: Common westward, becoming rare eastward, on dry prairies, gravel hill prairies, and dry fields; found in the prairie region from the Dakotas to northern Iowa, northern Illinois, and Michigan, northward.

Comments: The graceful feathery plumes resemble smoke at a distance; hence, the name. It is also called prairie avens. The Blackfeet boiled the plant in water to treat sore or inflamed eyes. A root tea was used as a mouthwash for canker sores and sore throat, and applied to flesh wounds. It was also scraped, mixed with tobacco, and smoked, to "clear the head."

PRAIRIE WILD ROSE
Rosa arkansana
Rose family (Rosaceae)

Description: A low-growing, prickly shrub, usually less than 2' tall, with reddish stems, alternate, compound leaves, and slender spines. The leaves are divided into 9–11 leaflets, each about 1½" long, broadest near the base, and sharply toothed along the margins. There are 2 prominent stipules along the base of the leaf stalks. Flowers appear on smooth stalks on the upper branches. Each flower is 1½–2" across, with 5 long-pointed, green sepals, and 5 broad, pink petals, each with a notch at the tip. There are numerous yellow stamens attached to the rim of the dome-shaped extension of the receptacle. The fruits are red, round "hips" about ⅜" long.

Bloom Season: Mid-spring–early summer

Habitat/Range: Common in wet, mesic, and dry prairies, hill prairies, sand prairies, savannas, pastures, old fields, and roadsides; found throughout the prairie region and westward.

Comments: Native Americans used prairie wild rose to treat convulsions, bleeding wounds, eye sores, and as a stimulant and tonic. A closely related species, early wild rose (*Rosa blanda*), has nearly spineless new branches, 5–7 leaflets per leaf, and pale pink flowers. Occasionally found in upland prairies, bottomland prairies, and sand prairies in the northern half of the prairie region.

CAROLINA ROSE
Rosa carolina
Rose family (Rosaceae)

Description: A low-growing, prickly shrub, usually less than 2' tall, with alternate, compound leaves and slender spines. The leaves are divided into 5–7 leaflets, each about 2" long, broadest in the middle, and sharply toothed along the edges. There are 2 prominent stipules along the base of the leaf stalks. Flowers appear on bristly stalks on the upper branches. Each flower is 2½–3" across, with 5 long-pointed, green sepals and 5 broad, pink petals, each with a notch at the tip. There are numerous yellow stamens attached to the rim of the dome-shaped extension of the receptacle. The fruits are red, round "hips" about ⅝" long.

Bloom Season: Mid-spring–summer

Habitat/Range: Common in mesic to dry prairies, hill prairies, sand prairies, savannas, pastures, old fields, and roadsides; found throughout the prairie region, but absent to rare in the northwestern part.

Comments: Also known as pasture rose, this low-growing woody shrub is technically not a wildflower, but its showy flowers can easily be mistaken for one. The fruit, known as rose hips, contains about 100 times more vitamin C than an orange.

PRAIRIE ROSE
Rosa setigera
Rose family (Rosaceae)

Description: A prickly shrub that acts more like a vine that can grow from 4–12' long, with short, stout spines that are not very numerous. The leaves are divided into 3, sometimes 5 leaflets, each about 2–3" long, slightly broader at the base, and with finely toothed margins. There are 2 prominent stipules along the base of the leaf stalks. Flowers appear on stalks that lack bristles. Each flower is about 2½–3" across, with 5 long-pointed green sepals and 5 broad, pink petals, each with a notch at the tip. There are numerous yellow stamens attached at the base of a small column of pistils in the center. The fruits are red, round "hips" about ⅜" long.

Bloom Season: Late spring–summer

Habitat/Range: Common in upland prairies, thickets at the edges of prairies, savannas, fencerows, and old fields; found throughout the prairie region, but absent in the northwestern part.

Comments: Also known as climbing wild rose. Prairie rose is sometimes cultivated, and has been used in horticultural crosses with European roses.

ROSE VERBENA
Glandularia canadensis
Vervain family (Verbenaceae)

Description: A low, spreading plant with hairy stems up to 2' long and 1' tall, with often several stems arising from the base and rooting at the lower nodes. The leaves are hairy, stalked, opposite, up to 4" long and 1½" wide, and usually divided into 3 or more lobes, with coarse teeth along the margins. The flowers are arranged in a flat-topped cluster, with each flower about 1" long and ½" wide, and shaped like a narrow tube, with 5 spreading lobes and notched tips. The flowers vary from pink to rose-purple to magenta.

Bloom Season: Spring–fall

Habitat/Range: Occasional in dry, rocky sites in prairies, savannas, woodlands, glades, pastures, and roadsides; found throughout the prairie region, but absent in the northwestern part, and rare in the northeastern part.

Comments: Also called rose vervain, and formerly known as *Verbena canadensis*. Another closely related species, Dakota verbena (*Glandularia bipinnatifida*), differs by having leaves 1½–2" long and lobes deeply cut to the midrib; flowers smaller, about ½" long; and found in rocky prairies and disturbed rocky ground in the western part of the prairie region.

ROUGH BUTTONWEED
Diodia teres
Madder family (Rubiaceae)

Description: Annual plants, somewhat creeping along the ground, with square, branching stems, up to 2' long. The leaves are opposite, stalkless, narrow, up to 1¼" long and ¼" wide, with pointed tips and a pronounced central vein. At the junction of the leaves, there is a pair of whitish, papery stipules with bristles along the edges. The flowers are small, about ¼" across, stalkless, and attached in groups of 1–3 at the axis of the leaf and the stem. The tubular flower has 4 pink petals and 4 small stamens.

Bloom Season: Summer–fall.

Habitat/Range: Common in dry prairies, sand prairies, and pastures in dry, usually acid soils, such as sand, or thin soil over sandstone; found throughout the prairie region, but absent in the northwestern part, and rare in the northeastern part.

Comments: A closely related species, large buttonweed (*Diodia virginiana*), has stems that spread across the ground, with hairs along the stem and white flowers ⅜" across; it occurs in wet prairies, depressions in sand prairies, wet soil along streams, and roadsides. Found in the southern part of the prairie region.

BLUE AND PURPLE FLOWERS

Symphyotrichum novae-angliae

This section includes flowers ranging from pale blue to deep indigo and from lavender to violet. Because purple flowers grade into pink flowers, that section should also be checked.

HAIRY WILD PETUNIA
Ruellia humilis
Acanthus family (Acanthaceae)

Description: Plants with hairy, squarish stems, often branched, usually less than 12" tall. The leaves are opposite, on very short stalks or stalkless, about 2" long and 1" wide, with long hairs along the veins and leaf margins. The showy, light lavender to purple flowers emerge from the leaf axils on the upper half of the plant. Each flower is up to 2½" long, tubular, and flaring to 5 broad lobes. The mouth of the flower is marked with dark purple lines.

Bloom Season: Late spring–early fall

Habitat/Range: Common in dry prairies and rocky open woodlands; found throughout the prairie region, but absent in the northwestern part.

Comments: The genus name, *Ruellia*, honors Jean de la Ruelle (1474–1537), French herbalist and physician to Francois I (1494–1547), who was king of France from 1515 until his death in 1547. The species name, *humilis*, means "low-growing." The individual flowers of hairy wild petunia open in the morning and fall off by evening.

LEAVENWORTH ERYNGO
Eryngium leavenworthii
Parsley family (Apiaceae)

Description: A thistle-like, hairless, spiny plant, 1½–3' tall, with somewhat waxy multibranched stems. The leaves are alternate, clasping the stem, up to 3" long and 1" wide, with short, stiff spines along the wavy margins, and leaves divided into narrow segments like the fingers of a hand. The flowers are in dense, rounded, purple cylinders at the tips of the branches, with 4–8 purple, spiny, leaf-like bracts at the base of the cylinder, and another 4–8 smaller purple to green spiny, leaf-like bracts at the top. There are numerous small flowers covering the cylinder, each with 5 white to purple petals and 5 bluish stamens.

Bloom Season: Midsummer–fall

Habitat/Range: Local in rocky prairies and pastures, and roadsides; found in the southwestern part of the prairie region in Kansas, Oklahoma, and Texas.

Comments: The unusual appearance of the column of flowers resembles a thistle or a small fuzzy pineapple. The dried flower heads are known to hold their color for several months. The genus name, *Eryngium*, comes from an ancient Greek name used by Theophrastus for a plant, which grew in Greece. The species name, *leavenworthii*, honors Melines Conklin Leavenworth, a US Army surgeon who collected plants in the South and West during the 1830s.

PURPLE MILKWEED
Asclepias purpurascens
Milkweed family (Asclepiadaceae)

Description: Slender plants with stout stems, up to 4' tall, with milky sap and opposite leaves. The leaves are thick, up to 8" long and 4" wide, tapering at each end, on short stalks, and with fine hairs on the underside. The smaller side veins are at right angles to the central vein, which is also typically red. The flowers are in large, round clusters at the top of the stem. Each deep-reddish-purple flower is about ¾", has 5 reflexed petals surrounding 5 upright hoods, each with a tiny, pointed horn arising from it. The fruit pods are about 6" long and ¾" thick, with fine hairs, and filled with numerous seeds, each with silky hairs at 1 end.

Bloom Season: Late spring–midsummer

Habitat/Range: Frequent in rocky, open prairie thickets, along prairie/woodland edges, savannas, and roadsides; found throughout the prairie region, but absent or rare in the western part.

Comments: Milkweeds have a long medical history, but they have also been used for food. The young shoots were cooked as an asparagus substitute. The flowers, buds, and immature fruits were cooked in boiling water; the water had to be changed to remove the bitter-tasting toxins. During World War II, the milky latex from milkweeds was tested as a rubber substitute, and the plumes of the seed heads were collected by schoolchildren and others as part of the war effort. The fluffy material was used as a substitute in life preservers when there was shortage of kapok, the silky down surrounding the seeds of the kapok tree of Africa and tropical America.

WESTERN DAISY
Astranthium ciliatum
Aster family (Asteraceae)

Description: A hairy, annual plant from 2–16" tall, sometimes branching near the base. The seeds germinate in the fall and produce small, flat basal leaves that overwinter. The stem leaves are alternate, up to 3" long and ½" wide, with the basal leaves sometimes withered by blooming time. The flowers vary in width, up to 1½" across; the petal-like ray flowers are lavender with white at the base, while the disk flowers are yellow.

Bloom Season: Spring

Habitat/Range: Common in dry prairies, glades, open woods, and along roadsides; found in the southwestern part of the prairie region.

Comments: An early-blooming aster, the western daisy often forms dense mats of flowers, especially along roadsides.

TALL THISTLE
Cirsium altissimum
Aster family (Asteraceae)

Description: A tall, branching biennial to short-lived perennial plant, up to 8' tall, with stems that have ridges along their length and are often covered with spreading hairs. The alternate leaves grow up to 18" long and 8" wide. The leaves are usually not lobed, but have coarse teeth along the leaf margins that end in spines. The undersides of the leaves have whitish, woolly hairs. The flower heads are at the ends of long stalks. The bracts at the base of the flower heads are flat and green, with a white stripe down the middle, somewhat resembling fish scales. Each bract has a ¼" long spine, with a short spine at the end of each bract. The flowers are tubular, about 1" long, with 5 narrow purple to pink lobes, each about ⅜" long.

Bloom Season: Midsummer–fall

Habitat/Range: Occasional in upland prairies, open woods, old fields, and along roadsides; found throughout the prairie region.

Comments: Thistles are an important part of the common goldfinch's nesting season. Considered late nesters, goldfinches wait until the seeds ripen in August and collect the downy filaments to line the bowls of their nests, which are surrounded by strands of plant material. Also, the thistle seeds are eaten by the adults and regurgitated to the young back at the nest.

FIELD THISTLE
Cirsium discolor
Aster family (Asteraceae)

Description: Stems branched near the top, somewhat hairy, spineless, up to 8' tall, with spiny leaves. The leaves are alternate, up to 9" long and 3" wide, divided into several narrow lobes that are often divided further, with small spines all along the edges, longer spines at the lobe tips, and leaf margins turned downward. The undersides of the leaves are densely covered with white hairs. The flower heads are 1½–2" across on individual leafy stalks. Each flower head has numerous overlapping, spiny, green bracts with a white stripe that resembles fish scales. There are numerous pinkish-purple disk flowers, each about 1¼" long, with 5 narrow lobes, and each about ¼" long.

Bloom Season: Midsummer–fall

Habitat/Range: Common in prairies that have had a history of grazing or some other disturbance, pastures, old fields, and roadsides; found in the prairie region, but rare or absent west of a line from Arkansas north to Minnesota.

Comments: Another thistle, prairie thistle (*Cirsium hillii*), is a much shorter plant, up to 3' tall, with leaves hairy underneath but not whitened, deeply lobed, and toothed along the edges with numerous spines. The large flower heads are 2–4" wide, with many overlapping, green, spiny bracts surrounding many small, pale purple disk flowers, each with 5 lobes. Found locally frequent in dry prairies, but declining over its range in the prairie region from Iowa to northern Indiana, and northward.

WAVY-LEAF THISTLE
Cirsium undulatum
Aster family (Asteraceae)

Description: Stems are erect, stout, arising from deep taproots, sometimes branched above, from 1–5' tall, with dense, white-woolly hairs along a grooved stem. The leaves are alternate, crowded, moderate to deeply lobed, 4–12" long and 1–4" wide, with wavy margins bearing yellowish spines, and densely white-woolly on the lower surface, less so on the upper surface. The flower heads are on individual stalks, 1–2" wide, with the bracts bearing a single spine at the tip. The heads are pinkish-purple to purple or white, with ray flowers absent and disk flowers numerous, each 1–1¾" long.

Bloom Season: Summer–fall

Habitat/Range: Common in dry prairies, pastures, roadsides, and open disturbed ground; found in the western part of the prairie region from North Dakota south to Texas, and rare to absent eastward.

Comments: Native Americans used the root as a food source and to make a tea to use as a wash to treat eye diseases. The Kiowa made a tea of the flowers, which they applied to heal burns and sores, and the Meskwaki made a tea from the root to cure stomachache. A closely related species, Flodman's thistle (*Cirsium flodmanii*), differs by having generally shorter stems (less than 2' tall), arising from horizontal roots. The upper leaf surface has lightly covered cobwebby hairs, while the lower surface is velvety white from a dense mat of hairs; the leaf margins have deep lobes that are triangular-shaped and extend to the leaf midrib. Found in moist prairies, meadows, and pastures in the northwestern part of the prairie region.

NARROW-LEAVED PURPLE CONEFLOWER
Echinacea angustifolia
Aster family (Asteraceae)

Description: A short, coarsely hairy plant, ½–2' tall, with mostly basal leaves and stem leaves widely spaced. Leaves are alternate, with long stalks at the base and stalkless along the stem, up to 8" long and ½–1½" wide, with smooth margins, and hairy and rough to the touch. The flowers are single at the end of stout, hairy stems, with 15–20 pink to light purple ray flowers, each ¾–1½" long, about ¼" wide, and with 3 slightly notched tips. In the center is a large, round to conical, orange to brown disk, with numerous 5-lobed disk flowers. The pollen on the anthers is white.

Bloom Season: Early summer–midsummer

Habitat/Range: Common in dry, especially rocky prairies, open rocky woodlands, and rocky slopes; found in the western part of the prairie region and further westward.

Comments: Also known as Kansas snakeroot and black Sampson, among other names. Narrow-leaved purple coneflower was the most widely used medicinal plant of the Plains Indians. Primarily the root, but also the entire plant, was used as a painkiller and for a variety of ailments, including toothache, coughs, colds, sore throat, and snakebite.

PALE PURPLE CONEFLOWER
Echinacea pallida
Aster family (Asteraceae)

Description: A stout-stemmed, showy plant, up to 3' tall, with coarse, bristly hairs on the stem and leaves. The leaves at the base are on long stalks, up to 10" long and 1½" wide, tapering at both ends, with parallel veins running along the length of the blade. The stem leaves are few, smaller, with short stalks. The flower heads are single on long stalks, with several drooping, pale purple petals, each about 3½" long, surrounding a purplish-brown, dome-shaped central disk. The pollen on the anthers is white.

Bloom Season: Late spring–midsummer

Habitat/Range: Common in mesic and dry prairies and savannas; found throughout the prairie region, but absent in the northwestern part, and rare to absent in the eastern one-fourth of the region.

Comments: Native Americans used the root to treat snakebite, stings, spider bites, toothache, burns, hard-to-heal wounds, flu, and colds. It is widely used today in pharmaceutical preparations.

PURPLE CONEFLOWER
Echinacea purpurea
Aster family (Asteraceae)

Description: A showy plant, up to 4' tall, with branching stems and rough hairs on the stems and leaves. The basal leaves are on long stalks, coarsely toothed, up to 6" long, broadest at the base, and tapering to a pointed tip. The stem leaves are alternate, on shorter stalks, coarsely toothed, and smaller. The large flower heads are at the ends of long stalks, and up to 5" across. The 10–20 purple, petal-like ray flowers surround a cone-shaped central disk. The cones are golden-red when in flower.

Bloom Season: Late spring–fall

Habitat/Range: Occasional in moist areas in prairies, savannas, and prairie/woodland edges; found through the prairie region, but rare to absent in the western one-fourth.

Comments: Native Americans used the root to treat snakebite, bee stings, headache, stomach cramps, toothache, and sore throats in people, and distemper in horses. Some tribes discovered that the plant was like a burn preventative, enabling the body to endure extreme heat. They use the plant's juice in sweat baths and in ritual feats, such as immersing hands in scalding water or holding live coals in the mouth. Purple coneflower is a long-blooming ornamental widely used in wildflower gardens.

BLUE LETTUCE
Lactuca tatarica
Aster family (Asteraceae)

Description: Plants with white latex, smooth, hollow stems, up to 3½' tall, with a deep rootstock and branching rhizomes. Leaves are stalkless, up to 8" long, linear, hairless, with smooth edges, and a whitish underside. The flowers are in branches at the top of the stem. Each flower is about 1" across, with 19–21 light blue petal-like ray flowers and no disk flowers.

Bloom Season: Summer

Habitat/Range: Occasional in dry prairies, loess hill prairies, and open, disturbed areas; found in the northwestern part of the prairie region, south to Nebraska, and introduced elsewhere.

Comments: Also known as *Lactuca pulchella*. Blue lettuce has a wide distribution. It is also found in Canada, Europe, and Asia.

ROUGH BLAZING STAR
Liatris aspera
Aster family (Asteraceae)

Description: A single-stemmed plant that is hairy or smooth, up to 4' tall, arising from a corm. The basal leaves are short-stalked and up to 16" long and 2" wide. The stem leaves are progressively shorter upward along the stem. The flower heads are alternately arranged and loosely spaced along a wand-like spike, up to 1½' long. The bracts on the head are rounded, with white to purplish papery tips. The flower heads are up to 1" across, with 16–35 small, purple disk flowers, each with 5 lobes and 2 conspicuous, purple, thread-like style branches.

Bloom Season: Midsummer–fall

Habitat/Range: Common in prairies, hill prairies, savannas, rocky open woods, and glades; found throughout the prairie region.

Comments: The Meskwaki used rough blazing star for bladder and kidney troubles. The Pawnee boiled the leaves and root together and fed the tea to children with diarrhea. Root tea was used as a folk remedy for kidney and bladder ailments, gonorrhea, and colic, and it was gargled for sore throats. The root was mashed and applied to treat snakebite.

CYLINDRICAL BLAZING STAR
Liatris cylindracea
Aster family (Asteraceae)

Description: There are few flower heads on this stiff, short-stemmed plant, which may grow up to 2' tall. The grass-like leaves are stalkess, smooth, up to 10" long and ½" wide, but becoming progressively smaller upward along the stem. The flower heads are alternate and cylindrical-shaped along the upper stem, about ½" across, and on short stalks. The bracts are smooth, flat, and not extending outward. The flower heads have 10–35 small purple disk flowers with 5 narrow, pointed tips that curl backward, and a long style with 2 thread-like, purple branches that protrude ½" from the flower.

Bloom Season: Midsummer–early fall

Habitat/Range: Occasional in dry prairies, sand prairies, hill prairies, savannas, rocky open woods, and glades; found in the eastern part of the prairie region, west to Minnesota and south to northern Arkansas.

Comments: The origin of the genus name, *Liatris*, is unknown, while the species name, *cylindracea*, means "cylindrical," for the shape of the flower head. There are 17 species of *Liatris* in the prairie region, and cylindrical blazing star ranks as being one of the shortest.

DOTTED BLAZING STAR
Liatris punctata
Aster family (Asteraceae)

Description: Growing up to 3' tall, these plants often have several unbranched, hairless stems arising from a common base. Leaves are numerous along the stem, alternate, up to 5" long and less than ¼" wide. The leaf margins usually have a row of tiny hairs and many tiny round dots on the underside. Flower heads are in dense wand-like spikes, each up to 1' long, with many cylindrical ½"-long heads. Each head is surrounded at the base by an overlapping series of flat-tipped, dotted bracts. The flower heads have 4–8 tiny lavender to reddish-purple disk flowers, each with 5 lobes and 2 long thread-like style branches.

Bloom Season: Midsummer–fall

Habitat/Range: Common to locally abundant in dry, often rocky prairies, sand prairies, hill prairies, rocky woodlands, and roadsides; found in the western part of the prairie region, east to central Iowa and northwestern Missouri.

Comments: The Kiowa considered dotted blazing star to be one of the "ancient" foods, and because of its ability to withstand drought, it was still an important part of their diet in the 1930s. A closely related species, narrow-leaved blazing star (*Liatris mucronata*), differs by lacking the row of tiny hairs along the leaf margins; it also lacks the tiny round dots on the underside of the leaf and on the bracts. Found in the southwestern part of the prairie region in similar habitat.

TALL BLAZING STAR
Liatris pycnostachya
Aster family (Asteraceae)

Description: Hairy, slender, unbranched spikes up to 5' tall, arising from a corm. The leaves are alternate, stalkless, and numerous, with the lower leaves sometimes over 1' long and up to ½" wide, gradually reducing in size ascending the stem. The numerous flower heads are in a long, dense spike, often over 1' long, at the top of the stem. Each small flower head is about ¼" across, with hairy, outward-curving bracts. There are 5–10 purple disk flowers, each with 5 lobes and 2 prominent thread-like style branches protruding from each flower.

Bloom Season: Midsummer–fall

Habitat/Range: Common in mesic to dry prairies; found throughout the prairie region, but infrequent to rare in the eastern one-fourth.

Comments: Also known as gayfeather. Edwin James, botanist for the Stephen Long expedition, reported from near St. Louis on June 27, 1819, that the gayfeather, "here called pine of the prairies, which was now in full bloom, has a roundish tuberous root, of a warm somewhat balsamic taste, and is used by the Indians and others as a cure of gonorrhea." Cultivated varieties are grown for the cut-flower market. The flowering spikes can be air-dried for use in winter arrangements.

SAVANNA BLAZING STAR
Liatris scariosa var. *neuwlandii*
Aster family (Asteraceae)

Description: A single-stemmed plant, 2½–5' tall, with moderate to dense hairs and numerous alternate, widely spread leaves arranged densely around the stem. The basal and lower leaves are stalked, about 12" long and 1½" wide, while the leaves ascending the stem are stalkless and less than 3" long. The flower heads are stalked and arranged along the upper part of the stem. The flower head at the tip of the stem is the first to bloom, and a descending order of blooming follows to the bottom, as is typical for other blazing stars. Each flower head is 1–2" across, with 25–80 purple disk flowers and no petal-like ray flowers. The two-branched styles in each disk flower extend outward, giving the flower heads a shaggy appearance.

Bloom Season: Midsummer–fall

Habitat/Range: Uncommon to rare in savannas and savanna/prairie borders; found in the prairie region from Missouri and northeastward.

Comments: As the common name implies, savanna blazing star is a classic savanna species. It doesn't compete well with prairie grasses, so it grows in partial shade in savannas, where it is less favorable for prairie grasses. This plant can be found moving into degraded prairies where the grasses are decreased. When fire is applied to the prairie, as a management tool, grasses increase while savanna blazing star decreases. In the prairie region, the decline in savannas directly relates to the decline of this very showy wildflower.

DENSE BLAZING STAR
Liatris spicata
Aster family (Asteraceae)

Description: Slender, unbranched, hairless, narrow spikes up to 4' tall, arising from a corm. The leaves are alternate, stalkless, and numerous, with the lower leaves up to 16" long and about ½" wide, gradually reducing in size up the stem. The numerous flower heads are in a long, dense spike, about 1' long, at the top of the stem. Each small flower head is about ¼" across, hairless, and having bracts with their tips flat against the head, often bluntly rounded. There are 4–8 purple disk flowers, each with 5 lobes and 2 prominent thread-like style branches protruding from each flower.

Bloom Season: Midsummer–early fall

Habitat/Range: Locally frequent in mesic to wet prairies and moist, sandy areas; found in the eastern half of the prairie region.

Comments: Dense blazing star is also known as marsh blazing star, button snakeroot, and prairie gayfeather. The Cherokee used the plant to relieve pain in the back and limbs, and the Menominee used it for a "weak heart." The plant was also used to treat swelling, abdominal pain, and snakebite. Currently, the plant is used for a sore throat by gargling, and as a tea; it is also used as an herbal insect repellent, and in potpourri.

SCALY BLAZING STAR
Liatris squarrosa
Aster family (Asteraceae)

Description: Often hairy, single-stemmed plants to 2½' tall, with narrow, somewhat rigid leaves. The lower leaves are up to 10" long and ½" wide, but are progressively smaller upward along the stem. The flower heads are few to solitary, each about ½" across, and emerging from the upper leaf axils. The bracts below the flower head overlap, with pointed tips that look spine-like or scaly. Each flower head has 20–40 small, purple disk flowers that are tubular, with 5 lobes and 2 prominent thread-like style branches protruding from each flower. The flower heads toward the top of the stem tend to be larger, with more disk flowers.

Bloom Season: Summer–early fall

Habitat/Range: Frequent in dry, often rocky prairies, savannas, open woods, and glades; found in the southern two-thirds of the prairie region, but rare or absent in the northern one-third.

Comments: Scaly blazing star was used as a diuretic, a tonic, and a stimulant. It was also used to treat gonorrhea, kidney trouble, and uterine diseases.

GLAUCOUS WHITE LETTUCE
Prenanthes racemosa
Aster family (Asteraceae)

Description: Tall, slender plants, up to 5' in height, with unbranched, hairless leaves and stems, and milky sap. The lower leaves are alternate, up to 10" long and 3" wide, with long, winged stalks. The middle leaves are mostly clasping the stem while the upper leaves are stalkless. The flowers are in tightly packed clusters along the upper portion of the stem. Each cylindrical flower head is about ½" long, with 9–16 lavender to purple, petal-like ray flowers. The purplish bracts and stems of the flower head are densely hairy.

Bloom Season: Midsummer–fall

Habitat/Range: Occasional in wet prairies and low ground-bordering streams; found in the northern half of the prairie region.

Comments: Also known as *Nabalus racemosus*. The stem has a white, waxy coating (glaucous), which accounts for part of the common name. One feature that easily distinguishes glaucous white lettuce from rough white lettuce (see p. 31) is that the former has basal leaves that persist at flowering, while the latter has basal and lowermost stem leaves usually withered or absent by flowering time. Also, glaucous white lettuce prefers low, wet ground, while rough white lettuce occurs in dry prairies and savannas. The bitter roots of this plant were once used to treat snakebite; hence, its other name, rattlesnake root.

SOUTHERN PRAIRIE ASTER
Eurybia hemispherica
Aster family (Asteraceae)

Description: A smooth-stemmed plant from 8–30" tall, with alternate, grass-like leaves up to 8" long and ¼" wide. Flower heads emerge from leaf axils and are clustered at the top of the stem, from 1–2" across, with 15–35 blue or violet, petal-like ray flowers surrounding 40–80 yellow disk flowers.

Bloom Season: Late summer–fall

Habitat/Range: Occasional in high-quality mesic to dry prairies, and less commonly open woodlands; found in the southern part of the prairie region from southeast Kansas and southwest Missouri, southward.

Comments: Formerly known as *Aster paludosus* subspecies *hemisphericus*. The showy flowers are noticeably larger than what might be expected for a plant of this size.

FLAX-LEAVED ASTER
Ionactis linariifolius
Aster family (Asteraceae)

Description: Plants with more than one stem emerging from a base, less than 2' tall, with stiff, roughish, minutely hairy leaves. The leaves are alternate, stalkless, narrow, up to 1½" long and ⅛" wide, and tapering to a fine point. Several flower heads are at the tops of stems on short individual stalks. Each flower head is up to 1¼" wide, with 10–20 satiny purple, petal-like ray flowers surrounding 20–40 yellow disk flowers.

Bloom Season: Late summer–fall

Habitat/Range: Occasional in sand prairies, and dry prairies, savannas, and dry, rocky woodlands in acid-based soils over sandstone; found in the eastern half of the prairie region.

Comments: Formerly known as *Aster linariifolius*. Another common name, stiff-leaved aster, references the leaves' stiffness and their tendency to break rather than bend when folded.

SMOOTH BLUE ASTER
Symphyotrichum laeve
Aster family (Asteraceae)

Description: Single-stemmed plants, up to 3' tall, with smooth leaves and a noticeable silvery to bluish-green cast to the leaves and stem. The leaves at the base of the stem are rounded and stalked, with a leafy fringe along two sides of the leaf stalk. The stem leaves are alternate and somewhat clasp the stem. There are several flowers on long stalks at the upper end of the stem. The flower heads are ¾–1½" across, with up to 25 bluish-purple, petal-like ray flowers surrounding a yellow disk.

Bloom Season: Late summer–fall

Habitat/Range: Occasional in mesic to dry prairies, hill prairies, and savannas; found throughout the prairie region, but less common in the southern part.

Comments: Formerly known as *Aster laevis*. The attractive silvery to bluish-green stem and leaves contrasting with the numerous bluish-purple rays and yellow disks have accounted for the many cultivated garden varieties that have been developed from this aster.

NEW ENGLAND ASTER
Symphyotrichum novae-angliae
Aster family (Asteraceae)

Description: Showy plants, up to 6' tall, with branching stems that have gland-tipped hairs toward the tip. The leaves are alternate, numerous, up to 4" long and 1" wide, hairy, with pointed tips and leaves clasping the stem. Several flower heads are clustered along the upper stems. The flower stalks and bracts at the base of each flower head are covered with gland-tipped hairs. Each head is about 1½" across, with over 40 bright purple, petal-like ray flowers surrounding a yellow disk. The flowers can also be pinkish-purple or pale lavender.

Bloom Season: Late summer–fall

Habitat/Range: Locally common in mesic to wet prairies, fens, edges of woods, old fields, pastures, and roadsides; found throughout the prairie region, but absent in Texas and Louisiana.

Comments: Formerly known as *Aster novae-angliae*. The Meskwaki burned the plant and blew the smoke up the nose of an unconscious person to revive him or her. Other tribes used root tea for diarrhea and fevers. This is the tallest aster in the prairie region, and is easily grown in gardens and wildflower plantings.

AROMATIC ASTER
Symphyotrichum oblongifolium
Aster family (Asteraceae)

Description: Fragrant, hairy plants, up to 2½' tall, with spreading branches. The leaves are alternate, crowded, hairy, up to 3" long and less than 1" wide, with clasping bases and a rough surface. The flower heads are at the end of short branches, with numerous, small, leaf-like bracts along their length. Each flower head is 1" across and has 20–40 purple, petal-like ray flowers surrounding 30–50 yellow disk flowers.

Bloom Season: Late summer–fall

Habitat/Range: Occasional in upland prairies, hill prairies, and glades; found throughout the prairie region, but rare east of Illinois.

Comments: Formerly known as *Aster oblongifolius*. Aromatic aster takes on a shrubby look with hundreds of attractive flowers when grown in the garden and given full sun. It continues to bloom well after the first frost. And, according to one reference, aromatic aster is used as a lotion for protection from witches!

SKY BLUE ASTER
Symphyotrichum oolentangiensis
Aster family (Asteraceae)

Description: This species has rough, slightly hairy stems, up to 3' tall. The leaves are alternate, thick, sandpapery on both sides, and lack teeth along the margins. The basal leaves have long stalks and are lance-shaped, narrowing to a pointed tip, with heart-shaped leaf bases, and up to 5" long and 2" wide. The stem leaves are much smaller and lack stalks. The flower heads are in spreading clusters at the tops of stems. Each head is about 1" across, with 10–25 blue, petal-like ray flowers surrounding 15–28 yellow disk flowers.

Bloom Season: Late summer–fall

Habitat/Range: Common in mesic to dry prairies, sand prairies, savannas, rocky upland forests, and glades; found throughout the prairie region.

Comments: Formerly known as *Aster oolentangiensis* and *Aster azueus*. John Leonard Riddell (1807–1865) was a science lecturer, botanist, geologist, medical doctor, chemist, microscopist, numismatist, politician, and science fiction author in the United States. He originally described this flower in 1835, and named it *Aster oolentangiensis* after the Olentangy River, where he found it near Worthington, Ohio. Riddell originally misspelled the name of the river with two O's, and that remains unchanged because the older species name had precedence.

WILLOWLEAF ASTER
Symphyotrichum praealtum
Aster family (Asteraceae)

Description: Plants up to 5' tall, often growing in dense colonies. The leaves are alternate along the stem, up to 5½" long and about ¾" wide, and about the same width along the length of the leaf. The lower surface has conspicuous net-shaped veins. Numerous flower heads are clustered in a pyramid-like column near the top. The flower heads are about 1" wide, with 20–25 pale lavender, petal-like ray flowers surrounding 20–35 yellow disk flowers.

Bloom Season: Late summer–fall

Habitat/Range: Frequent in wet prairies, moist depressions in upland prairies, fens, open thickets, and other moist places; found throughout the prairie region, but rare in the Dakotas and Michigan.

Comments: Formerly known as *Aster praealtus*. Willowleaf aster is named for its long, linear willow-like leaves. The species name *praealtum* means "very tall."

SWAMP ASTER
Symphyotrichum puniceum
Aster family (Asteraceae)

Description: Light green stems turning reddish-purple with age, up to 6' tall, with sparse to dense stiff white hairs in lines along its surface. The leaves are mostly dark green, often shiny, with short hairs underneath along the central vein. Leaves are 2–8" long and ¼–1¼" wide, with basal leaves having winged sheathing stalks that wither away by flowering time along with lower stem leaves. Stem leaves are stalkless, with bases that clasp the stem, and pointed tips. The flower heads are stalked, on branching clusters at the top of the stem, each 1–1½" across with 30–60 pale violet to bright blue-violet petal-like ray flowers, surrounding 30–70 yellow disk flowers.

Bloom Season: Late summer–fall

Habitat/Range: Occasional in wet prairies, fens, swamps, bogs, edges of moist woods; found in the prairie region from North Dakota to Iowa to Missouri eastward; also in Texas.

Comments: Formerly known as *Aster puniceus.* Swamp aster is also called purple-stemmed aster, red-stalked aster, red-stemmed aster, and glossy-leaved aster. This aster is similar to New England aster, but occurs in wetter sites, has hairs with fine lines along the stems, and lacks gland-tipped hairs. Native Americans used the roots of swamp aster to treat fever, colds, typhoid, pneumonia, and toothache.

SILKY ASTER
Symphyotrichum sericeum
Aster family (Asteraceae)

Description: Attractive plants with widely branching stems, up to 2½' tall. The leaves are alternate, somewhat stiff, up to 1¾" long and ½" wide, with soft, silky hairs that lie flat on both sides of the leaves, giving them a silvery-green color. Numerous flower heads are in an open cluster at the tops of stems. Each head is about 1¼" across, with 15–30 violet-purple, petal-like ray flowers surrounding 15–35 yellow disk flowers.

Bloom Season: Late summer–fall

Habitat/Range: Occasional in dry or sandy prairies, hill prairies, and glades; found throughout the prairie region, but rare in Arkansas, Indiana, and Michigan, and absent in Ohio.

Comments: Formerly known as *Aster sericeus*. Silky aster is very attractive, with its violet-purple rays contrasting intensely with the silvery-white foliage. Compared to most other American asters, the flowers appear disproportionately large for the plant's size. It is a good plant for dry, open spaces in native plant gardens, rock gardens, or butterfly gardens.

ARKANSAS IRONWEED
Vernonia arkansana
Aster family (Asteraceae)

Description: From 1 to several stems arise from the base to a height of 4', with willow-like leaves. The leaves are alternate, stalkless, up to 6" long and ½" wide, gradually tapering at both ends, and with small teeth along the margins. The flower heads are few in number but large, from ¾–1¼" across, with each head containing from 50–120 small, reddish-purple disk flowers. Petal-like ray flowers are absent. The bracts at the base of the flower head are long and curled, a distinctive character that is unique to this ironweed.

Bloom Season: Midsummer–fall

Habitat/Range: Common in upland prairies, bottomland prairies, savannas, fens, glades, stream banks, and gravel bars; found in the prairie region in Kansas, Oklahoma, Arkansas, and Missouri.

Comments: Formerly known as *Vernonia crinita*. The genus name honors botanist William Vernon, who collected in Maryland in 1698. The species name, *arkansana*, means "of Arkansas," indicating where it was first collected.

WESTERN IRONWEED
Vernonia baldwinii
Aster family (Asteraceae)

Description: Stems with relatively long, spreading, or often bent hairs, up to 5' tall. The leaves are alternate, up to 7" long and 2½" wide, broadest near the middle and tapering at both ends, densely hairy underneath, and toothed along the margins. The flower heads are numerous, up to ½" across, with up to 30 small, purple disk flowers. There are no petal-like ray flowers. A series of small, overlapping bracts with pointed, often spreading tips are at the base of the flower head.

Bloom Season: Summer–fall

Habitat/Range: Common in upland prairies, hill prairies, savannas, woodlands, glades, and pastures; found in the prairie region from Nebraska to Illinois and south; rare or absent in the northern and eastern parts.

Comments: A closely related species, tall ironweed (*Vernonia gigantea*; formerly *Vernonia altissima*), differs by having smooth to minutely hairy stems and leaves, with the bracts along the cup of the flower heads blunt instead of pointed, and not spreading. Common in wet prairies, fens, bottomland forests, swamps, pastures, and roadsides; found through the prairie region but absent in the northwestern part.

PRAIRIE IRONWEED
Vernonia fasciculata
Aster family (Asteraceae)

Description: Mostly unbranched, green to reddish-purple stems to 4' tall, with smooth, hairless stems and leaves. The leaves are alternate, up to 6" long and 1" wide, finely toothed along their edges, widest at the middle and tapering at both ends. Each leaf has numerous tiny pits on the underside. Flower heads are in a dense, rounded cluster at the top of the stem. Each flower head is about ¾" across, with 10–26 bright, reddish-purple disk flowers. There are no petal-like ray flowers. The bracts at the base of the flower heads are green to purplish-brown, flattened and rounded at the tip, somewhat resembling fish scales, and with white, cobwebby hairs around the edge.

Bloom Season: Midsummer–fall

Habitat/Range: Common in wet prairies and wet depressions in upland prairies, fens, marshes, and other moist places; found throughout the prairie region.

Comments: Also known as smooth ironweed because its stems, leaves, and flower heads are glabrous (smooth). The species name, *fasciculata*, is from the Latin word for "clustered, grouped together."

191

MISSOURI IRONWEED
Vernonia missurica
Aster family (Asteraceae)

Description: A densely hairy, single-stemmed plant, up to 6' tall. The stem has long, crooked, or often bent to tangled hairs toward the tip. The leaves are up to 8" long and 2½" wide, with long crooked hairs on the lower surface. The leaf margins range from coarsely toothed to entire. The flower heads are in clusters on several branches at the top of the stem. Each flower head is ½–¾" across, with 34–60 bright, reddish-purple disk flowers. There are no petal-like ray flowers. Numerous bracts, each rounded to a bluntly pointed tip, surround the flower head.

Bloom Season: Midsummer–fall

Habitat/Range: Common in dry and wet prairies, savannas, woodlands, glades, old fields, and pastures; found throughout the prairie region, but absent in the northwestern part.

Comments: The species name, *missurica*, is in reference to the Missouri River. Missouri ironweed is a good late-season nectar source. Butterfly visitors include monarchs, painted ladies, sulfurs, swallowtails, whites, and others. Like milkweeds, ironweeds are bitter to the taste, so herbivorous animals like white-tailed deer and cattle will avoid consuming it.

HAREBELL
Campanula rotundifolia
Bellflower family (Campanulaceae)

Description: Slender, erect to loosely ascending plants, up to 20" tall, with slender, alternate leaves. The basal leaves are long-stalked, almost round, with toothed edges and heart-shaped bases. The stem leaves are stalkless, up to 3" long and less than ½" wide, becoming grass-like on the upper stem. Flowers occur at the top of the plant on slender stalks, causing the flowers to node. Each flower is about ¾" long and pale blue to violet to bright purple. The cup-like flowers have 5 flaring, pointed lobes.

Bloom Season: Late spring–early fall

Habitat/Range: Local in dry hill prairies, open sandy woodlands, savannas, and cliffs; found in the northern part of the prairie region.

Comments: The common name, which is of European origin, may relate to the fact that this plant is sometimes found in areas inhabited by rabbits (hares). *Campanula rotundifolia* occurs throughout the northern United States, Canada, and southward in the intermountain region to near the Mexican border. It has a near-circumpolar distribution in the northern hemisphere, from about latitude 40 degrees N to about 70 degrees N, extending in Europe from northernmost Scandinavia to the Pyrenees and the French Mediterranean coast. It also occurs on the southern coasts of Greenland and on Iceland.

GREAT BLUE LOBELIA
Lobelia siphilitica
Bellflower family (Campanulaceae)

Description: Unbranched stems, up to 3' tall, with milky sap. The leaves are alternate, stalkless, up to 6" long and 1½" wide, widest in the middle and tapering at both ends, with teeth along the margins. The flowers are crowded along the upper part of the stem. Each flower is ¾–1½" long, deep blue, with pale stripes along the outside of the tube, and 2 lips. The upper lip is split into 2 upright lobes, and the lower into 3 spreading lobes with a white base.

Bloom Season: Midsummer–fall

Habitat/Range: Occasional in moist depressions in upland prairies, wet prairies, fens, along streams, and seepage areas; found throughout the prairie region.

Comments: The Meskwaki used great blue lobelia in love medicines. The roots were finely chopped and mixed into the food of a quarrelsome couple without their knowledge. This, the Meskwaki believed, would avert divorce and make the pair love each other again. Other tribes used root tea for syphilis and leaf tea for colds, fever, upset stomach, worms, croup, and nosebleed.

PALE SPIKED LOBELIA
Lobelia spicata
Bellflower family (Campanulaceae)

Description: Slender, smooth, single-stemmed plants, up to 3' tall, with milky sap, and ridges along the stem. The leaves are alternate, narrow, up to 3½" long and 1" wide, with teeth along the margins. The pale blue flowers are on short stalks that alternate along the stem. There is a small leaf-like bract at the base of each stalk. The flowers are less than ½" long, with 2 lips; the small upper lip has 2 lobes that are stiffly erect, while the broad lower lip has 3 larger spreading lobes.

Bloom Season: Mid-spring–summer

Habitat/Range: Common in prairies, savannas, glades, open woodlands, and old fields; found throughout the prairie region.

Comments: Native Americans used a tea of the plant to induce vomiting. Root tea was used to treat trembling by applying the tea to scratches made in the affected limb.

VENUS'S LOOKING GLASS
Triodanis perfoliata
Bellflower family (Campanulaceae)

Description: A slender, mostly unbranched, annual, up to 18" tall, with stems angled and hairs along the ridges. The leaves are roundish, about as long as they are broad, and clasp the stem with a heart-shaped base. There are teeth along the margins, and the veins are fan-shaped. Several star-shaped flowers arise from the leaf axils, stalkless, about ½" across, with 5 blue petals. Those flowers on the lower stalk do not open but produce the seed.

Bloom Season: Mid-spring–summer

Habitat/Range: Common in often gravelly or sandy soils in prairies, glades, open woodlands, pastures, old fields, and roadsides; found throughout the prairie region, but absent in the northwestern part.

Comments: The Cherokee took a liquid compound of the root for indigestion. The Meskwaki used it as an emetic (a substance that causes vomiting) to make one "sick all day long," and to smoke it at ceremonies. A closely related species, small Venus's looking glass (*Triodanis biflora*), has leaves that are longer than they are broad, and not clasping the stem, and only 1–2 flowers with petals at the top of the stem. Small Venus's looking glass occupies similar habitats and range as Venus's looking glass.

COMMON SPIDERWORT
Tradescantia ohiensis
Spiderwort family (Commelinaceae)

Description: Thin plants up to 3' tall, with smooth bluish to silvery-green stems and leaves. The arching leaves are alternate, up to 15" long and about 1" wide, and tapering to a long point, with a sheath that wraps around the stem. The flowers are in a tight cluster at the top of the stem. Each flower is about 1½" across, with 3 blue to purple, rounded petals and 6 yellow-tipped stamens covered with long, purple hairs.

Bloom Season: Late spring–midsummer

Habitat/Range: Common in mesic to dry prairies, savannas, woodlands, pastures, and roadsides; found throughout the prairie region, but absent in the Dakotas.

Comments: Common spiderwort was once thought to be a cure for spider bites. Native Americans used the stems as potherbs. Each showy flower lasts but a day.

VIRGINIA SPIDERWORT
Tradescantia virginiana
Spiderwort family (Commelinaceae)

Description: A smooth-stemmed plant, up to 16" tall, with 2–5 leaves along the stem. The leaves are up to 1' long, less than 1" wide, becoming wider toward the base to form a sheath that clasps the stem. The flowers are blue, purple, or reddish-purple, and occur in a cluster at the end of the stem just above 2 leaf-like bracts. Each flower is about 1" across with 3 rounded petals. There are 3 hairy, green sepals beneath the petals. Each flower has 6 bright yellow stamens with purple hairs along their length.

Bloom Season: Mid- to late spring

Habitat/Range: Occasional in sandy or rocky prairies, and rocky woodlands; found from Iowa to Missouri and eastward in the prairie region.

Comments: The Lakota made a jelly-like blue paint from the flowers, which was used for decorative purposes. A closely related species, long-bracted spiderwort (*Tradescantia bracteata*), has gland-tipped hairs on the sepals; occurs in upland prairies, sand prairies, and edges of woods; found in the prairie region from western Illinois and Wisconsin westward.

LEAD PLANT
Amorpha canescens
Bean family (Fabaceae)

Description: A small shrub, up to 3' tall, with grayish hairs on a stem that becomes woody with age. The leaves are stalked, up to 4" long, and divided into as many as 51 leaflets. The leaflets are covered with gray hairs, giving the plant a lead-gray color, which was thought to indicate the presence of lead ore below in the soil. Each leaflet is up ¾" long and ½" wide. The tiny purple flowers are in a spike-like mass along the upper part of the stem. Each flower has a single ¼"-long petal curling around 10 orange-tipped stamens.

Bloom Season: Late spring–summer

Habitat/Range: Occasional in high-quality mesic to dry prairies, savannas, glades, and rocky, open woods; found throughout the prairie region.

Comments: Native Americans used the dried leaves for smoking. A tea was made for treating pinworms and was used externally for eczema. The Omaha powdered the dried leaves and blew them into cuts and open wounds to help promote scab formation. A closely related species, indigo bush (*Amorpha fruticosa*), is a larger shrub, up to 10' tall, lacking hair, with 11–31 leaflets, each up to 2" long and over 1" wide. It is found in thickets along streams and in prairie draws throughout the prairie region.

GROUND PLUM

Astragalus crassicarpus var. *crassicarpus*
Bean family (Fabaceae)

Description: Plants usually with several trailing stems, up to 2' long, connected to a thick woody taproot. The leaves are hairy, up to 6" long and alternating along the stem on short stalks. Each leaf has 7–13 pairs of slightly folded leaflets, each ¾" long and ⅓" wide. The flowers are in small clusters at the ends of branches, with 5–25 flowers in each cluster. Each flower is about ¾–1" long and varies in color from purple and violet, to bluish or pinkish red. The upper petal is larger and flaring at the tip, below which are two side petals and a lower lip.

Bloom Season: Mid- to late spring

Habitat/Range: Locally frequent in dry prairies, loess hill prairies, and rocky woods; found in the western part of the prairie region, but absent in Wisconsin and Illinois eastward.

Comments: The fruits are succulent, shiny pods about 1" in diameter that become dry and hard when they age. They contain numerous small seeds. When ripe, the fruit has a reddish cast and was widely used for food by Native Americans and early settlers. They are said to taste like raw pea pods. A creamy white to greenish-yellow variety of ground plum (*Astragalus crassicarpus* var. *trichocalyx*) can be found on page 112.

BLUE WILD INDIGO

Baptisia australis var. *minor*
Bean family (Fabaceae)

Description: Smooth, branched, shrub-like plants, up to 4' tall. The leaves are alternate, divided into 3 leaflets, each less than 2" long. The flowers are on stalks and attached along a stem that stands well above the leaves. Each deep blue to purple flower is about 1" long, with a notched upper petal, 2 small side petals, and a middle keel-shaped lip. The seed pods are black, hairless, and about 2" long, with a pointed tip.

Bloom Season: Late spring–early summer

Habitat/Range: Occasional in upland prairies and glades; found in the prairie region from southeast Nebraska to northern Texas, east to northern Arkansas and Missouri.

Comments: Native Americans used root tea as an emetic (to induce vomiting) and a purgative (to clear the bowels). Externally, it was used as a wash for inflammations, cuts, wounds, bruises, and sprains, and in a compress for toothache. The Cherokee used the plant as a source of blue dye for cloth.

PURPLE PRAIRIE CLOVER
Dalea purpurea
Bean family (Fabaceae)

Description: Slender, leafy plants, up to 2' tall, with 1 to several stems arising from a common base. The leaves are divided into 3–9 shiny, narrow leaflets, each about 1" long and ⅛" wide. The flowers are densely packed in a cylindrical head, 1–2" long, at the tops of the branches, with the flowers opening in a circle around the head from bottom to top. Each reddish-purple flower is about ¼" long, with a large petal, 4 smaller petals, and 5 orange stamens.

Bloom Season: Late spring–early summer

Habitat/Range: Common in mesic to dry prairies, hill prairies, sand prairies, savannas, and glades; found throughout the prairie region.

Comments: Native Americans used the plant medicinally by applying a tea made from the leaves to open wounds. The Pawnee took root tea as general preventive medicine. The tough elastic stems were gathered to make brooms. A closely related species, silky prairie clover (*Dalea villosa*), has densely hairy leaves and stems, leaves with 9–25 leaflets, flowers pink to reddish-purple, densely packed in a 4"-long cylindrical head; found in sand prairies and pastures in the northwestern prairie region.

VIOLET BUSH CLOVER
Lespedeza frutescens
Bean family (Fabaceae)

Description: A bushy plant with weak stems that tend to lean, usually not more than 18" tall. The leaves are alternate, stalked, and divided into 3 somewhat oval leaflets. Each leaflet is about 1½" long and ¾" wide. The flowers are in sparse clusters at the ends of slender branches. Each violet- to rose-colored flower is about ⅜" long, with a spreading upper petal, 2 smaller side petals, and a protruding lower lip. The single seed pods are small, flattened, and up to ¼" long.

Bloom Season: Midsummer–early fall

Habitat/Range: Common in mesic to dry prairies, savannas, and glades; found in the southern part of the prairie region from eastern Oklahoma and Missouri eastward.

Comments: Formerly known as *Lespedeza violacea*. The seeds are eaten by songbirds, ruffed grouse, bobwhite quail, wild turkey, and greater prairie-chicken. The plants are eaten by white-tailed deer.

SLENDER BUSH CLOVER
Lespedeza virginica
Bean family (Fabaceae)

Description: A narrow-stemmed plant, up to 3' tall, with hairy, branching stems. The leaves are numerous, stalked, divided into 3 narrow leaflets, each of which is up to 1½" long and less than ¼" wide. The flowers are in dense clusters interspersed with leaves on the upper part of the stem. Each pink to purple flower is about ¼" long, with a spreading upper petal, 2 smaller side petals, and a lower protruding lip. The upper petal has a dark red blotch near its base.

Bloom Season: Late spring–early fall

Habitat/Range: Common in mesic to dry prairies, sand prairies, glades, savannas, and open woods; found throughout the prairie region, but absent in the northwestern part from Nebraska northward to the Dakotas and Minnesota.

Comments: A closely related species but extremely rare, prairie bush clover (*Lespedeza leptostachya*), is federally listed as threatened. The plants have a silver cast, with widely spaced, slender leaflets and open clusters of pale pink to creamy white flowers that bloom from midsummer to early fall. They occur in dry prairies and hill prairies with sandy or gravelly soils, from Iowa to northern Illinois, and north to southern Wisconsin and southern Minnesota.

WILD LUPINE
Lupinus perennis
Bean family (Fabaceae)

Description: Hairy-stemmed plants, up to 2' tall, with alternate, stalked, compound leaves. The leaves are hairy and divided into 7–11 leaflets, radiating from a central point. Each leaflet is up to 2" long and ½" wide, with round tips, and often with a sharp point at the apex. The flowers are in a spiked cluster up to 8" long. Each stalked blue or purple flower is about ½" long, with an upper fan-shaped petal that is often blue and white, 2 side petals, and an extended lower lip. Both upper and lower lips have darker blue veins running along their length. The seed pod is up to 2" long, hairy, and turns black when mature.

Bloom Season: Mid-spring–early summer

Habitat/Range: Locally common in sand savannas, sand woodlands, and somewhat degraded sand prairies where grasses are decreased; found in the northern part of the prairie region, from northern Illinois to Minnesota and eastward.

Comments: Wild lupine is the host plant for the Karner blue butterfly caterpillar. Habitat loss has led to the decline in wild lupine plants, the food larval source, and that has put the Karner blue butterfly on the federal endangered species list. Native Americans drank cold leaf tea of wild lupine to treat nausea and internal hemorrhage. A fodder was used to fatten horses and make them "spirited and full of fire." The seeds are considered poisonous.

SAMPSON'S SNAKEROOT
Orbexilum pedunculatum
Bean family (Fabaceae)

Description: A slender, sparingly branched plant up to 3' long, the leaves are alternate, stalked, and divided into 3 leaflets. Each leaflet is up to 3" long and ½" wide, with the center leaflet on a longer stalk. The flowers are in cylindrical clusters at the top of long stalks. Individual flowers are light blue to bluish-purple, about ¼" long, with a spreading upper petal, 2 smaller side petals, and a lower protruding lip. The fruits are hairy, flat pods less than ¼" long with wrinkled surfaces and a strongly curved beak at the end.

Bloom Season: Late spring–early summer

Habitat/Range: Common in acidic soils in dry upland prairies, sand prairies, savannas, rocky open woodlands, and glades; found in the prairie region from southeast Kansas to Ohio and southward.

Comments: Formerly known as *Psoralea psoralioides.*

PURPLE LOCOWEED
Oxytropis lambertii
Bean family (Fabaceae)

Description: A very short-stemmed plant with silky hairs and a stout taproot. The stem is reduced to a small crown at ground level where the leaves emerge. The leaves are on short stalks with 7–19 leaflets, each ¼–1½" long and less than ¼" wide. Flowers are on leafless stalks that combined are up to 8" tall. Each flower is silky-hairy, about ¾" long, with purple or rose petals. The upper petal forms a notched hood, while the side petals flank a pointed, keel-like lower lip.

Bloom Season: Mid-spring–early summer

Habitat/Range: Locally frequent in dry, rocky prairies, loess hill prairies, and open wooded slopes; found in the western one-fourth of the prairie region.

Comments: Like many species of locoweeds, purple locoweed accumulates and stores selenium from the soil, making it toxic to livestock if accumulated in substantial amounts. Although it is known to have deleterious side effects, the Navajo were known to make a tea for constipation, and they also ate it, parched or mushed, for food.

SILVERY SCURF PEA
Pediomelum argophyllum
Bean family (Fabaceae)

Description: A silvery-looking, bushy plant, up to 3' tall. The stems and leaves are covered with dense, shiny, white hairs that give the plant a silvery appearance. The leaves are alternate, on stalks up to 2" long, and compound, with each leaf consisting of 3–5 oval to narrow leaflets ½–2" long and ¾" wide, with all leaflets radiating from a single point. The flowers are in open spikes from upper leaf axils, with 2–8 deep blue to purplish-blue flowers whorled around the stem. Each flower is less than ¼" wide, with a flaring upper petal and 2 side petals flanking a protruding lower lip.

Bloom Season: Summer

Habitat/Range: Occasional in dry, rocky prairies, hill prairies, and open woodlands; found in the western part of the prairie region.

Comments: Formerly known as *Psoralea argophylla*. The Meskwaki used a tea from the root to cure chronic constipation. The Cheyenne made a tea from the leaves and stems to cure a high fever. Meriwether Lewis of the Lewis and Clark Expedition reported that "a decoction of the plant is used by the Indians to wash their wounds."

PRAIRIE TURNIP
Pediomelum esculentum
Bean family (Fabaceae)

Description: A much-branched plant, up to 18" tall, with long, white spreading hairs on the stem and leaves. The leaves are alternate, on long, hairy stalks, and fan-shaped, with 5 leaflets, each about 2" long. The undersides of the leaflets are densely hairy. The flowers are tightly clustered at the tops of stems. Individual flowers are about ½" long, dark bluish, with a flaring upper petal and 2 side petals flanking a protruding lower lip. The flowers turn from blue to white with age.

Bloom Season: Late spring–early summer

Habitat/Range: Occasional in dry prairies, often with rocky soil, glades, and open rocky woods; found in the prairie region from northern Arkansas to Wisconsin and westward.

Comments: Formerly known as *Psoralea esculenta*. The prairie turnip was considered the most important food of Native Americans who lived on the prairies. The plants were so valued that their presence influenced the tribes' selection of hunting grounds. The tuberous roots, which are said to taste like turnips, were also a favorite of the now-extinct Plains grizzly bear. The plant's medicinal uses included a root tea for treating sore throat, chest problems, and gastroenteritis.

SCURF PEA
Psoralidium tenuiflorum
Bean family (Fabaceae)

Description: A bushy plant, up to 3' tall, with gray-hairy stems. The leaves are alternate and stalked, with usually 3 leaflets, each up to 2" long and less than ½" wide. The flowers are in loose clusters on long stalks that arise from the leaf axils. Each flower is about ⅜" long, bluish-purple to purple in color, with a flaring upper petal and 2 side petals flanking a protruding lower lip.

Bloom Season: Late spring–summer

Habitat/Range: Occasional in mesic to dry prairies, savannas, glades, and sandy or rocky, open woods; found in the prairie region from Illinois to Iowa to South Dakota and southward.

Comments: Formerly known as *Psoralea tenuiflora*. The Lakota made a root tea to treat headache, and they burned the root as incense to repel mosquitoes. The Dakota took the tops of the plants and made garlands that were worn on very hot days to protect the head from the heat of the sun.

CLOSED GENTIAN
Gentiana andrewsii
Gentian family (Gentianaceae)

Description: Unbranched stems up to 2½' tall, with stalkless, smooth leaves that are opposite along the stem. The upper leaves are usually the largest, up to 5" long and 1½" wide, with pointed tips, parallel veins running down the leaf, and a fringe of small hairs along the margin. The flowers occur in 1–3 clusters along the stem, with a whorl of leaves and leaf-like bracts below each cluster. Each flower is about 1½" long, deep blue, with petals that remain closed except for a tiny, fringed opening at the top. Each flower has 5 lobes, with an interconnecting membrane between each lobe that extends slightly beyond the lobe, creating the fringed appearance.

Bloom Season: Late summer–fall

Habitat/Range: Infrequent in mesic prairies, seepage areas, fens, and moist areas in woodlands; found in the prairie region from Nebraska and Missouri to Ohio, and northward.

Comments: This plant is also called bottle gentian for the shape of the flowers. Bumblebees are the primary pollinators because they are strong enough to force their way into the tightly closed flowers. A closely related species, soapwort gentian (*Gentiana saponaria*), has the 5 lobes of each flower with an interconnecting membrane between each lobe that is of equal length, or slightly below, each lobe. This gentian is infrequent to rare in mesic sand prairies, sandy woods, and savannas; found in the prairie region, primarily in northeastern Illinois, northwestern Indiana, and Arkansas.

DOWNY GENTIAN
Gentiana puberulenta
Gentian family (Gentianaceae)

Description: Stout, unbranched stems, up to 12" tall, with shiny, pointed, opposite leaves. The leaves are without stalks, broadest toward the base, up to 2" long and 1" wide, with minute hairs along the margins. The showy flowers are in dense clusters of 3–10. Each flower is deep blue to bluish-purple, up to 1½" long and about as wide, with 5 spreading lobes that alternate with small fringed segments. The base of the petals is white with dark blue stripes or streaks.

Bloom Season: Late summer–fall

Habitat/Range: Locally frequent in mesic to dry prairies and savannas; found throughout the prairie region, but rare east of Illinois.

Comments: Downy gentian is one of the last flowers to bloom in the fall, even surviving the first frosts. The flowers can remain closed on overcast days, or can begin closing within minutes when shaded by a large passing cloud. The Winnebago and Dakota took root tea as a tonic. The Meskwaki used the root to treat snakebite.

STIFF GENTIAN
Gentianella quinquefolia
Gentian family (Gentianaceae)

Description: Annual or biennial plants, up to 16" tall, with 4-sided stems and several upper branches. The leaves are opposite, stalkless, up to 2½" long and 1" wide, broadest at the base, clasping the stem, and abruptly tapering to a pointed tip. The flowers are lilac to pale lavender to blue, tubular, upright, up to 1" long, and mostly closed at the top, with 5 bristle-tipped lobes.

Bloom Season: Late summer–fall

Habitat/Range: Infrequent in mesic to dry prairies, especially in calcareous soils, seepages, dry hill prairies, dry slopes, and rocky woodlands; found throughout the prairie region, but absent in the western part, from North Dakota southward to Texas.

Comments: Formerly known as *Gentiana quinquefolia*, this genus has now been reserved for the perennial gentians. Root tea was once used as a bitter tonic to stimulate digestion and weak appetite. Also used for treatment of headache, hepatitis, jaundice, and constipation.

FRINGED GENTIAN
Gentianopsis crinita
Gentian family (Gentianaceae)

Description: Annual or biennial plants up to 2' tall, stems hairless, slightly 4-angled, with few to several side branches. The leaves are opposite, stalkless, clasping the stem at their bases, up to 2½" long and ¾" wide, tapering to a pointed tip, hairless, smooth along the margins, and with a glossy surface. The flowers are on single, slender stalks, 2–7" long, near the top of the plant. The flowers are royal blue to blue-violet, trumpet-shaped, about 1" across, with 4 broadly rounded, spreading lobes that have long, delicate fringes around the edges.

Bloom Season: Late summer–fall

Habitat/Range: Uncommon in moist depressions in prairies, wet to moist sand prairies, fens, open wooded swamps, and stream banks; found in the northern part of the prairie region from Minnesota and Iowa, east from northern Illinois and Wisconsin to Michigan and Ohio, where it is rare.

Comments: Fringed gentian flowers open on sunny days, but generally remain closed on cloudy days. Ants are highly attracted to the nectar of these flowers because of their taste and nutritional value, so in response, some specialists believe the fringe along the petal lobes provides a measure of protection so that only pollinators like bees and bumblebees are allowed.

HAIRY PHACELIA
Phacelia hirsuta
Waterleaf family (Hydrophyllaceae)

Description: A branched, annual plant, up to 14" tall, with densely spreading hairs on the stems and leaves. The leaves are divided into 3–7 segments, with rounded lobes and dense hairs on both surfaces and along the margins. The basal leaves have stalks, but the stem leaves are attached directly to the stem. The flowers are about ¾" across, on short stalks, and in loose clusters at the tops of the stems. Each flower is often whitish at the base, with 5 lavender to blue rounded lobes.

Bloom Season: Spring–early summer

Habitat/Range: Occasional in dry prairies, sand prairies, and open woods; found in the prairie region from southeast Kansas, southwest Missouri, and southward.

Comments: The genus name, *Phacelia*, is from the Greek word for "bundle." The species name, *hirsuta*, is from the Latin for "hairy."

BLUE FLAG
Iris virginica var. *shrevei*
Iris family (Iridaceae)

Description: Spreading rhizomes produce clumps of basal leaves up to 3' long and 1" wide. The leaves are erect or arch out at the base, bluish-green to green, smooth, with parallel veins along the leaves and pointed tips. The flowers are on smooth, often waxy stems up to 3' tall, with 1–2 branches. There are 1–4 flowers on a stalk, with each flower up to 3–4" across, blue-violet, with yellow and white markings on the lower half of the petals. Each flower has 3 large, downward-curving sepals, 3 smaller, erect petals, 3 stamens, and 3 petal-like style branches within the flower. The fruit is a 3-angled capsule up to 3" long and 1½" wide.

Bloom Season: Late spring–midsummer

Habitat/Range: Locally frequent in wet prairies, marshes, fens, and roadside ditches; found throughout the prairie region, but absent in the Dakotas.

Comments: The Cherokee pounded the root into a paste that was then used as a salve for skin ulcers. A tea made from the root was used to treat ailments of the liver, and a decoction (boiling) of the root was used to treat "yellowish urine." It is considered to be one of the iris species used by the Seminole to treat "shock following an alligator-bite."

PRAIRIE IRIS
Nemastylis geminiflora
Iris family (Iridaceae)

Description: A low-growing plant with grass-like leaves and a showy, sky-blue flower. The leaves are up to 12" long and about ¼" wide. The flowers are from 1–2 per stem and up to 2½" across, with 6 petals that are actually 3 petals and 3 sepals; the latter are widest near the middle, narrow at the bases, and taper to pointed tips. The bases of the flowers are white and surround 3 yellow to orange stamens. Each flower opens once around midmorning and closes by midafternoon.

Bloom Season: Mid- to late spring

Habitat/Range: Uncommon in mesic to dry prairies, usually over limestone, glades, and other rocky sites; found in the prairie region from southeastern Kansas to Missouri and southward.

Comments: A closely related species, Nuttall's pleatleaf (*Nemastylis nuttallii*), has a taller stem, up to 8", narrower leaves less than ¼" wide, smaller flowers, less than 2" across, which are more purple in color and open in late afternoon and close during the night; occurs in prairies, glades, and dry upland woods; found in Missouri, Arkansas, and Oklahoma.

NARROW-LEAF BLUE-EYED GRASS
Sisyrinchium angustifolium
Iris family (Iridaceae)

Description: Small, clump-forming plants up to 12" tall, with winged stems, each about ⅛" wide, that appear to branch at the top. The grass-like leaves are green in shaded areas but appear bluish or grayish-green in the sun. The flower clusters are each attached on 1–4 stalks arising from 1 leaf-like bract. Each flower is deep blue-violet, with a yellow center, about ½" across, with 3 sepals and 3 petals, all looking like petals. The tips of the sepals and petals vary, from rounded with a hair-like point, to notched, to shallowly toothed.

Bloom Season: Late spring–early summer

Habitat/Range: Uncommon in mesic upland prairies and more frequent in prairie/woodland borders, savannas, bottomland forests, and stream banks; found throughout the prairie region, but absent in Nebraska and the Dakotas.

Comments: The deep blue-violet flowers of narrow-leaf blue-eyed grass give this species a distinctive look, along with its denser display of blooms. This plant makes for a popular addition to wildflower plantings and rock gardens.

PRAIRIE BLUE-EYED GRASS
Sisyrinchium campestre
Iris family (Iridaceae)

Description: Small, clump-forming plants, with stems not branching at the top, up to 12" tall, with pointed, upright, grass-like leaves. The flower stems are flat, about ⅛" wide, with 2 narrow wings, and typically longer than the leaves. Several flowers, each on a slender stalk, emerge from a long-pointed, leaf-like bract at the top of the stem. Each flower is light to dark blue or white (see p. 45 for white version) with a yellow center, about ½" across, with 3 sepals and 3 petals, all looking like petals. The tips of the sepals and petals vary, from rounded with a hair-like point, to notched, to shallowly toothed.

Bloom Season: Mid-spring–early summer

Habitat/Range: Common in dry upland prairies, savannas, rocky, open woods, and glades; found throughout the prairie region, but absent in North Dakota, and east of Illinois.

Comments: A similar species, eastern blue-eyed grass (*Sisyrinchium albidum*), has 3–4 leaf-like bracts surrounding a single flower cluster at the top of the stem. Flowers are white or pale violet; habitat is similar to prairie blue-eyed grass; found in the eastern half of the prairie region.

FALSE PENNYROYAL
Trichostema brachiatum
Mint family (Lamiaceae)

Description: Aromatic, annual plants less than 18" tall, with branching stems that are 4–sided and hairy on the upper part. The leaves are opposite and the pairs are at right angles to the one above and below. Each leaf is up to 2" long and ¾" wide, with short stalks, broadest in the middle and tapering at the end. Each leaf has parallel veins along its length and surfaces that are moderately to densely covered, with gland-tipped hairs. Flowers are stalked, with 1–3 flowers per cluster at the bases of upper stem leaves. Each flower ranges from pink to purple, is less than ¼" across, with petals fused at the base to form a tube that opens to 5 tiny lobes.

Bloom Season: Midsummer–early fall

Habitat/Range: Frequent in thin-soil areas of upland prairies, savannas, glades, and rocky pastures; found throughout the prairie region, but absent in North Dakota and rare in South Dakota and Nebraska.

Comments: Formerly known as *Isanthus brachiatus*; also known as fluxweed. According to *Culpeper's Complete Herbal* (1880) by English physician Nicholas Culpeper (1616–1654), fluxweed was used for stomach ailments, and it even has bone and sore healing properties.

WILD BERGAMOT
Monarda fistulosa
Mint family (Lamiaceae)

Description: The plants have a fragrant aroma and square stems, both characteristics typical of the mint family. The stems branch and are up to 5' tall, with the upper stem usually with fine hairs. The leaves are opposite, on short stalks, up to 5" long and 2" wide, widest at the base, narrowing to a long, pointed tip, and sometimes with fine teeth along the margins. The flowers are numerous in dense, round heads at the tops of the stems. The tubular, lavender flowers have 2 long lips, the upper narrow and hairy, the lower, broad and 3-lobed.

Bloom Season: Late spring–summer

Habitat/Range: Common in prairies, savannas, borders of glades, dry, rocky woods, pastures, old fields and along roadsides; found throughout the prairie region.

Comments: Many Native American tribes made tea from the flower heads and leaves to treat colds, fever, whooping cough, abdominal pain, and headache, and to act as a stimulant. The Lakota wrapped boiled leaves in a soft cloth and placed it on sore eyes overnight to relieve pain. Chewed leaves were placed on wounds under a bandage to stop the flow of blood. Wild bergamot is still used today in herbal teas.

BLUE SAGE
Salvia azurea var. *grandiflora*
Mint family (Lamiaceae)

Description: A slender, sometimes branched plant, up to 5' tall, with short hairs along the four-sided stems. The leaves are widely spaced along the stem, opposite, short-stalked, narrow, up to 4" long and 1" wide, with a few teeth along the margins. The flowers are in whorls along the upper stem, with up to 8 flowers in a whorl. Each flower is blue, with a white center, tubular, about 1" long, with 2 lips: The upper lip is narrow, hooded, and contains the two stamens, while the lower lip is broad, with 2 lobes.

Bloom Season: Summer–early fall

Habitat/Range: Common in dry prairies, savannas, and glades; found in the prairie region from Nebraska and Iowa southward, absent or escaped from cultivation elsewhere.

Description: The genus name, *Salvia*, comes from the Latin word, *salvere*, meaning "to feel well and healthy; to heal," which is the verb related to *salus* (health, well-being, prosperity, or salvation), in reference to the healing properties of some species in the genus. The species name, *azure*, means sky blue, for the azure-blue flowers. The attractive sky-blue flowers are pollinated by bumblebees.

SMALL SKULLCAP
Scutellaria parvula
Mint family (Lamiaceae)

Description: A short, slender plant, up to 8" tall, with a hairy, square stem. The leaves are opposite, stalkless, hairy, less than 1" long and about ¼" wide, lance-shaped, rounded at the base, and blunt-tipped. The flowers are opposite each other on short stalks that emerge from the leaf axils. Each flower is about ⅜" long, purple, hairy, with a tube ending in a small, hooded upper lip and a broad, lobed lower lip. The lower lip has a white center with purple spots.

Bloom Season: Late spring–midsummer

Habitat/Range: Common in upland prairies, savannas, open woodlands, glades, and pastures, often in sandy or rocky sites; found throughout the prairie region, but rare in the northeastern part.

Comments: The genus name, *Scutellaria*, comes from the Latin word *scutella*, meaning "a small dish or saucer," in reference to the shape of the persistent calyx after the flowers fade. The species name, *parvula*, means "little, small." The common name, skullcap, alludes to the resemblance of the calyx to miniature medieval helmets. The Meskwaki used small skullcap in the treatment of diarrhea.

WILD HYACINTH
Camassia scilloides
Lily family (Liliaceae)

Description: A stout-stemmed plant emerging from a bulb, growing up to 2' tall. The stem is bare, with long, narrow, grass-like leaves up to 1' long emerging from the base. The leaves are often partially folded along their lengths. At the top of the stem is a cluster 1¼–2" wide of up to 50 stalked flowers, each about 1" across, displaying 6 tepals (3 petal-like sepals and 3 petals) varying in color from pale blue to lilac and rarely, pure white. There are 6 yellow-tipped stamens.

Bloom Season: Mid- to late spring.

Habitat/Range: Common in mesic and dry prairies, open woodlands, glades, and rocky open slopes; found throughout the prairie region, but absent in the northwestern part.

Comments: A closely related species, prairie hyacinth (*Camassia angusta*), has stems up to 3' tall, flower clusters ¾–1¼" wide, 50–100 flowers in a cluster, and petals deep lavender to pale purple; occurs in mesic to dry upland prairies, savannas, sometimes in rocky areas; found in the southwestern portion of the prairie region, rare in the central part, and absent elsewhere.

WINGED LOOSESTRIFE
Lythrum alatum
Loosestrife family (Lythraceae)

Description: A smooth, loosely branching plant to 2' tall, with squarish stems that may support shallow wings or flaps of tissue. The leaves are opposite on the lower stem and alternate above, narrow, up to 2" long, progressively smaller toward the top, broadly round at the base, and pointed at the tip. The flowers, up to ½" across, arise singly from the upper leaf axils. Each flower has a narrow tube with 6 lavender to reddish-purple petals.

Bloom Season: Summer

Habitat/Range: Common in wet prairies, in depressions and seepage areas, and along streams in upland prairies; found throughout the prairie region.

Comments: The native winged loosestrife should not be confused with the introduced purple loosestrife (*Lythrum salicaria*) (see p. 243). Purple loosestrife is much taller, up to 4' high, hairy, with whorled or opposite leaves and tall spikes of red to purple flowers that appear in clusters.

BUSH'S POPPY MALLOW
Callirhoe bushii
Mallow family (Malvaceae)

Description: Plants with densely hairy stems, up to 30" tall. The basal leaves are on hairy stalks 4–9" long, with each leaf 1½–4" long, hairy, and divided into 5–7 narrow, deep finger-like lobes that are coarsely toothed. The stem leaves are 1–4" long, stalked, hairy, triangular shaped, with 3–5 lobes that are sparsely to coarsely toothed along the margins. The flowers are stalked, arising from leaf axils, cup-shaped, about 2–2½" across, with 5 reddish-purple petals, each about 1" long, and a central column containing stamens and styles.

Bloom Season: Summer

Habitat/Range: Occasional to rare in upland prairies, glades, and woodland edges; found in the prairie region from southeastern Kansas to western Missouri, Arkansas, and Oklahoma.

Comments: Bush's poppy mallow is named for Benjamin Franklin Bush (1858–1937), an American botanist and ornithologist credited with discovering the plant. Bush was an expert on the flora of Jackson County, Missouri, in which Kansas City is located. His lifelong research into the plant life of that area made it into one of the best-known botanical regions in the United States at that time. In addition to Missouri, he also traveled extensively throughout Arkansas, Oklahoma, and Texas.

FRINGED POPPY MALLOW
Callirhoe digitata
Mallow family (Malvaceae)

Description: A smooth, widely branching, spindly plant, up to 4' tall, with a whitish coating on the stems that can be rubbed off. The leaves are alternate, stalked, and divided into 5–7 narrow, deep finger-like lobes. Each lobe can be further divided and is usually less than ¼" wide. The flowers are on long stalks, with each flower 1½–2" across. The 5 petals are bright magenta, with ragged or fringed outer edges and a central column containing stamens and styles.

Bloom Season: Late spring–summer

Habitat/Range: Occasional in upland prairies, glades, and open areas; found in the prairie region from southwestern Missouri, Arkansas, and Oklahoma, to southwestern Kansas, where it is listed as rare.

Comments: The genus name, *Callirhoe*, honors the daughter of a minor Greek deity, Achelous, a river god. The species name, *digitata*, means "shaped like an open hand," referring to the leaves.

PURPLE POPPY MALLOW
Callirhoe involucrata
Mallow family (Malvaceae)

Description: A low-spreading plant with hairy branched stems up to 3' long. The leaves are alternate, stalked, 1½–3½" long, 1–3" wide, and deeply divided into 3–5 lobes, arranged like the fingers of a hand. The flowers arise from the junction of a leaf and a stem and are on stalks up to 8" long, and numerous. Each flower is cup-shaped, deep reddish-purple, about 2–2½" long, with 5 large petals surrounding numerous stamens and styles that are united into a column.

Bloom Season: Late spring–midsummer

Habitat/Range: Occasional in dry upland prairies, especially in sandy soil, glades, and open woodlands; found in the prairie region from Nebraska and Iowa southward.

Comments: The Dakota and Lakota dried the root and used it in a smoke treatment, inhaling the fumes from the smoldering root to treat head colds. The Dakota also boiled the root and drank the tea for internal pains, or used it externally to bathe aching body parts.

CLUSTERED POPPY MALLOW
Callirhoe triangulata
Mallow family (Malvaceae)

Description: Stems single or multiple from the base, weakly erect to ascending to prostrate, and 16–40" tall, or long. The stem and leaves are densely covered with star-shaped hairs. The basal leaves are stalked, up to 4" long, triangular-shaped, and with scalloped margins. The stem leaves are alternate, up to 4" long, becoming smaller along the upper stem, triangular-shaped, and with 3–5 shallow lobes. There are clusters of short-stalked flowers at the stem tips that arise from the upper leaf axils. Each flower is from 1–2½" wide, with 5 reddish-purple petals and a central column containing the stamens and styles.

Bloom Season: Summer

Habitat/Range: Uncommon to rare in sand prairies and sand savannas; found in the prairie region from eastern Iowa and Illinois to southern Wisconsin.

Comments: The genus name, *Callirhoe*, honors the daughter of a minor Greek deity, Achelous, a river god. The species name, *triangulata*, means "with three angles," referring to the lower leaves.

WILD FOUR O'CLOCK
Mirabilis nyctaginea
Four o'clock family (Nyctaginaceae)

Description: The stems are nearly square, somewhat hairy, branching, to 4' tall, with widely spaced opposite leaves. The leaves are short-stalked, with smooth margins, up to 4" long, and heart-shaped, with pointed tips. The flowers are in open-branched clusters at the tops of the stems. As many as 5 flowers are seated upon a shallow, green, cup-shaped platform, which is 5-lobed and ¾" across. Each flower is about ½" across with no petals and 5 pink to red sepal-like bracts, which form a spreading bell shape, with 5 notches and 3–5 yellow-tipped stamens. The flowers open in late afternoon.

Bloom Season: Late spring–early fall

Habitat/Range: A weedy species, occasional in upland prairies, especially in sandy soils, disturbed open ground, pastures, and roadsides; found throughout the prairie region, but spreading into Michigan and Ohio.

Comments: The Ponca chewed the root and spit it into wounds to heal them. The Pawnee ground the dried root and applied it as a remedy for sore mouth in teething babies. Some tribes pounded the root and used it to treat swellings, sprains, and burns. The plant is considered poisonous. A closely related species, white four o'clock (*Mirabilis albida*), has narrow leaves without stalks, and white-lilac to pinkish flowers; occurs in prairies, sand prairies, glades, and dry disturbed sites; found throughout the prairie region, but rare in the eastern half.

ROUGH FALSE FOXGLOVE
Agalinis aspera
Broomrape family (Orobanchaceae)

Description: An annual, slender-stemmed plant, 8–24" tall, with slightly rough stems and short, stiff hairs. Leaves are opposite, stalkless, and narrow, 1–1½" long and less than ⅛" wide, with sharp-pointed tips and smaller leaf clusters in the leaf axils. The flowers are bell-shaped, reddish to deep purple, with prominent lobes, minutely hairy, and ¾–1" long. The throat of the flower has 2 pale yellow lines and reddish or purplish spots.

Bloom Season: Late summer–fall

Habitat/Range: Occasional in dry upland prairies, hill prairies, sand prairies, and open woods; found in the prairie region from Oklahoma, Missouri, and Illinois, northward.

Comments: Another species, eared false foxglove (*Agalinis auriculata*), has moderately to densely hairy stems and leaves, with leaves up to 2" long and ¾" wide, and 1–2 small, outward-pointing lobes near their rounded bases. Each flower is densely hairy and ¾–1¼" long; uncommon in dry to mesic prairies and savannas; widely scattered across the prairie region, but absent in the northwestern part.

FASCICLED FALSE FOXGLOVE
Agalinis fasciculata
Broomrape family (Orobanchaceae)

Description: Stems ridged to 4-sided, with moderate to dense hairs, 2–3' tall, and somewhat bushy, with numerous short side branches. The primary leaves have clusters (or fascicles) of secondary leaves arising from their bases. Leaves are linear, somewhat arching, up to 1½" long and less than ⅛" wide, with pointed tips, smooth edges, and a prominent vein along the middle. The showy flowers are on short stalks at the leaf junctions, or at the tips of stem branches. The flowers are pink to purplish-pink or purple, up to 1" across, with hairs along the flaring tubular portion and the 5 lobes. The lobes are fringed along the margins and joined above a whitish throat, with purple to reddish-purple spots.

Bloom Season: Late summer–fall

Habitat/Range: Occasional in mesic to dry upland prairies, open woodlands, and sandy, open ground; found in the prairie region from southeastern Kansas, east to southern Illinois, and southward.

Comments: Another species similar in appearance, purple false foxglove (*Agalinis purpurea*), differs by being an annual, with smooth to slightly hairy stems, and clusters (or fascicles) of secondary leaves absent or shorter than the primary leaves; frequent in wet prairies, moist sand prairies, sand savannas, and openings in sandy woodlands; found throughout the prairie region, but rare in Kansas and Nebraska, and absent in the Dakotas.

SLENDER FALSE FOXGLOVE
Agalinis tenuifolia
Broomrape family (Orobanchaceae)

Description: A much-branched annual plant, less than 2' tall, with narrow ridges along the main stem. The leaves are opposite, very narrow, up to 3" long and often less than ⅛" wide, with smooth edges. The upper leaves have smaller secondary leaves emerging from the same axils. Single flowers arise from the leaf axils on stalks about ½" long. Each rose-purple flower is less than ½" long and ¾" across and funnel-shaped, with a short tube opening to 5 rounded lobes. There are purple spots and 5 hairy stamens in the mouth of the flower.

Bloom Season: Midsummer–early fall

Habitat/Range: Occasional in mesic to dry prairies, sand prairies, savannas, glades, and moist sandy areas; found throughout the prairie region, but rare in Oklahoma.

Comments: Like other members of the genus *Agalinis*, slender false foxglove is *hemiparasitic* (half or partially parasitic) on a variety of host plants, particularly grasses and sedges. Foxgloves use a special structure called *haustoria* to connect its roots with those of its host plants, in order to obtain nutrients; in addition, the plant also has green tissues, and performs photosynthesis.

BLUEHEARTS
Buchnera americana
Broomrape family (Orobanchaceae)

Description: Typically a single-stemmed plant, hairy, up to 3' tall. Leaves are from 2–4" long, opposite, stalkless, broadest at the base, and tapering to a pointed tip, hairy, with a few coarse teeth along the margins. Flowers are in pairs along a spike at the tip of the stem; each reddish-purple flower is about ⅝" across and about ½" long, tubular, with 5 widely spreading lobes.

Bloom Season: Summer–early fall

Habitat/Range: Occasional in mesic to dry prairies, glades, and savannas; found in the prairie region from Kansas and Missouri south, and rare in Illinois.

Comments: The genus name, *Buchnera*, is in honor of Johann Gottfried Büchner, an 18th-century German botanist. Like the slender false foxglove (see p. 222), bluehearts are hemiparasitic, meaning they are able to grow independently without a host, but grow more strongly with a host. They also attach to their host plant by the parasitic roots called haustoria.

BLUE TOADFLAX
Nuttallanthus canadensis
Plantain family (Plantaginaceae)

Description: Annual to biennial plants with smooth, slender stems, up to 18" tall, with trailing offshoots at the base that display rosettes of leaves that stay green all winter. The leaves are alternate on the upper stem and opposite or whorled below, narrow, and up to 1" long and ⅛" wide. The light blue to blue-violet flowers are in a loose cluster along the upper part of the stem. Each flower is about ½" long, with 2 lips: The upper lip has 2 lobes, and the lower lip has 3 lobes. A long, down-curved spur emerges from the back of the flower.

Bloom Season: Mid-spring–summer

Habitat/Range: Occasional in sandy soils, including sand prairies, glades, and savannas; found throughout the prairie region, but absent in Nebraska and the Dakotas.

Comments: Formerly known as *Linaria canadensis*. A closely related species, southern blue toadflax (*Nuttallanthus texanus*), has larger flowers (up to 1" long). It shares a similar bloom season and habitat and range as blue toadflax, but it is more common in the western part of the prairie region.

COBAEA BEARDTONGUE
Penstemon cobaea
Plantain family (Plantaginaceae)

Description: A finely hairy plant up to 3' tall, with opposite leaves. The leaves near the base of the plant are up to 6" long and up to 2" wide, strongly to weakly toothed along the edges, and stalked, but the upper leaves are stalkless and clasp the stem. The flowers are stalked and in 4–8 clusters, each with 2–6 flowers along the upper part of the stem, with a pair of small leaves below each cluster. Each flower is large, tubular, and inflated, up to 2¼" long, with 2 spreading lips divided into 2 upper lobes, and 3 lower lobes. The flowers appear in varying shades of purple, white, or pinkish, with purple lines and white blotches inside. The flower also has gland-tipped hairs along the outside and in the mouth.

Bloom Season: Mid-spring–early summer

Habitat/Range: Occasional in dry prairies, rocky hillsides, and pastures; found in the prairie region from southeastern Nebraska and western Missouri, southward.

Comments: There is a form of cobaea beardtongue found in rocky, open glades of southwestern Missouri and northwestern Arkansas that is particularly vibrant. Its bright purple flowers give it the reputation of being the showiest of all the beardtongues (see inset), and it is often featured in wildflower catalogs.

LARGE BEARDTONGUE
Penstemon grandiflorus
Plantain family (Plantaginaceae)

Description: A stout, unbranched, waxy plant, up to 3' tall, often with a bluish-green color. The leaves are opposite, thick, stiff, stalked below, stalkless and clasping above, 1–6" long and ½–2" wide. The flowers are stalked and in 2–6 clusters, each with 2–3 flowers along the upper part of the stem, with a pair of small leaves below each cluster. Each bluish-lavender to pale blue flower is tubular, inflated, and hairless, about 2" long, with 2 upper lobes and 3 lower lobes. The mouth of the flower has faint reddish to magenta lines.

Bloom Season: Mid-spring–midsummer

Habitat/Range: Locally common in dry prairies with sandy to loamy soils, and hill prairies; found in the western part of the prairie region, introduced or escaped from cultivation eastward.

Comments: The Pawnee drank a tea made from the leaves for chills and fever. The Kiowa made a tea from the boiled roots as a cure for stomachache. The Dakota boiled the root and used it to treat pains in the chest.

CAROLINA LARKSPUR
Delphinium carolinianum
Buttercup family (Ranunculaceae)

Description: The stems of this plant are wand-like, with soft hairs, and up to 3½' tall. The stalked leaves are mostly on the lower half of the stem. The leaves are fan-shaped, with 3–7 narrow segments that are often divided once or twice again. The short-stalked flowers are alternately arranged along the upper stem. Each flower is about 1" long and shaped like a cornucopia, consisting of 5 white to blue or purple, petal-like sepals, with the upper sepal curved back and upward in a long, tubular spur, 2 lateral, spreading sepals, and 2 lower sepals. There are 4 smaller petals, with the upper 2 petals extending backward into the sepal spur, while the other 2 petals are each split into 2 hairy lobes.

Bloom Season: Late spring–early summer

Habitat/Range: Frequent in upland prairies, savannas, and glades; found in the western part of the prairie region eastward to western Wisconsin and western Illinois.

Comments: Most of the prairie plants belong to subspecies *virescens*, with flowers white, pale blue to bright blue, with leaf stalks ⅛" long, and with most basal leaves present at flowering time. Subspecies *carolinianum* has flowers pale to deep blue or purple, or blue and white, with leaf stalks ¼–½" long, and with most basal leaves absent at flowering time. Both subspecies occupy similar habitat and range, but subspecies *carolinianum* is less common, or absent in the western edge of the prairie region.

BLUETS
Houstonia caerulea
Madder family (Rubiaceae)

Description: A small, mat-forming winter annual, with stems usually less than 6" tall. The leaves are opposite, few in number, mostly at the base, spatula-shaped, less than ½" long, and narrowed to a stalk almost as long as the leaf. The flowers are at the ends of stalks, about ½" across, sky-blue and tubular, with 4 pointed lobes and a yellow center.

Bloom Season: Spring

Habitat/Range: Occasional, sometimes locally abundant in sand prairies, sand savannas, sandstone glades, and sandy areas along streams; found in the prairie region from Oklahoma and Arkansas to Wisconsin and eastward.

Comments: Formerly known as *Hedyotis caerulea*. Bluets are also known as azure bluets and Quaker ladies. The flower's yellow center is distinctive among bluet species.

SMALL BLUETS
Houstonia pusilla
Madder family (Rubiaceae)

Description: A small, mat-forming winter annual, with stems usually less than 4" tall. The leaves are opposite, few in number, mostly at the base, and less than ½" long. The blue, pink, or sometimes white flowers are at ends of stalks, about ¼" across, with a tubular shape, 4 pointed lobes, and a reddish-purple center.

Bloom Season: Late winter–mid-spring

Habitat/Range: Locally common in open, sandy soils of prairies, woodlands, glades, pastures, and lawns; found in the southern half of the prairie region from Texas to Kansas, and east from Iowa, to Illinois, and Indiana.

Comments: Formerly known as *Hedyotis crassifolia*. Small bluets often form a carpet of blue in yards and cemeteries in early spring.

BLUE VERVAIN
Verbena hastata
Vervain family (Verbenaceae)

Description: Tall, slender plants, up to 6' tall, with rough hairs and branching stems. The leaves are opposite, stalked, up to 7" long and 2" wide, pointed, and coarsely toothed along the margins. The larger leaves are crowded along narrow spikes at the top of the stem, with 2 opposite lobes at the base of each leaf. Each blue to purplish-blue flower is about ⅜" long and ¼" across, with 5 spreading, rounded lobes.

Bloom Season: Summer–fall

Habitat/Range: Common in wet prairies, fens, and other wet areas, especially where the soil is disturbed; found throughout the prairie region, but rare in Texas.

Comments: The Omaha used the leaves for a beverage tea. The Meskwaki used the root as a remedy for fits. The Chippewa took the dried, powdered flowers as a snuff to stop nosebleed. During the American Revolution, doctors used blue vervain to induce vomiting and to clear respiratory tracts of mucus. Early settlers used a leaf tea as a spring tonic known as "simpler's joy" (*simpler* is an old term for an herbalist).

NARROW-LEAVED VERVAIN
Verbena simplex
Vervain family (Verbenaceae)

Description: Short, slender plants, 12–18" tall, hairy, with ridges along the stem. The leaves are opposite, stalkless, somewhat hairy, narrow, up to 3½" long and 1" wide, with sparse teeth, and tapering at both ends. The flowers are crowded along a spike at the top of the stem. Each flower is dark lavender to purple, small, about ¼" long, with a short tube and 5 spreading, rounded petals.

Bloom Season: Late spring–summer

Habitat/Range: Common on upland prairies, glades, other open rocky sites, pastures, and open disturbed areas; found throughout the prairie region, but rare or absent in the northwestern part, and absent in Texas.

Comments: A similar species, creeping vervain (*Verbena bracteata*), is an annual or biennial that produces several hairy, spreading stems up to 12" long, forming a low mat on the ground. The hairy leaves are toothed or lobed. The small flowers are purplish-blue. Common in disturbed portions of upland prairies, old fields, pastures, and long roadsides; found throughout the prairie region.

HOARY VERVAIN
Verbena stricta
Vervain family (Verbenaceae)

Description: Stout, densely hairy plants, up to 4' tall, branching in the upper half. The leaves are opposite, with very short stalks, gray-hairy, broadly rounded, up to 4" long and 2½" wide, and toothed along the margins. The flowers are crowded along 1 to several narrow spikes at the top of the plant. Each purple to purplish-blue flower is about ⅜" long and ¼" across, with 5 spreading, rounded lobes.

Bloom Season: Summer–early fall

Habitat/Range: Common in degraded upland prairies and hill prairies, old fields, pastures, and along roadsides and other disturbed sites; found throughout the prairie region.

Comments: The genus name, *Verbena*, comes from a Latin name used for some plants in religious ceremonies and also in medicine. The species name, *stricta*, means erect or upright. Hoary vervain is one of the showiest of the vervains because of its larger flowers and exceptionally hairy stems and leaves, giving the plant a silvery cast. Cattle and other herbivores generally avoid this plant because of its hairy nature and bitter taste.

JOHNNY-JUMP-UP
Viola bicolor
Violet family (Violaceae)

Description: A small, slender, annual plant, up to 6" tall. The leaves are alternate, the lowermost nearly circular, the upper ones narrower, up to ¾" long, rounded, and on long stalks. At the base of each leaf there is a deeply divided leaf-like stipule. The flowers are on stalks arising from the axils of leaves. The flowers are violet, lavender, or white, up to ¾" long, with 5 petals. The base of the petals is white, with a beard of hairs and purple lines. There is usually a yellow throat that is best developed on the lower petal.

Bloom Season: Spring

Habitat/Range: Common in disturbed upland prairies, margins of hill prairies, glades, savannas, pastures, fallow fields, gardens, lawns, and open disturbed areas; found in the prairie region from Nebraska to Ohio and southward.

Comments: Formerly known as *Viola rafinesquii*. Johnny-jump-up was once considered to have originated from Europe but is now accepted as part of the native flora, although it has weedy tendencies. The flowers look like miniature pansies, often forming dense carpets in lawns and cemeteries. The common name refers to the quick growth of this plant in the spring. As in other members of the violet family, Johnny-jump-up contains quantities of methyl salicylate (oil of wintergreen) in its taproot.

BIRD'S FOOT VIOLET
Viola pedata
Violet family (Violaceae)

Description: Small, sparse violets, up to 6" tall, with leaves and flowers emerging from the same base. The leaves are ¾–1½" long and wide, with narrow, deeply cut, segments resembling a bird's foot, and are often further divided into smaller lobes. The bare flower stems extend above the leaves and are sharply curved at the top, each with a single flower. The flowers are about 1½" across, with 5 petals; the lowest petal is white at the base, with purple lines. The orange stamens form a column in the center of the flower. There are two color variations, 1 with all 5 petals pale lilac or lavender, the other with the upper 2 petals deep velvety purple and the lower 3 petals pale lilac to lavender.

Bloom Season: Spring; also in fall

Habitat/Range: Common in rocky or sandy soils in prairies, hill prairies, sand prairies, savannas, and glades; also in black soil prairies; found throughout the prairie region, but less frequent in the northwestern part.

Comments: It has been reported that compared to other violets, the more horizontal position of the flowers of bird's foot violet are more attractive to butterflies and skippers, which makes it easier for them to land on. The caterpillars of various fritillary butterflies feed on the foliage and flowers of prairie violets. One specific fritillary, the regal fritillary, may prefer this violet species over others as a food source. The regal fritillary population has been rapidly declining over the past 50 years in the prairie region due to habitat fragmentation, degradation, and destruction of prairies. Unfortunately, this practice is greatly reducing all plant and animal species that depend upon prairies for their existence.

PRAIRIE VIOLET
Viola pedatifida
Violet family (Violaceae)

Description: Small plants, up to 6" tall, with individual leaves and single flowers on stalks emerging from the base of the plant. The leaves are 1–3" long and wide, with each leaf divided into 3 deeply lobed, narrow segments that are further divided into smaller segments. The slightly irregular flowers barely appear above the leaves on single stalks. The purple to blue-purple flowers are about ¾" across, with 5 slightly irregular petals. The 3 lower petals are white near the base, with the 2 side petals having a tuft of white hairs and the lower petal with dark purple lines. The stamens are arranged in a tight group within the flower.

Bloom Season: Spring; also in fall

Habitat/Range: Local in dry prairies, hill prairies, and savannas; found throughout the prairie region but rare in Indiana, Michigan, and Ohio.

Comments: Prairie violet is similar in appearance to bird's foot violet, but differs in having the leaf segments further divided into narrower lobes; flowers about ¾" across compared to 1½" across for the latter; and tufts of hairs at the base of the 2 side petals, while the latter lacks hairs.

ARROW-LEAVED VIOLET
Viola sagittata
Violet family (Violaceae)

Description: Plants up to 6", with single flowers arising on stalks above the leaves. The leaves, which emerge from the base on long stalks, are up to 3" long and about 1½" wide, shaped like an arrowhead with small lobes generally toward the base. The flowers are ¾ to 1" across, with 5 blue-violet to purple petals that are white at the base. The 3 lower petals have white tufts of hairs at their base, with the lowest petal also showing dark purple veins.

Bloom Season: Spring–early summer

Habitat/Range: Common in dry to moist prairies, sand prairies, and open woodlands; found throughout the prairie region, but absent in Nebraska and the Dakotas.

Comments: Arrow-leaved violet's species name, *sagittata*, is derived from the Latin word, *sagitt(a)*, meaning "an arrow," referring to the leaves, the shape of which easily distinguishes it from the other violets.

COMMON BLUE VIOLET
Viola sororia
Violet family (Violaceae)

Description: The plant forms a mound of leaves and flowers on usually hairy stalks, less than 6" tall. The leaves are less than 3" across, about as wide as or wider than long, rounded at the base, with rounded teeth along the margins, and often hairy on both surfaces. The flowers are on long smooth (or hairy) stalks, with each flower about ¾" across, with 5 bluish-purple to purple petals. The base of the petals is white, with a beard of hairs and purple lines.

Bloom Season: Spring–early summer

Habitat/Range: Occasional in upland prairies, savannas, and glades, and more frequent in rocky or dry, open woods, wooded slopes along streams, pastures, lawns, and disturbed areas; found throughout the prairie region.

Comments: The plants have been used as salad ingredients, as cooked greens, soup thickener, tea, and candy. A closely related species, Missouri violet (*Viola missouriensis*), has leaf blades that are triangular-shaped, longer than wide, flat at the base, sharply toothed along the margins, and with a lighter shade of blue-violet flowers, each about ½–¾" across; occurs along the borders of wet prairies and bottomland forests, upland forests, marshes, and other wet areas; found throughout the prairie region, but absent in the Dakotas and Ohio.

WEEDS

As the tallgrass prairie region began to be settled by Europeans—and later, by Asians, hundreds of years ago—they brought with them either deliberately or accidentally seeds and plants from their homeland. Over time, hundreds of these often-aggressive nonnative species have become established in the tallgrass prairie. Their presence has led to the degradation of many prairies by overcrowding and outcompeting native prairie plants. Many of these nonnative species are more in harmony and not as aggressive in their European and Asian native environments because the animals that feed upon them are present. This section includes some invasive weeds that one can encounter in tallgrass prairies.

QUEEN ANNE'S LACE
Daucus carota
Parsley family (Apiaceae)

A biennial with a large taproot and stout, branching, hairy stems to 4' tall. Both basal and stem leaves are large and finely divided on long, hairy stalks. Tiny, white flowers, each with 5 tiny petals, are tightly grouped in clusters, which in turn form a larger umbrella-shaped cluster about 4" across. In the center, there is often 1 purple flower. As the flowers fade, the feather-like stalks curl into a tight bird-nest shape supporting numerous oval, bristly, dried fruits that are up to ⅛" long. Introduced from Europe, this abundant weed can be found in degraded, grazed, or unburned prairies; also found in pastures, old fields, along roadsides, and open disturbed areas. It is also known as wild carrot.

WILD PARSNIP
Pastinaca sativa
Parsley family (Apiaceae)

A stout, smooth-stemmed, biennial plant to 5' tall, with grooves along the stem. The leaves are alternate and divided into leaflets each up to 3" long that are round and lobed, with teeth along the margins. The flower heads are large, up to 5" across, on long stalks, and shaped like an umbrella. Numerous yellow flowers, each with 5 petals and 5 stamens, are borne on slender stalks. A common weed, native to Europe, found in disturbed portions of upland prairie, pastures, fallow fields, old fields, roadsides, and open, disturbed sites.

MUSK THISTLE
Carduus nutans
Aster family (Asteraceae)

A sturdy biennial with a spiny, winged stem, up to 7' tall. First year's leaves spread over the ground, radiating out from a central core, and overwinter, sending up branching stems the second year. Leaves are alternate, up to 10" long, 4" wide, smooth, deeply lobed, with spiny tips. The flower heads are about 2" across, solitary, nodding at the ends of very long stalks, with numerous reddish-purple flowers. A common weed, native to Europe and Asia, which can spread into upland prairies from adjacent roadsides, old fields, pastures, and open, disturbed sites.

CANADA THISTLE
Cirsium arvense
Aster family (Asteraceae)

Plants spreading to form large colonies from deep lateral roots that send up new stems up to 4' tall that are spineless. Leaves are alternate, spiny, lobed, and 2–7" long. There are numerous pale pink flowers, each less than 1" across, with bracts at their bases that emerge with non-spineless tips. Male and female flowers are on separate plants, unlike other thistles in the region. A common weed native to Europe, Asia, and North Africa, and found to invade prairies in the northern half of the prairie region.

BULL THISTLE
Cirsium vulgare
Aster family (Asteraceae)

A biennial plant growing from a fleshy root, with much-branched, stout, hairy stems and narrow-spiny-margined wings, from 2–5' tall. The leaves extend along the stem as spiny wings. Basal leaves are 4–16" long, and the stem leaves are 1–6" long, deeply lobed with crinkled margins and spines. Flower heads are reddish-purple to purple, 1–1½" wide, and covered with numerous long, yellow-tipped spines at their bases. A common weed native to Europe, Asia, and North Africa and found to invade prairies throughout the prairie region.

OX-EYE DAISY
Leucanthemum vulgare
Aster family (Asteraceae)

Plants are often multistemmed to 2½" tall, with basal leaves round to spoon-shaped, toothed, and on stalks. The stem leaves are widely spaced, narrow, deeply cut along the margins, and lack stalks. The flower heads are up to 2" across, with about 30 white, petal-like ray flowers surrounding a central disk of numerous bright yellow, tubular disk flowers. A common weed, native to Europe and Asia; found in fields, pastures, roadsides, and open, disturbed areas that can invade disturbed or degraded, often unburned prairies.

COMMON TEASEL
Dipsacus fullonum
Teasel family (Dipsacaceae)

A tall, stout biennial with very prickly, branched stems, up to 8' tall. The leaves are opposite and stalkless or sometimes slightly fused to the stem at the very base, up to 12" long, broadest at the base, narrowing to a pointed tip, with rounded teeth along the margins and lacking prickles, except underneath along the mid-vein. The pink to lavender 4-lobed flowers are densely packed along a cylindrical head at the top of long stalks. A similar weed, cut-leaved teasel (*Dipsacus laciniatus*), has opposite leaves that form a cup-like structure around the stem, long, narrow lobes along the margins, and white flowers. Both are common weeds that are native to Europe and rapidly increasing in the prairie region; found in fields, pastures, roadsides, and open, disturbed ground that can invade degraded, often unburned prairies.

LEAFY SPURGE
Euphorbia virgata
Spurge family (Euphorbiaceae)

Stems are single or multiple from the base, hairless, often branched above the midpoint, up to 3' tall, and forming colonies from rhizomes. The leaves are alternate, narrow, 1–3" long, and pointed at the tip. The upper stems have a branched array of paired, yellow round bracts surrounding a small cluster of greenish-yellow flowers. A common weed, native to Europe and Asia; found in prairies, pastures, fields, disturbed soil, and very difficult to eradicate. According to the organization Flora of North America, populations long thought to be *Euphorbia esula* are more appropriately treated as leafy spurge (*Euphorbia virgata*), although some believe that both occur in North America. *Euphorbia virgata* differs by having a somewhat pointed tip at the end of a leaf that is long and narrow along its length, while *Euphorbia esula* has a rounded tip at the end of a leaf that is wider above the middle.

CROWN VETCH
Securigera varia
Bean family (Fabaceae)

Densely spreading plants, up to 4' long, with branched, smooth stems. The leaves are alternate and divided into 15–25 leaflets. Each leaflet is up to ¾" long, narrow, abruptly pointed at the tip, lacking hairs, and smooth along the margins. The flowers are in dense clusters (like a crown), on long stalks arising from the axils of the leaves. Each flower is about ½" long, with 5 pink and white petals arranged to form a typical bean-family flower. A common, aggressive weed that has often been planted to control erosion, it has been found to actually *increase* erosion. This is because it provides no cover in contact with the ground, so the soil remains bare even though there is dense foliage above it. Native to Europe, Asia, and Africa, this weed has been commonly planted along roadsides and has escaped into prairies, glades, forests, edges of streams and gravel bars, fields, and disturbed sites. Formerly known as *Coronilla varia*.

SERICEA LESPEDEZA
Lespedeza cuneata
Bean family (Fabaceae)

A single-stemmed plant, up to 5' tall, with many erect, leafy branches, which are green to ashy in color. The stem has flattened hairs along its length. The leaves are divided into 3 leaflets, each from ¼–1" long. The lower 2 leaves have stalks, with the end leaflet stalkless, or nearly so. The flowers are in clusters of 2–3 in the upper leaf axils. The flowers are about ¼" long and are a pale creamy color with conspicuous purple or pink markings in the center of the fan-like upper petal. A common aggressive weed native to eastern Asia, it was first introduced into the United States in the early 1900s to aid in soil erosion control. It has become a major nuisance and is difficult to eradicate; found to invade prairies, woodlands, and gravel bars in streams; also along roadsides and in disturbed open ground. The common name "sericea" comes from the Latin *sericatus*, meaning "clothed in silken hair," describing its downy foliage.

BIRD'S FOOT TREFOIL
Lotus corniculatus
Bean family (Fabaceae)

A sprawling plant, up to 2' long, with branching stems upright toward the tips. The leaves are divided into 5 leaflets, each up to ¾" long, with 2 lower leaflets some distance below the 3 upper leaflets. The flowers are clustered on a long stalk that arises from a leaf axil. The flowers are golden yellow, about ¾" long, and arranged in the pattern typical of members of the bean family. The seeds form in slender, upright pods. A native of Europe, this common weed has been planted along roadsides to reduce mowing, and has sometimes overseeded into prairie pastures.

WHITE SWEET CLOVER
Melilotus albus
Bean family (Fabaceae)

This legume, depending on conditions, grows as an annual or biennial. The branching, smooth stems can be found up to 6½' tall. The leaves are alternate, grayish-green, divided into 3 leaflets, with each leaflet about 1" long, oval, rounded at the tip, and finely toothed. The flowers are white, fragrant, about ⅜" long, and clustered on 4" stalks. A very common, aggressive native of Europe and Asia, it has been found to invade prairies and is difficult to eradicate; also occurs along roadsides, fields, and open disturbed ground. Some botanical authorities consider white sweet clover to be a different color form of yellow sweet clover, and believe that both should be called *Melilotus officinalis*. In fact, white sweet clover has distinct characteristics that differentiate it from yellow sweet clover, including being slightly larger in size, with grayish-green foliage and a network of raised nerves on the surface of the fruits, and blooming about two weeks later.

YELLOW SWEET CLOVER
Melilotus officinalis
Bean family (Fabaceae)

This legume, depending on conditions, grows as an annual or biennial. The branching, smooth stems can be found up to 5' tall. The leaves are alternate, green, divided into 3 leaflets, with each leaflet about 1" long, oval, rounded at the tip, and finely toothed. The flowers are yellow, fragrant, about ⅜" long, and clustered on 4" stalks. Very common, aggressive; native of Europe and Asia; found to invade prairies and difficult to eradicate; also occurs along roadsides, fields, and open disturbed ground. Some botanical authorities consider yellow sweet clover and white sweet clover to be the same species (*Melilotus officinalis*), but yellow sweet clover has distinct characteristics, including being slightly smaller in size, with green foliage and a network of flat nerves on the surface of the fruits, and blooming about two weeks earlier.

RED CLOVER
Trifolium pratense
Bean family (Fabaceae)

Much-branched stems, up to 2' tall, occurring in open clumps, with widely spaced leaves. The leaves are alternate, divided into 3 rounded leaflets up to 2" long and ¾" wide, stalkless, with sparse hairs along the margins, which are sometimes finely toothed. There is typically a V-shaped pattern on the leaf surface. The pinkish-red flowers are in round, dense clusters about ¾–1" across. Very common; native of Europe and Asia; planted as a forage or cover crop that often escapes into disturbed or degraded prairies, where it can be very persistent.

WHITE CLOVER
Trifolium repens
Bean family (Fabaceae)

Low-growing plants with fibrous roots and sometimes short rhizomes. Stems are 4–12" long and rooting at the nodes. The leaves are alternate and divided into 3 broadly oval to nearly round leaflets, each about ½" in diameter, with finely toothed edges. Sometimes there is a white crescent across the middle of the leaflets. The flowers are round, about ½" across, white, and on smooth stalks about 3" long. Very common; native of Europe and Asia; planted as a forage or cover crop that often escapes into disturbed or degraded prairie, where it can be very persistent.

PURPLE LOOSESTRIFE
Lythrum salicaria
Loosestrife family (Lythraceae)

Hairy, square-stemmed branching plants, up to 5' tall, with opposite leaves, but occasionally in whorls of 3 or 4. The leaves are stalkless, about 4" long and 1" wide, smooth along the margins and slightly hairy. The flowers are purple or pinkish-purple and densely packed in spikes up to 20" long. Each flower is about ½–¾" across, with 6 petals that have a wrinkled appearance and a dark vein down the middle. A common, aggressive weed; native to Europe and Asia; planted as an ornamental and escaped into wetlands, including marshes and fens. Purple loosestrife could also invade wet prairies that contain depressions with standing water.

GLOSSARY

alternate—Placed singly at different heights on the stem or axis (*see* "opposite") (*see* p. 6, figure 2).

annual—A plant completing its life cycle—from seed germination to production of new seeds—within a year, and then dying.

anther—The pollen-bearing part of a stamen (*see* p. 8, figure 8).

axil—The angle between the upper part of a leaf and the stem from which it grows.

banner—The usually erect, spreading upper petal in many flowers of the bean family (Fabaceae) (*see* p. 9, figure 9).

basal—At the base or bottom of; generally used in reference to leaves at the base of the plant (*see* p. 4, figure 4).

biennial—A plant that completes its life cycle in two years, normally not producing flowers during the first year.

bract—A reduced or modified leaf, often associated with flowers (*see* p. 8, figure 10).

bristle—A stiff hair, usually erect or curving away from its attachment point.

bulb—An underground plant part derived from a short, usually rounded shoot that is covered with scales or modified leaves.

calyx—The outer set of flower parts, composed of the sepals, which may be separate or united; usually green (*see* p. 8, figure 8).

capsule—A dry fruit that releases seeds through splits or holes.

clasping—Surrounding or partially wrapping around a stem or branch.

cluster—Any grouping or close arrangement of individual flowers that is not dense and continuous.

compound leaf—A leaf that is divided into two or more leaflets, each of which may look like a complete leaf but which lacks buds. Compound leaves may have leaflets arranged along an axis like the rays of a feather or radiating from a common point like the fingers on a hand (*see* p. 7, figures 6, 7).

corm—A fleshy, bulb-like base of a stem, usually underground.

corolla—The set of flower parts interior to the calyx and surrounding the stamens, composed of the petals, which may be free or united; often brightly colored (*see* p. 8, figure 8, and p. 9, figure 10).

disk flowers—Small, tubular flowers in the central portion of the flower head of many plants in the aster family (Asteraceae) (*see* p. 9, figures 10, 11, 12).

disturbed—Referring to habitats that have been impacted by actions or processes associated with human settlement, such as ditching, grading, or long intervals of high-intensity grazing.

erect—Upright; standing vertically or directly perpendicular from a surface.

escape—A plant that has been cultivated in an area and subsequently spread from there into the wild.

family—A group of plants having biologically similar features—such as flower anatomy, fruit type, and so on—and common ancestry, such as the family Liliaceae, encompassing lilies, onions, wild hyacinths, and trilliums.

fen—A specialized wetland permanently supplied with mineralized groundwater.

flower head—As used in this guide, a dense and continuous group of flowers, without obvious branches or space between them; used especially in reference to the aster family (Asteraceae) (*see* p. 9, figures 10, 11, 12).

fruit—The ripened ovary of a flowering plant, containing seeds.

genus—A group of related species, such as the genus *Solidago*, encompassing the goldenrods (*see* "specific epithet").

glade—An opening in the forest with bedrock at or near the surface and drought-resistant plants.

gland—A bump, projection, or round protuberance, usually colored differently than the object on which it occurs, and often sticky or producing sticky or oily secretions.

herbaceous—Having the character of an herb, which is a plant lacking persistent woody parts above the ground.

hood—The curing or folded, petal-like structures interior to the petals and exterior to the stamens in milkweed flowers (*Asclepias* species); because most milkweeds have reflexed petals, the hoods are typically the most prominent feature of the flowers.

hooded—Arching over and partially concealing or shielding.

horn—A small, round, or flattened projection from the hoods of milkweed flowers (*Asclepias* species).

keel—A sharp lengthwise fold or ridge, referring particularly to the two fused petals forming the lower lip in many flowers of the bean family (Fabaceae) (*see* p. 9, figure 9).

leaf— A flat outgrowth of a stem capable of manufacturing food for the plant and usually green (*see* Photosynthesis).

leaflet—A distinct, leaf-like segment of a compound leaf.

lobe—A segment of an incompletely divided plant part, typically rounded; often used in reference to leaves.

margin—The edge of a leaf.

mesic—Referring to a habitat that is well-drained but generally moist through most of the growing season.

midrib—The central or main vein of a leaf.

node—The portion of the stem where one or more leaves are attached; buds are commonly borne at the node, in the axils of the leaves.

opposite—Paired directly across from one another along a stem or axis (*see* "alternate") (*see* p. 6, figure 1).

ovary—The portion of the flower where the seeds develop; usually a swollen area below the style (if present) and stigma (*see* p. 8, figure 8).

palmate—Lobed, veined, or divided from a common point, like the fingers of a hand (*see* p. 7, figure 6).

parallel—Side by side, approximately the same distance apart for the entire length; often used in reference to veins or edges of leaves.

perennial—A plant that normally lives for three or more years.

petal—An individual segment or part of the corolla, often brightly colored (*see* "corolla") (*see* p. 8, figure 8).

photosynthesis—The process in which the energy of sunlight is used by organisms, especially green plants, to synthesize carbohydrates from carbon dioxide and water, releasing oxygen as a by-product.

pinnate—A compound leaf where smaller leaflets are arranged along either side of a common axis (*see* p. 7, figure 7).

pistil—The seed-producing, or female, unit of a flower, typically consisting of the ovary, style, and stigma; a flower may have one to several separate pistils (*see* p. 8, figure 8).

pod—A dry fruit that splits open along the edges.

pollen—The fine, dust-like grains discharged from the male part of the flower and typically necessary for seed production.

prickle—A small, sharp, spine-like outgrowth emerging from the outer surface.

ray flowers—The flowers on the flower heads of members of the aster family (Asteraceae) that have a single, strap-shaped corolla, resembling one flower petal; ray flowers may surround the disk flower in a flower head; or, in some species, such as dandelions, the flower heads may be composed entirely of ray flowers (*see* p. 9, figures 10, 12).

recurved—Curved backward or outward.

reflexed—Abruptly bent or curved downward.

rhizome—An underground stem, usually lateral, and producing shoots and roots.

root—An underground organ that anchors a plant in the soil and absorbs water and nutrients.

rosette—A dense cluster of basal leaves from a common underground part, often in a flattened, circular arrangement.

sepal—An individual segment or part of the calyx; typically green, but sometimes enlarged and brightly colored (*see* p. 8, figures 8, 9).

shrub—A persistent woody plant with several stems from the base.

simple leaf—A leaf that has a single leaf-like blade, although this may be lobed or divided (*see* p. 7, figure 5).

specific epithet—The second portion of a scientific name, identifying a particular species; for instance, in wild geranium, *Geranium maculatum*, the specific epithet is *maculatum*.

spike—An elongated, unbranched cluster of stalkless or nearly stalkless flowers.

stalk—As used in this guide, the stem supporting the leaf, flower, or flower cluster (*see* p. 7, figure 5).

stalkless—Lacking a stalk; a stalkless leaf is attached directly to the stem at the leaf base.

stamen—The pollen-producing, or male, unit of a flower, typically consisting of a long filament with a pollen-producing tip (the anther) (*see* p. 8, figure 8).

stigma—The portion of the pistil receptive to pollination; usually at the top of the style, and often appearing fuzzy or sticky (*see* p. 8, figure 8).

stipule—A bract or leafy structure occurring in pairs at the base of the leaf stalk.

style—The portion of the pistil between the ovary and the stigma; typically a slender stalk (*see* p. 8, figure 8).

succulent—Thickened and fleshy or juicy.

tepals—Sepals and petals entirely or nearly alike

tendril—A slender, coiled, or twisted filament with which climbing plants attach to their support.

toothed—Having small lobes or points along the margin (as of a leaf).

tubular—Narrow, cylindrical, and tube-like.

variety—A group of plants within a species that has a distinct range, habitat, or set of characteristics.

vine—A plant with long, flexible stems trailing on the ground or climbing on other plants.

whorl—Three or more parts attached at the same point along a stem and often surrounding the stem; usually referring to leaves (*see* p. 6, figure 3).

winged—Having thin bands of leaf-like tissue attached edgewise along the length of a stem or leaf stalk.

wings—The two side petals flanking the keel in many flowers of the bean family (Fabaceae) (*see* p. 9, figure 9).

winter annual—An annual plant that begins its growth from seed in the fall and produces basal leaves that overwinter.

TALLGRASS PRAIRIE DIRECTORY

This directory provides telephone numbers and websites of state and federal agencies and private organizations that administer high-quality prairies in the tallgrass prairie region that are open to public visitation. The Nature Conservancy chapters are well represented throughout the prairie region; their telephone numbers are listed, but they do not provide direct access to their state websites. One must first go to the national website and find the pull-down menu titled "Choose a Location"; then, scroll down and find the state you are wanting. That link will take you to the state chapter.

There is an excellent resource available for finding prairies, savannas, and grasslands throughout the United States, Canada, and Mexico. It is called *Prairie Directory of North America* by Charlotte Adelman and Bernard L. Schwartz. Listed by state and county, it is the most extensive list of prairies available, with well over 1,000 prairies, savannas, and grasslands represented, along with their contacts.

ARKANSAS

Arkansas Game and Fish Commission (877-836-4612); www.agfc.com
Arkansas Natural Heritage Commission (501-324-9619); www.naturalheritage.com
The Nature Conservancy, Arkansas Chapter (501-633-6699); www.nature.org

ILLINOIS

Illinois Department of Natural Resources (217-782-6302); www.dnr.illinois.gov
Illinois Nature Preserves Commission (217-785-8686); www.dnr.illinois.gov/INPC
Midewin National Tallgrass Prairie (815-423-6370); www.nationalforests.org
The Nature Conservancy, Illinois Chapter (312-580-2100); www.nature.org

INDIANA

Indiana Department of Natural Resources (317-232-4200); www.in.gov/dnr
Indiana Division of Fish and Wildlife (317-232-4200); www.in.gov/dnr/fishwild
Indiana Division of Nature Preserves (317-234-1064); www.in.gov/dnr
The Nature Conservancy, Indiana Chapter (317-951-8818); www.nature.org

IOWA

Iowa Department of Natural Resources (515-725-8200); www.iowadnr.gov/

Iowa Natural Heritage Foundation (515-288-1846); www.inhf.org/

The Nature Conservancy, Iowa Chapter (515-244-5044); www.nature.org

KANSAS

Kansas Department of Wildlife and Parks (785-296-2281); www.ksoutdoors.com

The Nature Conservancy, Kansas Chapter (785-233-4400); www.nature.org

Tallgrass Prairie National Preserve (620-273-8494); www.nps.gov/tapr

MICHIGAN

Michigan Department of Natural Resources (517-284-7275); www.michigan.gov/dnr

Michigan Nature Association (866-223-2231); https://michigannature.org

The Nature Conservancy, Michigan Chapter (517-316-0300); www.nature.org

MINNESOTA

Minnesota Department of Natural Resources (651-296-6157); www.dnr.state.mn.us

Minnesota Scientific and Natural Areas (651-296-6157); www.dnr.state.mn.us/snas

Minnesota Wildlife Management Areas (651-296-6157); www.dnr.state.mn.us/wmas

The Nature Conservancy, Minnesota Chapter (612-331-0750); www.nature.org

MISSOURI

Missouri Department of Conservation (573-751-4115); https://mdc.mo.gov

Missouri Prairie Foundation (888-843-6739); www.moprairie.org

Missouri State Parks (800-334-6946); https://mostateparks.com

The Nature Conservancy, Missouri Chapter (314-968-1105); www.nature.org

NEBRASKA

The Nature Conservancy, Nebraska Chapter (402-342-0282); www.nature.org

Nebraska Game and Parks Commission (402-471-0641); http://outdoornebraska.gov

Prairie Plains Resource Institute (402-694-5535); www.prairieplains.org

NORTH DAKOTA

The Nature Conservancy, North Dakota Chapter (612-331-0700); www.nature.org

North Dakota Game and Fish (701-328-6300); https://gf.nd.gov

OHIO

The Nature Conservancy, Ohio Chapter (614-717-2770); www.nature.org
Ohio Department of Natural Resources (614-265-6565); www.ohiodnr.gov
Division of Natural Areas and Preserves (ODNR) (614-265-6561); http://naturepreserves
.ohiodnr.gov

OKLAHOMA

The Nature Conservancy, Oklahoma Chapter (918-585-1117); www.nature.org
Oklahoma Department of Wildlife Conservation (405-521-3851); https://wildlifedepartment
.com
Oklahoma Tourism and Recreation Department (405-230-8400); www.go-oklahoma.com/
Oklahoma-Tourism-and-Recreation-Dept-OK/#

SOUTH DAKOTA

The Nature Conservancy, South Dakota Chapter (612-331-0700); www.nature.org
South Dakota Game, Fish and Parks (605-223-7660); https://gfp.sd.gov

TEXAS

Native Prairie Association of Texas (512-772-4741); http://texasprairie.org
The Nature Conservancy, Texas Chapter (512-623-7240); www.nature.org
Texas Parks and Wildlife Department (512-389-4800); https://tpwd.texas.gov

WISCONSIN

The Nature Conservancy, Wisconsin Chapter (608-251-8535); www.nature.org
Wisconsin Department of Natural Resources (888-936-7463); https://dnr.wi.gov
State Natural Areas (WDNR) (888-936-7463); https://dnr.wi.gov/topic/Lands/naturalareas

SELECTED FURTHER READING

Adelman, Charlotte, and Bernard Schwartz. 2013. *Prairie Directory of North America*, 2nd ed. New York: Oxford University Press. (A comprehensive source for locating North American public prairies, grasslands, and savannas in the United States, Canada, and Mexico.)

Betz, Robert. 2011. *The Prairie of the Illinois Country*. Westmont, IL: DPM Ink. (An extensive amount of information on the history, climate, soils, plants, vertebrate and invertebrate fauna, prairie remnants, and restoration of the tallgrass prairie in Illinois.)

Farrar, Jon. 2011. *Field Guide to Wildflowers of Nebraska and the Great Plains*, 2nd ed. Iowa City: University of Iowa Press. (A guide to the wildflowers of the Great Plains, including the western tallgrass prairie region.)

Freeman, Craig, and Eileen Schofield. 1991. *Roadside Wildflowers of the Southern Great Plains*. Lawrence: University Press of Kansas. (A guide to Kansas wildflowers, including the southwestern tallgrass prairie region.)

Great Plains Flora Association. 1986. *Flora of the Great Plains*. Lawrence: University Press of Kansas. (A technical manual for the identification of plants in the Great Plains, including the western tallgrass prairie region.)

Kilde, Rebecca. 2000. *Going Native: A Prairie Restoration Handbook for Minnesota Landowners*. St. Paul: Minnesota Department of Natural Resources. (An account of all aspects of prairie restoration and plantings.)

Kindscher, Kelly. 1987. *Edible Wild Plants of the Prairie*. Lawrence: University Press of Kansas. (Information on many edible prairie plants and their preparation, use, and history.)

———. 1992. *Medicinal Wild Plants of the Prairie*. Lawrence: University Press of Kansas. (Information on many medicinal prairie plants and their preparation, use, and history.)

Kurtz, Carl. 2001. *A Practical Guide to Prairie Reconstruction*. Iowa City: University of Iowa Press. (An introduction to prairie restoration, written from the author's personal experience.)

Ladd, Doug, and Frank Oberle. 2005. *Tallgrass Prairie Wildflowers*, 2nd ed. (Falcon Guide). Guilford, CT: Globe Pequot Press. (A guide to tallgrass prairie wildflowers, grasses, sedges, rushes, and weeds; also information on prairie plantings and restorations.)

Madson, John. 1982. *Where the Sky Began*. Boston: Houghton Mifflin. (A classic book about the prairie world.)

———. 1993. *Tallgrass Prairie*. Helena, MT: The Nature Conservancy / Falcon Press. (A coffee table–style book with narration and photographs that capture the grace and beauty of the tallgrass prairie.)

Packard, Stephen, and Cornelia Mutel, eds. 1997. *The Tallgrass Restoration Handbook*. Washington, DC: Island Press. (A comprehensive account of ecological restoration in the tallgrass region, including practical suggestions and lists of tallgrass prairie plants by state.)

Runkel, Sylvan, and Dean Roosa. 1989. *Wildflowers of the Tallgrass Prairie: Upper Midwest*. Ames: Iowa State University Press. (A guide to tallgrass prairie wildflowers that occur in the northern states of the prairie region.)

Swink, Floyd, and Gerould Wilhelm. 1994. *Plants of the Chicago Region*, 4th ed. Indianapolis: Indiana Academy of Science. (A checklist of the plants of the Chicago region, with keys, notes on local distribution, ecology, and taxonomy, including tallgrass prairie plants.)

Transeau, Edgar. 1935. "The Prairie Peninsula," *Ecology* 16: 423–437. (The classic account of the eastern part of the tallgrass prairie, along with an analysis of its climate and environment.)

Vance, Fenton, James Jowsey, and James McLean. 1984. *Wildflowers of the Northern Great Plains*. Minneapolis: University of Minnesota Press. (A guide to wildflowers in the northern Great Plains, which extend into Canada, and include the northwestern part of the tallgrass prairie region.)

Weaver, J. E. 1954. *North American Prairie*. Lincoln, NE: Johnsen Publishing Co. (The classic study of prairies and the dynamics of their plant life.)

Wilhelm, Gerould, and Laura Rericha. 2017. *Flora of the Chicago Region: A Floristic and Ecological Synthesis*. Indianapolis: Indiana Academy of Science. (A guide to plants of the Chicago region, along with illustrations, dot distribution maps, and taxonomic keys, including tallgrass prairie plants.)

INDEX

ABOUT THE AUTHOR

After completing master's degrees in botany and zoology at Southern Illinois University, Carbondale, Don Kurz spent the next 34 years working to inventory, acquire, protect, and manage natural areas, endangered species sites, and other special features in the Midwest, including prairies. For 22 years he was employed by the Missouri Department of Conservation, where he held various supervisory positions in the Natural History Division, including that of Natural History Chief, which he held until his retirement from the department in 2002.

Don is now a part-time writer and nature photographer specializing in landscapes, wildlife, insects, and plants. His photos have appeared in calendars and magazines such as *Natural History*, as well as numerous wildflower books, including Falcon Publishing's *Tallgrass Prairie Wildflowers* and *North Woods Wildflowers*. He is also the author of Falcon Publishing's *Ozark Wildflowers* and *Scenic Routes and Byways: The Ozarks, including the Ouachita Mountains*, along with the Missouri Department of Conservation's *Shrubs and Woody Vines of Missouri, Shrubs and Woody Vines of Missouri Field Guide, Trees of Missouri*, and *Trees of Missouri Field Guide*. His other guides published by Tim Ernst Publishing are *Arkansas Wildflowers, Illinois Wildflowers*, and *Missouri's Natural Wonders Guidebook*.